Contents

Norms in Human Development

The distinction between norms and facts is long-standing in providing a challenge for psychology. Norms exist as directives, commands, rules, customs and ideals, playing a constitutive role in human action and thought. Norms lay down 'what has to be' (the necessary, possible or impossible) and 'what has to be done' (the obligatory, the permitted or the forbidden), and so go beyond the 'is' of causality. During two millennia, norms made an essential contribution to accounts of the mind, yet the twentieth century witnessed an abrupt change in the science of psychology where norms were typically either excluded altogether or reduced to causes. The central argument in this book is twofold. Firstly, the approach in twentieth-century psychology is flawed. Secondly, norms operating interdependently with causes can be investigated empirically and theoretically in cognition, culture and morality. Human development is a norm-laden process.

LESLIE SMITH is Professor Emeritus, Lancaster University and is currently based in the Lake District as a freelance researcher.

JACQUES VONÈCHE is Professor Emeritus, University of Geneva and Director of the Archives Jean Piaget, Geneva.

Norms in
Human Development

Edited by

Leslie Smith and Jacques Vonèche

CAMBRIDGE
UNIVERSITY PRESS

CAMBRIDGE UNIVERSITY PRESS
Cambridge, New York, Melbourne, Madrid, Cape Town, Singapore, São Paulo

CAMBRIDGE UNIVERSITY PRESS
The Edinburgh Building, Cambridge CB2 2RU, UK
Published in the United States of America by Cambridge University Press,
New York

www.cambridge.org
Information on this title: www.cambridge.org/9780521857949

First published 2006

Printed in the United Kingdom at the University Press, Cambridge

A catalogue record for this book is available from the British Library

ISBN-13 978-0-521-85794-9 hardback
ISBN-10 0-521-85794-5 hardback

Figures

Tables

Contributors

MARK H. BICKHARD, Henry R. Luce Professor of Cognitive Robotics and the Philosophy of Knowledge, Department of Psychology, Lehigh University, USA

LUTZ H. ECKENSBERGER, Professor Dr Head of the Centre for Education and Culture, German Institute for International Educational Research, and Chair for Psychology, Johann Wolfgang Goethe University, Frankfurt-am-Main, Germany

VITTORIO GIROTTO, Professor of Psychology, Department of Arts and Design, University IUAV of Venice, Italy

MICHEL GONZALEZ, Dr, Research Affiliate, Laboratoire de Psychologie Cognitive, University of Provence & CNRS, France

MONIKA KELLER, Dr, PD, Max Planck Institute for Human Development, Berlin, Germany

RICHARD F. KITCHENER, Professor of Philosophy, Colorado State University, USA

HENRY MARKOVITS, Professor of Psychology, University of Quebec, Montreal, Canada

PETER C. M. MOLENAAR, Professor of Methodology, Department of Human Development and Family Studies, Pennsylvania State University, USA

LESLIE SMITH, Professor Emeritus, Lancaster University, and freelance researcher, Lake District, UK

ELLIOT TURIEL, Professor, Graduate School of Education, University of California, Berkeley, USA

JACQUES VONÈCHE, Professor Emeritus, University of Geneva, Director, Archives Jean Piaget, Geneva, Switzerland

Acknowledgments

Leslie Smith and I want to express our gratitude to a number of persons and institutions who have made this book possible: the Board of Trustees of the Jean Piaget Archives in Geneva for many different grants; the Swiss National Science Foundation for a conference grant anticipating this book; the British Academy for its Overseas Conference Grants; Marylène Bennour for tremendous work tiding us over difficult moments as well as doing the job of research associate in the process; Silvia Parrat-Dayan, Maria del Rio Carral, Katalin Haymoz and Mathieu d'Acremont who assisted us in various capacities. As to our own always amicable collaboration on this book, we part company. Les sees its origin in things that I wrote a quarter of a century ago before he started to read Piaget at all, clinched by a conversation in my office in 1991 and followed by numerous exchanges at the Jean Piaget Archives in Geneva. He seems to think that without my expertise and commitment this book would not have been produced at all. For my part, I am very much indebted to Les for the incredible amount of energy, talent and faith he put into this project and its implementation. This book owes so much to his intelligence and leadership that I am a bit ashamed to co-sign it with him.

JACQUES VONÈCHE

1   Norms in human development: introduction

Leslie Smith

1   Introduction

The central issue is both general and well known as being problematic. It concerns the relation between the factual and the normative, between 'what is the case' on the one hand, and 'what has to be done' or 'what has to be' on the other. This issue is fundamental and recognized to have a direct relevance to contemporary neuroscience (Changeux, 2000; Damasio, 2003) and to current philosophy (Goldman, 2001; Nozick, 2001; Putnam, 2002). The particular version of the question at issue in this book is normativity in developmental psychology (DP).

The question 'Can DP deal with normativity?' has a standard answer 'No'. In outline, the argument for this answer runs like this. DP is an empirical science whose domain of investigation comprises developmental facts for description and explanation. Since norms are not facts, normativity does not fall within DP's domain of investigation. Further, normativity is itself a complex notion, suitable for philosophical, but not scientific, investigation. Philosophers have identified two classes of norms, concerning 'what has to be' and 'what has to be done'. Neither amounts to 'what is the case', so neither is in the scientific domain. The conclusion seems inescapable. DP does not deal with normativity, nor is normativity on DP's list of outstanding problems. Chemistry long ago parted company from alchemy. Astronomy long ago ceased to address the question of whether human destiny was written in the heavens. So too, this answer runs, DP ought to leave normativity out.

And there's the rub – *DP ought to leave normativity out*. The term *ought* along with comparable terms such as *has to, must, may, can, must not, should not* are normative. If DP is the science of the human mind and action, its silence about this reflexive requirement binding on itself is awkward. Cannot DP make some contribution here? The answer 'Yes' to this question has its own argument that, in outline, runs like this. The normative requirement – *DP ought to leave normativity out* – does not exhaust the class. Far from it, and other members of the class are ubiquitous in the lives of individuals in their societies. If DP has nothing to say about the members of this class, DP is not comprehensive. Norms are used by people and groups to make commitments. These commitments are directives in the regulation of action and thought. Individuals think and act both in terms of them and on account of them. The use of normative capacities has causal consequences without normativity being itself reducible to causality. That is why norms are suitable for inclusion in DP's domain of investigation. The failure to address normativity in DP would amount to a fundamental omission. In short, DP ought to include normativity in its stock of problems.

Since these two arguments have contrary conclusions about DP and normativity, they cannot both be right. The main aim in this Introduction is to address this problem head-on. The challenge ahead is to show that normativity is something to be taken seriously in DP, and in allied disciplines too. This challenge is addressed in four parts. The main outcome is that the initial question 'Whether DP can deal with normativity' can be replaced by a better successor 'How can developmental psychology deal with normativity?'

2   Why normativity is left out of developmental psychology

To the question 'Can the science of developmental psychology deal with normativity?' the standard answer is 'No'. This answer has a twofold rationale, one based on the empirical nature of science, the other on its demarcation from normativity.

2.1   *Fatal ambiguity: natural and normative laws of thought*

Psychology is the science of the mind, in much the way that physics is the science of matter. So there seems to be a way forward after all, namely a psychology of the laws of thought on the model of physics and the laws of nature. Although physics and psychology differ as to their domains – the physical and the mental respectively – they are similar with regard to the laws true of these different domains. These laws are natural laws based on factual evidence about causality. Just as physics is the search for the laws of nature explanatory of the physical world, so too is psychology the search for the laws explanatory of the mental world. In the case of psychology, these laws are laws of thought. The search for these laws of thought is sufficiently inclusive to cover normativity, and not merely causality.

The problem is that the natural and the normative are not the same thing at all. Indeed, there is a fatal ambiguity in the very notion of 'laws of thought' which was elegantly identified by Gottlob Frege, the founder of modern logic, at the start of the twentieth century.

> What is fatal is the double meaning of the word 'law'. In one sense a law asserts what is; in the other it prescribes what ought to be (but the) expression 'law of thought' seduces us into supposing that these laws govern thinking in the same way as laws of nature govern events in the external world.   (Frege, 1964, p. 12)

Even if natural laws are descriptions of 'what is the case', normative laws are not descriptions in this sense. Further, normative laws are laws about 'what ought to be done' or 'what ought to be the case'. So the parallel between physics and psychology breaks. Under this argument, what is looming is a forced choice for psychology between causality and normativity. The 'laws of thought' could be causal laws about the mind, or they could be normative laws about the mind. But they could not be both at once.

   This forced choice can be elaborated. The suggestion was that psychology can be 'just like' physics. It is innocuous for a *physicist* to say that something is forbidden in *physics*. Thus Stephen Hawking recently contrasted Newton's and Einstein's theories, making the point that one of these theories embodied something forbidden. *Forbidden* is a normative notion. For example, if Newton's theory has the consequence that gravitational forces are instantaneous in their effects throughout the universe in being dependent on transmission faster than the speed of light, such a consequence is 'something that was *forbidden* by relativity' (Hawking, 2001, p. 14 – my emphasis). Note well: Hawking was not saying that the natural laws of Newton's physics stated a prohibition, i.e. stated that something *should not be*. Rather, he was saying that a physicist presented with two theories with contrary implications about 'what is the case' in the physical world should choose one and reject the other. Similarly, if psychology is like physics, an empirical science of psychology would describe 'what is the case' in the mental world. Normative commands and prohibitions would be absent from psychological theories about the mind. True: they could be manifest in the thinking of real psychologists in much the way that they are manifest in the thinking of real physicists. But that is exactly the point at issue! So interpreted, no theory in psychology dealing with the laws of thought would have anything to say about normativity. It would focus exclusively on natural laws about the mind, leaving out 'what has to be' and 'what has to be done'. Yet the psychologist would all the same realize that something was forbidden. The tension here is acute in DP aimed at a comprehensive model of the mind. Despite a normative realization being in the mind of the psychologist, normativity would be 'left out' of psychological theory.

In short, normativity would be left out of DP in much the way that perpetual motion machines are 'left out' of physics.

2.2   *Developmental psychology as an empirical science*

As a branch of psychology, DP has three features. First, it is an empirical science. Second, it investigates human minds and actions through the lifespan from infancy to adulthood in individual and socio-cultural contexts. Thirdly, it provides descriptions of sequences as changes through time under social conditions, and explanations by reference to their change-mechanisms. For present purposes, the key feature is the first one. If DP is an empirical science, its *modus operandi* is that of any science and so two conditions apply:

- DP's laws are natural laws
- DP's laws are factually testable

Both conditions fit a widely accepted account of empirical science (Popper, 1968). Although this account of science has attracted critical commentary, neither condition is materially affected (Kuhn, 2000; Laudan, 1996). On this view of science, DP proceeds in the same two steps, one by devising universal laws of nature, the other by testing them in terms of their factual consequences. But norms are out of step twice. Normative laws are not natural laws, and so norms do not figure in the first step. Nor are they in the second step: norms are not facts, and so do not figure in empirical testing.

Facts are facts open to observation and experimentation. They serve in empirical testing directed on the causality of natural laws. Further, if these laws are causal laws, the relevant facts are causal facts. Indeed, testability in science strictly requires that all testing is factual testing. But normativity is not like this at all. First, the relation between norms and facts is problematic. Second, norms are used to make reflective judgments about facts.

The problematic relation between facts and norms

What is this relation? Two main candidates are entailment in logical deduction, and causality in science. Yet neither fits the relation between facts and norms.

The relation is not entailment. The argument that norms are not necessitated by facts alone was famously stated in 1739 by David Hume. The main point behind this argument is widely accepted (MacIntyre, 1998; von Wright, 1983). Dissenting views have been expressed about how, contrary to first impressions, normativity can be introduced into apparently non-normative premises, but these views do not alter the basic Humean point (Searle, 1969; Bickhard, 2003). Hume's argument was that facts are statements about what *is the case*. As such, they are different from norms about what *ought to be* the case or what *ought to be done*. Therefore, some explanation is owed as to why 'is' premises are sufficient for the deduction of an 'ought' conclusion.

This slide is imperceptible; but is, however, of the last consequence. For as this *ought*, or *ought not*, expresses some new relation or affirmation, 'tis necessary that it shou'd be observe'd and explain'd; and at the same time that a reason should be given, for what seems altogether inconceivable, how this new relation can be a deduction from others, which are entirely different from it.

(Hume, 1965, Bk III, Pt I, §I)

Remarking ironically that nobody ever provides such an explanation, Hume recommended his readers to follow suit – something they *should* do, if you will. Simply put, Hume's Rule is that *ought* cannot be derived from *is*. For example, suppose you are a director with limited resources insufficient to assist all groups, and have been presented with reliable evidence. This evidence is evidence about what is the case for use in making a decision about which group should be given assistance, and by implication which group given none. Suppose the evidence states:

members of group *A* regularly out-perform members of group *B*

Two conclusions can be drawn from this evidence in this context:

(A) Extra educational assistance should be given to group *A*
(B) Extra educational assistance should be given to group *B*

Notice that (A) and (B) are both normative, both lay down what *should* happen. But neither conclusion is necessitated by the evidence. Indeed, (A) and (B) are contraries in this context since a forced choice is made between them. Yet in logic, contrary conclusions could not be entailed by the same premises – in this context, (A) rules out (B), and (B) rules out (A). So there is no entailment here from this evidence to (A) or to (B). The way out is also clear. Either inference can become valid, if it is combined with a normative premise. This premise might be explicitly stated; more frequently, it would remain unacknowledged. For example, the same evidence along with

(A1) Scarce funding ought to be used to maximize excellence
(B1) Scarce funding ought to be used to compensate inequalities

entails (A) and (B) respectively. But (A1) and (B1) are both normative. Both contain an *ought*. And that is exactly the point. Hume's Rule amounts to the heuristic: if someone makes a commitment to one norm, there is always another norm behind it, rationally speaking. But no norm is necessitated by facts alone.

Causality as the relation between facts and norms fares no better. Hume's analysis of causality is decisive on this, too. As well, there is an added complication about transitivity. Four criteria of cause–effect relationships were stated by Hume (1965, Bk I, Pt III, §15):

- contiguity in space and time
- temporal priority of cause over effect
- constant conjunction of cause–effect
- universality of same cause–same effect

If norms are effects in causal sequences, all four are violated. Norms are not in space. New norms can be issued prior to any evidence about new circumstances. Constant conjunction is breached due to human frailty – weakness of the will is such that people may fail to think or act rationally in any particular case. Finally, universality is violated since the same facts do not generate the same norms – witness the contraries (A) and (B) in response to the same evidence.

As well, there is an added complication about transitivity. All causal sequences

if $X \rightarrow Y$ and $Y \rightarrow Z$, then $X \rightarrow Z$

are transitive. This is because propositional implication is transitive (Sainsbury, 1991). Thus the so-called Bruce effect occurs as the blockage of a female mouse's pregnancy by exposure to the sexual activity of a second male in that 'genes affect proteins, and proteins affect X which affects Y which affects Z which . . . affects the phenotypic character of interest', in this example the outcome of the second male's sexual activity on the female mouse's pregnancy (Dawkins, 1999, p. 232; the 'Bruce effect' is cited on p. 229). But normative sequences are non-transitive – sometimes the inference goes through, sometimes not. And this means that if a sequence is not transitive, it is not causal. For example, suppose your training has led to your acceptance of the tenets of evolutionary psychology, i.e. norms are causally produced by Darwinian mechanisms (Bjorklund & Pellegrini, 2002; Changeux, 2000). You also live during World War II in a country occupied by the Nazis who 'make you' accept their view that Nazis are a superior race due to the working of biological causality. A Jewish family is hiding in your house with the Gestapo at the door, so you risk your own death by concealing them. In such a case, are you obliged – that is, caused – to hand them over to the Nazis? Not so! You may well believe that you are not obliged to do things which preserve a species that produced the Nazis (Korsgaard, 1996, p. 15). Further, your belief may have a rational basis. If so, the rationale behind your belief would be non-causal. In short, causality is too weak a relation to be productive of normativity.

In general, the relation between facts and norms is neither of the two obvious candidates. It is neither entailment nor causality. This means that no exclusively causal model of the mind can be explanatory of the norms issued and used by people in their action and thought. Nor will any exclusively formal model of the mind fare any better.

Norms are used to make reflective judgments about facts

This leads to the second point that norms are used to make reflective judgments about facts. Any fact at all is open to normative judgment or reflection on that fact, whether as a confirming endorsement or as a critical challenge. Making a normative judgment in and of itself does not, and cannot, change causal facts. But facts can be scrutinized and evaluated by human agents who always have the ability to give – or to refrain from giving – their assent to them. Human agents can as well challenge the facts in taking a stand which can be a bold and creative step forward. Here are two examples:

King Canute

The use of a normative capacity does not amount to miracle-making, and so cannot suspend causal laws. Even so, normative judgments can be made about causal regularities. King Canute was exemplary. Endlessly told by his obsequious courtiers that his regal powers had no limits, he issued the command – a normative matter – that his throne was to be placed in front of the incoming tide. He then declared:

I command you to come no further! Waves, stop your rolling!   (Baldwin, 2005)

The king did this precisely to remind his courtiers about the scope and limits of normative action and thought. Effectively, he was pointing out that his courtiers should acquire a better understanding of the interaction of causal and normative laws. Yet for all that, his judgment was normative.

Martin Luther King

Invited to address the American Psychological Association in 1967, he issued a series of normative judgments:

you who are in the field of psychology have given us a great word. It is the word maladjusted [*sic*]. It is a good word [with its implication that] destructive maladjustment *should* be destroyed. But on the other hand, I am sure that we all recognise that there are some things in our society, some things in our world, to which we *should* never be adjusted. There are some things concerning which we *must* always be maladjusted, if we are to be people of good will . . . We *must* never adjust ourselves to racial discrimination and racial segregation . . . We *must* never adjust ourselves to the madness of militarism, and self-defeating effects of physical violence.   (King, 1968, 185)

The psychological findings at issue were causal regularities. Yet the judgments expressed about them were explicitly normative. The address made clear that psychology had provided a service in its investigation of the causal basis of maladjustment. All the same, a normative view was expressed that there are some things to which everybody should be maladjusted, including racism and militarism. This amounted to a normative challenge to the prevailing state of things in society. It is well known that these normative admissions turned out to be historically important, a paradigm case of normative judgment which actually did result in social change.

In short, normative judgments are made by people in reflecting on their beliefs and actions. Norms play a regulative role in the making of human judgments (Brandom, 2000; Ricoeur, 2000). Since these judgments are normative, they are not causal.

Summary

If DP is an empirical science in the search for natural laws and their explanation through causal theories, norms would be absent from its domain of investigation. This is because facts and norms are independent of each other. Natural laws and normative laws of thought are not the same thing. Norms are neither necessitated by nor causally generated from facts alone. Rather, norms serve to make reflective judgments about the prevailing facts. The options open to DP under this view of its scientific status are twofold. One option is to ignore normativity altogether. The other is to reduce normativity to causality. These options are now taken up, with a third option identified in §5.

3   How norms are currently interpreted in the science of psychology

The argument in §2 has been well taken in psychology, and in the social sciences generally. Both options have had distinguished sponsors. This is evident in the commitment to four interpretations of normativity which amount to the dominating position in psychology. Note well: in its own terms, each member of this quartet is valid. Even so, none goes to the core of normativity. This quartet is now reviewed in two parts, one identifying the four interpretations in psychology generally, the other their applicability to DP. It is worth stating that the discussion in this section is subject to a major qualification that a dominating position is not a universality.

3.1   Four non-normative interpretations of norms in psychology

Four interpretations are set out. In its own terms, each is intelligible and valid. Even so, severally and jointly, they miss the main plot about norms.

Behaviourism: norm as non-entity

In this interpretation, norms are either disregarded as being beyond the psychological frame of reference, or denied to exist for psychological explanation at all.

Behaviourism is the branch of empiricist psychology with an ABC ontology of observables – antecedents, behaviour, consequences. Behaviourism then subdivides. The tolerant version – methodological behaviourism – concedes the existence of non-observables, which are then ignored (Watson, 1930). The radical version – metaphysical behaviourism – denies that non-observables such as knowledge, consciousness and values are there at all (Skinner, 1974). Normativity is a member of this same class of excluded non-entities. Skinner used the example of instructions on a vending machine. The directive is: 'to operate, place coin in the slot and pull plunger beneath item wanted' (p. 120). Skinner's gloss on this is that directions do not impart knowledge or convey information; instead, they describe 'behaviour to be executed and state or imply consequences' (p. 120).

Yes: people learn – they learn how to operate a vending machine, place coins in slots, pull levers, and so on. Behavioural sequences such as these can be observed. Even so, this is like *Hamlet* without the Prince of Denmark. A directive is not just a behavioural regularity, but is instead a norm (Ross, 1968; von Wright, 1963). The term *how to* is normative in meaning – learning how a machine works and learning how to work the machine are not the same thing, in that one is descriptive, and the other is normative (Simon, 1981). Anyone who wanted to gain by legal means an item on sale in the vending machine would *have to* – normative requirement – comply with the directive. If the item wanted was freely available, the machine would have malfunctioned – another normative notion. Quite simply, both forms of empiricism have the same consequence – normativity is left out, either in fact or in principle.

Psychometrics: norm as average

In this interpretation, norms are taken into account as what is descriptively or statistically normal, typical or average.

Norms have an explicit place in psychological measurement, notably in psychometrics. A norm in this sense refers to what is typical or average with a view to the interpretation of scores, i.e. in norm-referenced testing.

Psychological tests have no predetermined standards of passing or failing; performance on each test is evaluated on the basis of empirical data. For most purposes, an individual's score is interpreted by comparing it with the scores obtained by others on the same test . . . a norm is the normal or average performance.   (Anastasi, 1982, p. 24)

So characterized, a norm identifies a descriptive tendency. If a series of tests form a longitudinal series, norm-referenced scores map out how far an individual has progressed along 'the normal developmental path' (p. 71). If the scores gained by person *P* are all average scores in this sense, then *P*'s performance is normal.

Normality in this descriptive sense is not normality in a normative sense. Descriptively, a normal performance is the performance of the average person. Yet it can always be asked: is it normal to be normal? Normal performances can and do change. Sometimes the change is upwards, such as the 'Flynn effect', consisting in the five to twenty-five points' increase in intelligence test scores over generations (Neisser, 1998), and sometimes downwards, such as the half to a full standard deviation decrease in scores on Piagetian tests over a generation (Shayer, 2007). Descriptive normality is evidently mobile, but not its normative counterpart in the question: 'Is that normal – does it have to be so?' Take another case: recent polls continue to attest the belief of most US adults that biological life is due to intelligent design, not to evolution. Further, these twenty-first-century adults hold comparable beliefs about the content of the biology curriculum in schools (Mooney, 2003). So the beliefs of these US adults are normal; and they are also non-normal. The whiff of contradiction is dispelled by the distinction between descriptive and normative normality. Their beliefs are normal, i.e. commonly held; but that has no bearing on whether the beliefs are normal, i.e. these are the right, or true, beliefs to hold about evolution. A psychological interpretation reliant on descriptive normality alone has left out something fundamental. Indeed, probability is itself a normative notion (cf. Girotto & Gonzalez, this volume, Chapter 10).

Social psychology: norm as social regularity

This interpretation is a variant of the previous one. It differs in making explicit the incidence of cases by reference to a social group. A norm sets out what is common to or typical in a social group.

Sociology shares with psychology the aspiration of being an empirical science. A case in point is the explanation of the suicide of individuals in social groups. Philosophers had argued that suicide is morally wrong on the grounds that the principle underlying the action of killing oneself could not be consistently universalized, and so could not be a categorical imperative (Kant, 1785). A categorical imperative is a particular type of norm. But a sociological explanation of suicide would be non-normative just because, for science, norms

> do not exist. [Instead] every sociological phenomenon, just as every biological phenomenon . . . can assume a different form for each particular case. Among these forms exist two kinds. The first is common to the whole species . . . Other forms exist which are exceptional . . . Those facts which appear in the most common forms we shall call normal, and the rest morbid or pathological.
>
> (Durkheim, 1901, pp. 87, 91)

As in psychometrics, a norm is a description of what is common in a group of people in contrast to the exceptional or morbid which is individually specific.

This interpretation amounts to the social version of methodological behaviourism. In consequence, it shares the self-limiting consequence of psychometrics in being officially precluded from distinguishing 'what is common in some group' from 'what ought to be common in that group'. Yet under Durkheim's account, the latter is not the stuff of science. Evidently, the President of Harvard University was siding with this interpretation in stating that recent advances in behavioural genetics, rather than socialization theory, had now established normality distributions for human attributes such as

> height, weight, propensity for criminality, overall IQ, mathematical ability, scientific ability [since there is] a difference in the standard deviation, and variability of a male and a female population. (Summers, 2005)

He also made a significant admission, that this evidence 'ought to influence the way one thought about other areas where there was a perception of the importance of socialization'. This admission is normative in a non-descriptive sense. Left unexplained was the basis of this normative judgment in behavioural genetics, currently regarded as a non-normative science.

Social psychology: norm as social control

In this interpretation, norms are directives from other people in authority, investigable in psychology by reference to their effects in social action.

The elegant summary contained in the title of a famous book, *Obedience to authority*, carried the implication that norms are just that. On this view, social action corresponds to behavoural compliance, that is 'the action of a subject when he or she goes along with his peers'. This compliance is social, behavioural and observable. Obedience requires compliance but goes beyond this in being 'the action of the subject who complies with authority' (Milgram, 1974, p. 113). The rationale for this proposal is twofold. One is biological: individual actions not conducive to the preservation of a species would not have evolved. The other is cybernetic: a self-regulating system maintains hierarchical checks on its own actions. Accordingly, obedience requires the adoption of an agentic state:

a person is in a state of agency when he defines himself in a social situation in a manner that renders him open to regulation by a person of higher status.

(Milgram 1974, p. 134)

The basic point is the same. For Milgram (1992, p. 37), norms are the grounds of everyday activity, which are neither made explicit nor codified.

Au contraire, norms often are made explicit – this is taken up in §4 below. More than this, and despite his contribution as translator of Genevan text (Inhelder & Piaget, 1958), Milgram did not take on board a key distinction previously stated by Piaget in 1950 when he asked this question about human reasoning:

is reasoning an act of obedience, or is obedience an act of reason?

(Piaget, 1995, p. 60)

Humans can be trained to be obedient, and their learning has a causal basis, even when this is obedience to an authority. But obedience can also be rational in being based on normative reason. These are not the same thing at all. Although Milgram's interpretation has gone beyond methodological behaviourism by requiring norms to be issued by authorities, this is to let the cat out of the bag. What is the basis of such authority – is this a causal or normative matter? And individuals lower down the hierarchy – can they develop to be in a position of authority? Was not mighty Caesar once a child?

The relevance of this quartet is this. The dominant position in the social sciences generally is such that norms are interpreted in one of four valid ways, none of which reflects the core of normativity. In consequence, this core is left out of account in either of two ways. It is either written off as non-existent, or is confined to the margins.

3.2   Non-normative interpretations of norms in DP

At issue now is whether this conclusion about psychology generally applies to DP in particular. The answer is Yes, subject to the caveat in §3.3 below.

Major textbooks

Regular commentary on recent work in DP abounds (Bornstein & Lamb, 1992; Cole, Cole & Lightfoot, 2005; Flavell, Miller & Miller, 1993; Gardner, 1982; Goswami, 2002; Damon, 1998; Siegler, 1991; Slater & Muir, 1999). Typically, norms are left out, not even listed in the Index. Alternatively and in the very few cases where they gain an entry in the Index, the entry is brief and confined to one or more of the four standard interpretations above. Main issues are typically identified for attention or resolution in future work. The issues selected are valid and important in their own right, including:

- formulation of precise models for broad empirical use
- setting their limits in the integration of developmental diversity
- accounting for biological–cultural interactions
- specification of change-mechanisms
- extent of plasticity in interventions and fortuitous experiences
- individual differences and general regularities
- relations between organismic and mechanistic standpoints

But normativity is not a member of this class.

Experimental DP

A widely held commitment is made to the methodological benefits arising from controlled studies directed on the causality at work in human development. This commitment is explicitly elaborated in surveys of empirical methods in which experimental designs are accorded highest priority, and is often mandatory. Norms make their default appearance as statistical normality, norm-referencing, norm-of-reaction, and the like – see §3.1 above. No account is taken of the methods appropriate to the investigation of normativity in any other sense. Yet if normativity is at work in human development, it is an issue in its own right and of fundamental importance – it is not mere 'noise', nor an epiphenomenon. Normative commitments can be made autonomously.

How could these normative regulations be investigated under controlled conditions as causal regularities?

Concept of development

Midway through the twentieth century, the same tendency was manifest in a key text (Harris, 1957). This text included papers by an eminent philosopher of natural science, Ernest Nagel, along with leading developmentalists, notably Heinz Werner. Neither addressed the contribution of normativity in human development. Fair enough: no single work can deal with everything. Yet this proved itself to be a significant omission. Elsewhere in the same book, the makings of the main problem can be found. On the one hand, aspects of children's development can be measured longitudinally, for example their physical height and weight, and also their mental characteristic so that 'an individual could be compared with a so-called normal or average child' (Anderson, 1957, p. 228). This is the descriptive sense of norm above. On the other hand, comparative studies attested cultural diversity in that human values are not universal, and this has led some developmentalists to search for 'a normative . . . metacultural "best"' (Spencer, 1957, p. 221). The term *normative* is used here in its normative sense, *not* in any of the four senses in §3.1 above.

Recent perspectives

Two recent perspectives in DP have their basis in evolutionary psychology and neuroscience. Despite their major differences, they share the principle that DP is an empirical science directed on the explanation of causal facts. Since these are the only facts in town, normativity is excluded from their town plans for DP in the two ways identified in §3.1 above.

In the evolutionary psychology of human development, a weaker variant is set out:

> evolutionary developmental psychology, we believe, serves as a metatheory for developmental psychology. [We] do not argue for a form of genetic determinism, but rather hold that evolved mechanisms interact with the local environment to produce a particular pattern of behaviour.
>
> (Bjorklund & Pellegrini, 2002, pp. 334–5)

A metatheory has a superordinate function, subsuming all theories falling under it. This leaves open which theories these are. Since this metatheory is causal, norms could figure in this account only as one of the four interpretations in §3.1 above. This position seems to leave open the possibility of its non-comprehensiveness in that other aspects of development are not covered by it. In fact, this is expressly ruled out by a stronger counterpart:

nothing about the mind makes complete sense except through evolution.
(Plotkin, 1997)

The use of *evolution* is pretty clear and is to be interpreted as biological causality. In short, norms are either ignored or reducible to causality in that 'ought', in the final evolutionary analysis, really amounts to 'is'.

The same two variants appear in neuroscience. Under the weaker variant, the brain is a causal mediator linking genes and the mind:

the mind and body are parallel and mutually correlated processes, two faces of the same thing. Internal to them is a mechanism for representing body events in the mind with an asymmetry in the mechanism in that the body shapes the mind's contents more than the mind shapes the body's contents, despite their mutual mirroring.   (Damasio, 2003, p. 217)

Correlation does not mean the identity of mind and brain. By implication, other entities such as norms are non-identical with the brain. So on this variant, norms really are there, and they could in principle exist, even though they are not identical to brains. The stronger variant rules this out: evolutionary processes are fourfold covering species over paleontological time, individuals in the epigenesis of neural connections, culture in epigenetic but extracerebral social history, and personal thought in psychological time. The causal basis of these four processes is put like this:

the fundamental idea is that each of these evolutions is embedded in the others and proceeds in accordance with a general scheme of variation-selection-amplification. This is the schema that Darwin used.   (Changeux, 2000, p. 239)

Since norms are neither facts nor causes in this Darwinian sense, they are excluded from official consideration in this perspective. Quite simply

the brain is a physical system [such that] our neural circuits were designed by natural selection to solve problems that our ancestors faced during our species' evolutionary history.   (Cosmides & Tooby, 2004)

The implication is clear. Causal processes are the sole processes for psychological investigation. If norms exist, they do so in the causal nexus.

Summary

In short, normativity in its core sense has gone AWOL in both psychology generally and in DP, where the dominant position remains king.

So much is manifest in four interpretations of norms as behavioural transactions, descriptive averages, social incidences or social controls. The interpretation in this quartet is entirely descriptive and so either non-normative or only marginally normative.

3.3   Caveat: dominance is not universality

There is an important qualification to enter about this conclusion. A dominant position is not a universality. Indeed, the conclusion is historically invalidated – it is only in recent times that normativity has been pensioned off (cf. Vonèche, this volume, Chapter 2). Second, even in recent times, the dominant position has been accepted neither in all accounts, nor by all dominant psychologists – including developmental psychologists. Rather, the point at issue is this. First, the dominating position has become the default position. The onus has been on others to show how any other position about norms can be made good. And this is too rarely taken on. Second, the default position has been widely, even if not universally, accepted in framing ideas and evidence. There is an actual, or incipient, reductionism at work, whereby norms are converted into facts in the causal nexus. This reductionism is inadequate in view of omission. It leaves out the distinguishing characteristic of norms. In DP, norms are either accepted to exist but disregarded in scientific explanation, or they are regarded as phantoms denied to exist at all. Third, the main target is DP defined exclusively in terms of causality. An exclusively causal psychology is not enough, necessary but not sufficient. Normativity is in the reckoning, and goes beyond causality. This does not, of course, mean that normativity 'kicks out' causality. Rather, normativity 'kicks in' requiring co-attention with causality. The reason why now follows.

4   Why leaving normativity out of DP will not do

The reason why leaving normativity out of DP will not do is because norms exist, and they do so in the thought and actions of individuals in society. Reality is more than the world of physics. Norms are real, and they are there. Norms are not open to direct observation like Mount Everest, nor even inferred like black holes, nor are they constructs like the Equator. To the contrary: norms regulate action and thought, and are imposed by intelligent agents on an otherwise norm-free world. Such a view is long-standing, traceable to this discussion of legal norms interpreted as moral entities:

now as the original way of producing physical entities is creation, so the way in which moral entities are produced can scarcely be better expressed than by the word *imposition*. For they do not arise out of the intrinsic nature of the physical properties of things, but they are *superadded, at the will of intelligent entities*, to things already existent and physically complete, and to their natural effects.

(Pufendorf, 1703 – my emphasis)

On this view, normativity is neither physical nor mental and yet part of reality for all that. Norms are not the same as causal regularities. Rather, norms exist as the regulatory commitments of intelligent agents capable of reflecting on what they think and do. A paradigm case concerns moral norms.

Normative concepts exist because human beings have normative problems. And we have normative problems because we are self-conscious rational animals, capable of reflection about what we ought to believe and to do . . . we can still always ask: but is this really true? and must I really do this.

(Korsgaard, 1996, pp. 46–7)

Normative concepts are used in dealing with moral problems. They are manifest as commitments made in human action and thought, both individual and social. Crucially, norms are not confined to morality. Many accounts of normativity tend to focus solely on morality (Changeux, 2000; Korsgaard, 1996; Putnam, 2002). Yet norms can be used in any domain of action and thought:

our ordinary understanding of states and acts of meaning, understanding, intending, or believing something is an understanding of them as states and acts that *commit* or *oblige* us to act and think in various ways. [It follows that] the challenge is to explain what sort of practical capacity the relevant kind of understanding consists in.   (Brandom, 1994, pp. 13/89 – author's emphasis)

A normative commitment in action and thought amounts to a duality. In part, it enables there to be *causal regularity* covering 'what is the case'. In part as well, it requires there to be a *normative regulation* about 'what has to be' or 'what has to be done'. Although norms as causal regularities have been investigated in the default position in DP, the open question is how to address normative regulation as well.

Three taxonomies of norms are now illustrated along with their defining criteria. Normativity is a complex notion, resistant to definition (Brandom, 2000; Horty, 2001; Putnam, 2002; Ross, 1968; von Wright, 1963). Even the terminology is diverse with reference made to norms, directives, imperatives, and the like. Instantiation is another matter. It is much easier to give examples of normativity. This task is now taken on. These taxonomies have either two (Kant, 1800), or three (Brandom, 2000), or six (von Wright, 1963) categories. It is sufficient for the argument that any one category is admitted to be a genuine category of norms, i.e. that at least one category is non-empty. This is sufficient because then the question arises: if there is at least one category of norm at work, what follows about human minds for explanations in DP? If other, or even all eleven, categories are admitted, so much the better.

4.1   Two categories

- what has to be
- what has to be done

These categories, but not the examples, are due to Immanuel Kant, amounting to his rules of thought and action respectively. Under this analysis, human understanding gives rise to objective thought, human willing to universalizable action, always provided the corresponding norms are activated. Further, these norms or rules were regarded as rules of logic but in a wider sense than in modern logic.

> Logic gives us rules in regard to the use of understanding, and practical philosophy in regard to the use of willing, which are the two powers from which everything in our minds arises.
>   (Kant, 1780, p. 41; cf. Kant, 1800, paras. 170–1; Longuenesse, 1998)

Since these rules are logical, they are also necessary, and so not merely causal regularities (see Kitchener, this volume, Chapter 4; Molenaar, this volume, Chapter 9).

Since norms concern 'has to' their properties can be characterized in modal logic which provides formal models in two ways. One is the deontic modality of obligation in that 'ought', 'may' and 'should not' correspond to that which is obligatory, permitted and forbidden (Horty, 2001; Ross, 1968; von Wright, 1983). The other is the alethic modality of necessity in that 'must', 'can' and 'must not' correspond to that which is necessary, possible and impossible (Cresswell & Hughes, 1996; Marcus, 1993; Sainsbury, 1991). The vernacular expression 'has to' provides an intriguing crossover point (Smith, 1993; von Wright, 1983).

Norm as 'what has to be'

The numbers 1, 2 and 3 form a series such that the next number in the same proportion is 6. In Spinoza's analysis, there are three ways to understand this – perceptual belief, learned algorithm and autonomous reason. For Spinoza, only the last reflects the normative properties of the proportion in that the proportion in these numbers had to be so, and could not be otherwise.

(Spinoza, 1963)

Spinoza's point was that necessary knowledge is dependent on the use of reason, not on observation nor learned rules. Spinoza was *not*, of course, saying that it is the human use of reason that is necessary – in fact, most folks rely on the other two types of understanding. Rather, Spinoza was saying that an understanding of the necessity in this proportion – the 'has to be' – requires the capacity to use reason.

Norm as 'what has to be done'

As a member of the Catholic Church, Martin Luther was summoned to Worms in Saxony in 1521, and asked to explain his attack on the Catholic religion. He was specifically asked why his own judgment was superior to the judgment of others. Luther answered:

I do not accept the authority of popes and councils, for they have contradicted each other – my conscience is captive to the word of God. I cannot and I will not recant anything, for to go against conscience is neither right nor safe. Here I stand, I cannot do otherwise.   (Bainton, 1950, p. 144)

This answer is twofold. First, Luther claimed that other Catholics have contradicted themselves, the implication being that nobody is rationally obliged to accept a contradiction. Second, Luther was captive to his own conscience, the implication being that he could not do otherwise because what his conscience commanded was obligatory. That is, his action was something which he had to do. In short, Luther set out reasons with a binding force on his action, something which he 'had to do'.

4.2   Three categories

- prudential norms
- institutional norms
- unconditional norms

This taxonomy and examples are due to Robert Brandom (2000, ch. 2). They are acknowledged to be indicative rather then complete. This means that each category is a normative category, but there may well be other categories. Brandom's own interpretation is to regard each of these as deontically valid in being implicit commitments and entitlements of discursive practices. This means that, under his position, normativity has an essential link with language. His analysis thereby runs into problems with biological normativity (see Bickhard, this volume, Chapter 3).

Prudential norms
From an observational premise, a normative inference can be drawn:

It is raining

I shall open my umbrella

In this inference, premises are shown above, and conclusion below, the line which marks the inference – the 'therefore'. One explicit premise is shown. It may be combined with other premises such as:

I want to stay dry
Only opening my umbrella will keep me dry

which are implicit in one of two ways. One is that they may be acknowledged by the agent but regarded as too obvious to state. The other way is that they may be unacknowledged by the agent who could make them explicit, if asked. The use of *shall* in the conclusion can be interpreted in two ways. In one way, it is a prediction about an effect soon to occur in this causal context. In the other, it is an obligation about what the agent has to do in this causal context. The latter is deontic. To the question 'OK, it is raining – but why are you going to open your umbrella?', this agent could reply 'because I have to'. This agent may be allergic to becoming wet, or just does not want to run the risk of getting a chill. A prudential inference is an individual inference 'up to this agent' – other agents may prefer to get wet. Still, for this agent, the inference is a deontic obligation, and an inference binding too on any other agent who accepts these premises.

Institutional norms
Whereas prudential reasoning is individually instantiated, reasoning in this category is socially instantiated, 'up to this institution' – other institutions may have different commitments.

I am a bank employee going to work

I shall wear a necktie

Once again, *shall* has a dual role as prediction and obligation. It is compatible with other possibilities, such as:

I shall not wear a clown costume

Typical premises are:

My employer has a dress code for employees
The dress code requires the wearing of neckties at work
I am a current employee

Recall here Frege's fatal ambiguity in §2.1 above. The conclusion is not necessitating in the way in which the law of gravity necessitates the falling to the ground of an unsupported body. The inference is necessitating in a deontic sense: the conclusion is binding on this agent who is required or obliged to dress appropriately, and other employees too. Crucially, the agent actually has to draw this conclusion as a deontic 'therefore' in action, even if not in thought. Compare the last day of the employment when the code is still binding: will this agent still draw this conclusion? Contrast on the same day when the same agent trips on a flight of stairs: will the law of gravity be suspended?

Unconditional norms

In contrast to the previous categories, these norms are universal, binding on every individual and all institutions:

Repeating the gossip would harm someone to no purpose

I shall not repeat the gossip

The dual role of *shall* here is primarily as obligation, with prediction as its consequence. If *shall* were to be regarded as a true/false prediction in the previous categories, that would leave unexplained why it is an obligation here. Well-known problems can arise. Is the premise false – maybe repeating this gossip does have a purpose? Is there a conflicting premise – maybe a promise to 'tell all' about this person? The former is a challenge to this particular inference: if the premise is false, the conclusion does not have to be drawn in this case (MacIntyre, 1998). The latter is a challenge to the over-riding nature of this conclusion – a dilemma is a dilemma just because two obligations collide in circumstances where only one of them can be acted on (Mason, 1996). Neither challenges the main point, that deontic inference can be a valid inference.

4.3   Six categories

- rules of games
- regulations
- directives
- customs
- ethical norms
- ideal rules

This taxonomy – though not the examples – is due to G. H. von Wright (1963; cf. Smith, this volume, Chapter 5).

Norms as rules of games

It is one thing for a ball to be in motion on a field; another for a group of people to kick a ball on a field; it is something else again for this activity to be a rule-governed game such as football. The rules of soccer include enabling rules and rule-violation.   (Blank, 2002)

LAW 1

The field of play must be rectangular.

LAW 14

The kicker deliberately handles the ball before it has touched another player: a direct free kick is awarded to the opposing team.

The normativity of Law 1 is explicit in the use of the term *must*, laying down requirements about the shape of the pitch. This rule is constitutive or determinative: any activity played on a square or oval is not, and cannot be, soccer. Similarly with Law 14: although no modal term is used to state this law, it is all the same constitutive and necessary in character: a player who deliberately handles the ball has broken a rule of soccer, and this violation merits compensation as a direct free kick.

Norms as regulations

One class of norm are regulations such as the norms about human safety on construction sites:

---

* *Children must not play on this site*
* *No unauthorized persons allowed on this site*
* *Safety helmets must be worn in this area*

Often such norms are presented graphically and linguistically. Animals and people too can be causally trained to conform to them. Only normative agents can comprehend their binding force as commands. Commands, orders, regulations are central to individuals in societies. Legal norms codifying obligations, permissions or prohibitions have a high salience in almost all societies. Regulations retain their force even if they are idiosyncratic, such as the norms at a European seminar to which Tom Stoppard was an invited guest:

here everything is free, you can do exactly what you want – but don't touch that painting! And don't move that chair! You can come to breakfast whenever you wish; it is served between 8 a.m. and 8.30.   (Nadel, 2002, p. 133)

Regulatory norms require an authority to issue them, and subjects to whom they are addressed.

Norms as directives

In this category are means-end norms, which are typically stated as a conditional linking an antecedent and consequent ($A \rightarrow C$). Even so, distinctions are drawn by von Wright (1963, pp. 9–11): in his analysis of the three examples that follow, the first and last are normative in distinct ways, while the middle example is not normative. (For psychological research on conditional reasoning, see Markovits, this volume, Chapter 11; Smith, this volume, Chapter 5.)

Technical directive: its antecedent is about something wanted, and its consequent is about something that must or must not be done to gain this. One and the same person has both the desire and action-plan. This norm is categorical:

If you want to make the hut habitable, you ought to heat it

Anankastic proposition: its antecedent and consequent are propositions independent of human desires and actions. That is, both antecedent and consequent are descriptive propositions. The use of the term *ought* is convertible into a descriptive counterpart, and so is not normative:

If the house is to be made habitable, it ought to be heated
Unless the house is heated, it will not be habitable

Hypothetical norm: this is a mixed conditional with a descriptive antecedent and normative consequent which lays down prescribed, permitted or prohibited action in particular circumstances. Although terms such as *ought* or *may* are often used to state such norms, their normativity is also left implicit in other cases, for example in commands:

If the dog barks, don't run

Norms as customs

Every society has customs and traditions manifest as habits and practices, either unique to that society or with a family resemblance to counterparts in other cultures. Either way, a custom lays down what is obligatory, permitted or forbidden in that social world. Customs have an origin in time, and may be terminated too. Norms as customs can be similar to rules of games, and also to commands. They differ in that they are typically not codified in writing, their issuing authority is unknown and they can be disregarded without penalty. In 1903, the first Tour de France cycling race was held, and LeTour (2005) is now an international rule-governed sport. It also has distinctive customs. In 2001, the race leader was Lance Armstrong. His main rival was Jan Ullrich who, in descending the Col de Peyresourde, misjudged a bend at 50 mph, crash-landing into a field. 'We're all going to wait for him,' said Armstrong, and they did. At Luz-Ardiden in 2003, the situation was the reverse. With Ullrich just ahead on an ascent, Armstrong collided with a spectator, landing on the road.

> Tour etiquette dictated that the leaders wait for me to catch up, just as I had waited for Ullrich [in 2001]. The Tour was supposed to be won by the strongest rider, not the luckiest, and the consensus in the peloton was that no one *should* profit from a freak accident.   (Armstrong, 2003, p. 240 – emphasis added)

Note Armstrong's use of *should*. Tour etiquette had a temporal origin in the twentieth century; it applies to action, but also to thought; and it is normative, laying down 'what has to be done' when mishaps befall race leaders. As such, this custom is normative – it is not merely descriptive in that Ullrich in 2003 was initially not inclined to wait, though he eventually did. Contrast the norms in Formula 1 motor racing: if a leading driver has an accident, competitors seize their chance to take the lead. Not so in LeTour. Implicated here as well is a key distinction between 'normative pressure' which is causal, and normative autonomy (von Wright, 1983). Customs are normally learned, passed on through the generations. They can as well be internalized and invoked autonomously.

Ethical norms

Norms in morality are well known in laying down obligations, permissions and proscriptions (Korsgaard, 1996; Nozick, 2001; Putnam, 2002). For example, moral norms can be addressed to

> humans – promises have to be kept
> children – you may play in the park
> students – plagiarism is never permissible

Unlike normative customs, ethical norms are commonly regarded as atemporal and cross-culturally universal. It is worth noticing that moral norms really are normative, but that they are the sole type of norm in none of the three inventories reviewed here. The importance of ethical norms is not in doubt (see Eckensberger, this volume, Chapter 6; Keller, Chapter 7; Turiel, Chapter 8).

Norms as ideal rules

These norms are ideal in laying out what it is to be someone or something, which attributes ought to be possessed by a good mother, for example, or a good film. What the rule then states is the set of attributes determining the relevant goodness. This determination is normative, not causal, as in the case of rules of games. Norms as ideal rules are distinct from ethical norms – theft is immoral, and yet a good thief has attributes which a bad thief lacks. Attributes conferring goodness are regarded as virtues which can be learned (von Wright, 1968). It is in this sense that a virtue epistemology is directed on the abilities, powers and acquired habits contributory to a person's achieving their cognitive aims, for example in the search for true rather than false beliefs (Axtell, 2000). This category of norm takes the review full circle to the first Kantian category 'what has to be' in contrast to ethical norms about 'what has to be done'.

Summary

This discussion had a limited aim, namely to review taxonomies with either two, three or six categories of norms. Evidently, some categories are common to each inventory, notably ethical norms. Others were unique to the inventory, such as prudential norms. The question as to which inventory is 'the right one' or how to combine these separate inventories is not pursued, nor is the question of supplying a formal analysis of norms. Rather, it is sufficient that any one category is accepted as a valid and non-empty category. If other, even all, categories are accepted, then so much the better. Further, the three taxonomies were simply three taxonomies without any claim that they are exhaustive.

The main conclusions are twofold. One is ontological: if there are norms in at least one category, then norms exist, norms are part of reality. The other is methodological: if norms are part of reality, a more inclusive DP is required to replace the ersatz normativity in §3 with the real normativity here in §4.

5   How DP can be inclusive of normativity

What is required in DP is the reconnection of causality and normativity without losing sight of its factual status as a science. The challenge is to show how to do this.

A general way to do so is by recourse to recent accounts of normativity, and several are to hand (Brandom, 2000; Habermas, 1992; Korsgaard, 1996; Putnam, 2002; Ricoeur, 2000; von Wright, 1983). These accounts contain subtle analyses with generic implications for psychology. They are not, however, empirically elaborated with special reference to human development.

A particular way forward is available in Piaget's model with its explicitly developmental focus. In Piaget's first book, action was presented as a unit of analysis in which norms as ideals are invoked in any intentional action whose performance is a fact, thereby deforming that ideal. 'Action necessarily deforms the ideal in virtue of its mixture of fact and norm' (Piaget, 1918, p. 116; for commentary, see Smith, 2003). This principle was elegantly restated as the requirement that any cognitive activity is always directed on the intentional object that is its goal, where this goal is assigned a value by its agent (Piaget, 1953, p. 9; for commentary, see Brown & Weiss, 1987). The same view was again restated in his periphery–centre model of developmental change (Piaget, 1976, pp. 334–45). As an ideal, the goal of an action amounts to a norm or ideal rule intrinsic to the action (cf. von Wright's taxonomy in §4.3). Further, the relation between an intentional action and its goal or object is itself normative, even though the performance of the action is an empirical matter (Brandom, 1994). As well, Piaget's model is empirical in being 'a psychology of normative facts' (Smith, this volume, Chapter 5; see also Smith, 2002, 2003). Almost all of the chapters ahead make use of Piaget's model, either as a reference-point, or for analytical elaboration, or for critical assessment.

There are other models of human development as well, and these include the ten chapters ahead. They have a common starting-point in two respects. One is in going beyond the descriptive interpretations of norms in §3 above. The other is in setting out ways in which DP can contribute to the explanation and justification of normativity in human development. As to the nature of these several contributions, they part company. Normativity is a tractable problem, but it is also huge and complex. As such, it is amenable to the complementary approaches adopted by these ten chapters grouped in three parts:

Part I Norms and development in epistemology

Chapter 2: Jacques Vonèche provides an insightful survey of normativity in accounts of the human mind over two millennia. His starting-point is arrestingly simple. Normativity has made some contribution to the dominant accounts over this long period in many different ways. By contrast, developmental psychology during the twentieth century has been instrumental in the exclusion of normativity in its accounts. This exclusion is due to the default assumption that development is nothing but change over time. The tension between these two positions is acute. A feast with rich pickings was on offer in most of the past accounts; by contrast, the cupboard in the default position is bare. Even if the former cannot all be right – many past accounts were contraries – the latter must be wrong. This means that the default assumption is a dead-end. The way ahead is evidently to take heed of a rich past in the identification of a successor assumption in which developmental psychology is necessarily a normative discipline.

Chapter 3: Mark Bickhard elaborates his argument that normativity is intrinsic to any developmental process. In human development, normativity is not a mono-track affair, but is instead operative on multiple tracks at different, hierarchically related levels. His model is sophisticated and shown to be amenable to subtle analysis. Its main principle is that normativity is operative in and intrinsic to agency with the key properties of being self-maintenant, recursive and emergent. Triggered by what an agent finds in the environment, new actions amount to conditional indicative relations of interactive potentiality. As such, these actions are essentially interactive with modal and normative properties. They are non-reducible to causal regularities. Under this argument, action is not under the causal outcome of representations and the like 'in the mind'. Rather, normative direction in what is done is itself an interactive process of change that can amount to amelioration and novelty. This argument generalizes to cover the key aspects of human development such as learning, motivation, emotion and value. Crucially, it has the clear implication that a process devoid of normativity is simply non-developmental. This implication undermines most accounts of human development in the twentieth century.

Chapter 4: Richard Kitchener focuses on a recent revolution in philosophy concomitant to the cognitive revolution in psychology, namely naturalistic epistemology. A naturalistic epistemology has to confront a dilemma. As a naturalistic discipline, the epistemology will be committed to the methods of science; as an epistemology, this science will be committed to the analysis and justification of normativity. The dilemma is how to combine both in one account. His conclusion is that Piaget's model provides the basis of the resolution of this dilemma. Under this interpretation, Piaget's model is a mediating position that deals with the emergence of norms from facts. In turn, emergence is interpreted as a relation of supervenience. On this view, the meaning and function of norms is both to make possible and to develop cooperation between individuals in a social group, for example in formulating directives and then making commitments to them about how information can, should or should not be acquired and transmitted.

Chapter 5: Leslie Smith revisits the argument that DP interpreted as an exclusively causal science of human development is deeply flawed. His argument is in two steps: a negative analysis exposing the flaw and a positive identification of a better rationale for DP. The negative argument concerns why psychology cannot be a causal science just like physics. Its main principle is that Frege's critique of psychologism was sound in its own terms in two respects. One is that causality and normativity could not be the same thing. The other is that, even so, the joint focus on both in one model is not excluded. Piaget's developmental epistemology is just such a model, and this leads to the positive argument. Piaget's model is interpreted as a unitary model directed on both causes and norms. Four principles are presented, dealing with dual access to norms, the use and consciousness of norms, multiple norms manifest in dilemmas, and normative reasoning as modal reasoning. This model is also empirical, amounting to a psychology of development as normative facts. Further, this model is empirically investigable, and is shown to stand up to evaluative scrutiny using currently available evidence.

Part II   Norms in moral and social development

Chapter 6: Lutz Eckensberger elaborates in detail a perspective based on action theory with a specific focus on the relation between norms and facts. This perspective is presented with insight and analytical care. Under this analysis, intentional actions have goals that entail standards, i.e. norms, while actions have outcomes, i.e. factual effects. As well, this perspective is resolutely empirical with evidence arising from a major project in which the norms in moral judgments were displayed in decontextualized dilemmas, fictitious dilemmas and biographical interviews. Their factual use was investigated by means of different methods at several levels. Some were epistemic covering knowledge of context and information-seeking, while others were affective in dealing with coping and defence strategies related to the individual's self-concept. His interpretation of the findings shows that although moral judgments are never based on 'pure structure', that is on norms alone, levels of moral reasoning do influence the interpretation of these facts.

Chapter 7: Monika Keller addresses a core issue in normative development, namely the interplay between universality on the one hand, and individual or cultural differences on the other. Her position has its basis in action theory directed on a central distinction between reasoning about moral obligations and interpersonal responsibilities by children and adolescents in Iceland and China. In turn, reasoning was investigated through the consequences of norm violations, notably with regard to moral emotions, and about decision-making in an everyday moral conflict situation. Under this argument, an empirical check

is required between the universality of norms and their use both longitudinally and cross-culturally. The findings are extensive. They include
cultural similarities in the developmental sequences of the concepts of
social and moral reasoning, and cultural differences between children
concerning the role of self-interest, interpersonal responsibilities and
moral feelings. An interesting interaction was the culturally specific
interpretation of close friendship relationships that were themselves constrained by trends in modernization. Since this trend had become manifest in a short time-span, interesting conclusions emerge as to the jointly
universal and yet socially dynamic aspects of normative development.

   Chapter 8: Elliot Turiel sets out his argument about norms in human
development with special reference to morality. Two main contentions
are evident. One is that human thinking in the moral domain includes
the understanding of norms. The other is that in the development of
children's understanding, norms are divided through domains in social
realms. Taken together, these principles are incompatible with accounts
seeking to reduce normative understanding to biological or social mechanisms. They also rule out any homogeneity such as a 'norm of norms' in
that norms are not and should not be applied consistently across situations. An engaging feature of this position about normativity is its direct
basis in the study of psychological development in children. Central
features of this study include influences due to a multiplicity of social
experiences; adjustments and coordinations in social decision-making;
individual reflection on social conditions and cultural practices; opposition and resistance to unfairness, including manifestations whereby one
norm is used to compensate for inequities arising from the application of
some other norm; and autonomous choices made both in the everyday
lives of people and in moments of high drama in human history.

Part III   Norms in cognitive development

Chapter 9: Peter Molenaar sets out a normative difference in contrasting
two positions in test-theory. One is the default position in psychometrics
where norms are defined at the level of populations. By contrast, norms
are defined at the level of individual persons in idiographic psychology,
interpreted in terms of time series analysis techniques with applications
to nonlinear and chaotic dynamics. His argument is twofold. His general
argument is that this contrast is itself a manifestation of the key tenet of
logical positivism, that reality comprises facts and non-facts, such that
science focuses on facts with the consequence that non-facts are non-
scientific. The objection to this tenet is that it is false. His particular
argument is the demolition of the default position in test-theory under

which a score is partitioned into the true score and measurement error. In turn, his argument runs, this partitioning requires that repeated measurements are independent without affecting the measurement of the person. But this is to assume that if an arbitrarily large number of people are measured once, all differences are equal. His preferred assumption is contrary to this, namely that if one person is measured repeatedly for an arbitrary number of times, heterogeneity is built into the test system. The key premise is that this preferred assumption permits there being a score true of the individual on the basis of the sequential dependence of scores of that individual. This argument has massive implications for psychological research on learning and development, hitherto largely based on the untenable assumption.

Chapter 10: Vittorio Girotto and Michel Gonzalez exploit a novel twist about the norms of chance. If there are rules of chance, they have always been in operation. Yet such rules are norms the human knowledge of which emerged only in the seventeenth century with the development of the probability calculus. Their empirical argument concerns the un-availability of this knowledge to two groups, namely young children and fourteenth-century adults. Evidence of successful mastery is reported in both groups. Their interpretation of this evidence is in terms of one version of the extensional competence view, that even though untutored individuals have not been taught the rules of the probability calculus, they have the capacity to make evaluations in conformity with these rules. Indeed, naive individuals appear to be able to infer the probability of an event by considering and enumerating the ways in which it may or it may not occur. There is an extensional equivalence between the norms of chance and these individuals' evaluations of chance. The key premise is that this equivalence turns on one and the same set of norms. Training in the rules of chance is excluded, and yet the intuitions of these two groups fit the norms. This success is either luck – a matter of chance! – or it is norm-based. Their argument in favour of the latter is incompatible with the position in evolutionary psychology, according to which reasoning about the chance of single events is dependent on training in the probability calculus.

Chapter 11: Henry Markovits has a particular concern with conditional reasoning, a paradigm case of normativity in the cognitive domain. Under his argument, conditional reasoning is well defined in terms of logical norms, while children's development is itself normative in being directed on the formation of better levels of reasoning. Complementary to these normative claims is the appeal to causal mechanisms invoked in cognitive psychology. His position is contrasted with alternatives that rely either on non-normative heuristics with an evolutionary rationale;

or on the study of individual differences dealing with the improvement of available abilities rather than the development of new ones; or on slimmed-down versions of mental models theory. His preferred alternative has two main parts. One consists in reflective abstractions in a Piagetian sense in that older children are enabled to construct internal representations of action structures that reflect some key underlying properties of these actions. The other is based on their manipulation, achieved by retrieval efficiency directed on the generation of alternatives to the antecedent in a conditional, and by the capacity to inhibit information about the actual world notably in fantasy contexts. His conclusion is that norms in formal logic represent basic structural properties of the real world that are gradually reconstructed at more abstract levels by the workings of the basic processes of the mind.

Summary

Our book deals with fundamental questions about normativity in human development and normativity:

  i. *developmental psychology and normativity*: can an empirical science of human development deal with normativity?
 ii. *evidence-base*: is this augmented or diminished when normativity is taken into account?
iii. *psychological theory*: does the combination of causality and normativity provide a degenerative or productive problem-shift?

Our short answers proposed to these questions are:

  i. yes – there could be no human development without normativity
 ii. yes – the evidence-base is augmented
iii. yes – the problem-shift is productive with important work still to be done

We make no claim that our answers are the last word. But in our view, they are distinctive answers on both theoretical and empirical grounds.

Part I

Norms and development in epistemology

2 The implicit normativity of developmental psychology

Jacques Vonèche

Introduction

Any developmental psychology is necessarily normative, because it deals, in one way or another, with perfection and perfectibility. The importance of this principle has been lost in the default position taken in developmental psychology in the twentieth century.

Development as mere passage of time

In the most objectivistic and empiricistic view of development, development is merely the measure of change over time. But even in such a simplistic conception of development, not any change qualifies for development. To be developmental a change has to improve something over the previous state of affairs or, negatively, to regress from the previous state to qualify as a regression. Thus, the idea of progression (be it regression or progress) is necessarily associated with the concept of development. The trouble with this view of development is that it confuses progress with recency, since the passage of time is the only factor of development. Hence, the later the better. This mechanical approach presents an epistemologically dangerous consequence for empiricism. If progress is due to the work of the clock, then the end of history, or the end of the world or even the end of evolution will happen in a world close to perfection, if not already perfect. The ultimate hour will be the accomplishment of a mechanical form of eschatology: in a way, a secularized version of the second coming of Christ for the last judgment. Perfection and time are one. Perfection happens to be a mere incrementation similar to the augmentation of a bank account that increases with the passage of time. But if development is identified with anything that changes with time, then, since everything changes more or less with time, everything is developmental in nature – which is inane. Because of this inanity, psychologists of the strictly mechanical obedience have decided to deny any value to change by reducing any apparent

change to a mere semblance, reality being made out of endless external arrangements and rearrangements of homogeneous and featureless
elements, excluding, by the same token, development and novelty from
the realm of reality.

In this context, it will be instructive to take stock of the philosophical
heritage.

The philosophical heritage

Development as logos

At the other extreme of the range of epistemological positions is the
'eschatological–perfectibilistic' philosophy of Hegel, according to which,
through a continuous dialectical process of thesis, antithesis and synthesis, ceaselessly repeating itself, reason progresses necessarily towards its
end-state of domination over the world. This view has inspired the
genetic–rationalistic approach in developmental psychology. But this
current of thought has a long history that needs to be told here to
understand its scope.

Mind, transcendence and reality according to Plato

This tradition can be traced back to Plato. For Plato as well as for
Aristotle (or even Pythagoras before them) the mind is transcendent,
because it strikes eternity, divinity and other immutable entities making
truth the coincidence between eternal reality and mind via the Ideas,
thus setting the mind above the rest of the actual world which is ever
changing, transient in its total caducity. Truth is an absolute norm
for Plato in the same way that the distinction between Good and Evil
is an absolute commandment for the author of the Hebrew Genesis.

In both cases, this is accomplished by a logical displacement from
the object aimed by thought to the thought aiming at it and its agent,
the mind. By this process, the very art of thinking opens a horizon
of transcendence in an immanent universe. This general view is further
elaborated by Plato in his theory of the eternity of the mind as a
hierarchical structure similar to Freud's distinction among id, ego and
superego, since, at the level of the id, Plato places pathos (παθος)
governed by a sort of pleasure principle; at the level of the ego he places
thumoeides (θυμοιεδες) or personal emotions; and he places reason
(λογος) at the superior level. Psychological pathology is supposed to
stem out of an imbalance among these three structures. Moreover, the
higher levels of functioning are irreducible to lower ones and knowledge

is the result of an active process from the part of the mind as evidenced in Plato's theory of anamnesis. This theory constitutes a formal rejection, at the methodological level, of inductivism in its simplest form that assumes that theoretical concepts are achieved by the mere examination of their concrete instances or direct abstraction. The theory also means that hypotheses to account for or explain phenomena cannot be on the same level as the phenomena to be explained or accounted for by the hypotheses set forth, because this would amount to selecting (on what basis?) one element of a totality and endowing it with a special ontological status (reality, for instance) and seeking to show that it generates all the others.

This methodology has been typical of behaviourism, but it is also used in other domains of social sciences to stigmatize as ideological, epiphenomenal appearances those behaviours that are far from irreproachable in the investigator's eyes.

Aristotle, mind, genesis, epigenesis and categories

Aristotle was one of the first thinkers to emphasize that understanding past history could cast some light on the present situation and predict the future (Russell, 1946). He made genesis the central category of his way of thinking. He distinguished development from growth by calling growth continuous, and quantitative changes and development (γενεσις) those that are discontinuous and qualitative. He introduced the notion of epigenesis to account for the relations between an organism and its environment and for the emergence of novel structures and modes of operation in the course of development. He was also one of the first to insist on individuation, differentiation and self-actualization as the marks of developmental progression. He suggested as well that all existing forms could be ordered hierarchically from the lowest and most inferior ones to the highest and most advanced. Moreover, he was one of the proponents of the idea of a comparative developmental analysis when he showed that less advanced stages of development in more advanced organisms could be usefully compared to more advanced stages in less advanced organisms. He was the first philosopher to consider that human beings are composed of different levels of organization among which the highest were irreducible to inferior ones. He conceived of the mind not as separate and distinct from the body but as embodied in it as the principle governing motility, sensitivity and understanding ('vegetal', 'animal' and 'rational', 'soul') which is strikingly close to the modern views of phenomenology and Piaget.

Methodologically, Aristotle insisted upon the over-determination of behaviour which led him to distinguish different forms of causality and between causality and reason. He opposed, for the first time, 'physical' and 'dialectical' explanations. He considered as physical an explanation of anger either in terms of a hot substance around the heart or as caused by the boiling of blood. A dialectical explanation of anger would be the desire to render suffering for suffering. The same distinction can be made for an object: a house could be considered as a shelter (dialectical explanation) or as a mass of bricks, stones and wood (physical explanation). He also advocated the temporal priority of wholes over parts and of the organisms (unities) over their components. Similarly, he argued against those who believed that they could account for the functioning of concrete organisms by way of the factors in which these unities could be analysed, thus indicating the superiority of dialectical explanations over physical ones and, by way of consequence, of abstract models over physiological ones.

But his teleology led him to consider that all is well in the universe considered as a wonderful success story, complemented as it was by his science of genera according to which when a stone falls, it reaches the 'natural place' of all stones and thereby realizes the essence of the genus 'stone'. Note how close this is to socio-biology, vitalism and Piaget's early (Bergsonian) ideas about a clear distinction between geometrical order or dead order (laws) and biological order (genera) which transmits the vital impetus, the motor of evolution that will lead the organism towards its end-point, goal or τελος. This vital impetus is power (ἐνεργεια) versus act and thus form versus matter. Once again, notice the similarity with Piaget's opposition between form and content and his emphasis upon formal causes under the guise of implications.

Aristotle's other major methodological contribution that greatly influenced Linnaeus, Cuvier, Darwin, Freud and Piaget, was the introduction of the comparative method in science as exemplified in D'Arcy Thompson's book *On growth and form* (1942) and von Wright's *Practical reason* (1983).

Descartes and the mind–body separation

Descartes introduced the idea that mind and body were radically different and that there was a parallelism between the two entities. The body is material and, as such, because of the equality between cause and effect, it cannot create the mind, since it is inferior to the mind.

This view led him to a form of dualism that will be reflected in psychology in what is known, among psychologists and epistemologists, as the psychophysical parallelism in which the series of mental events co-occur with the series of physical events in one-to-one correspondence.

Monists reject Descartes's position on the ground that the mind is itself matter or, at least, stems out of matter. But this argument rests entirely on the assumption that the mind is located in the brain and that the brain is a bodily structure exclusively.

The argument does not hold any water for the dualists, because 1) the locus of mind is not necessarily the brain: it could be argued, for instance, that culture or society is the locus of mind; 2) even if we agreed with the view that the brain is the locus of mind this would be what the French call 'une vue de l'esprit', i.e. materialism is a product of the workings of the mind and, thus, we are back to Plato and Aristotle: should not the products of our refined analyses be considered as the real thing or the original state of affairs?

Locke and Leibniz: growth by contiguity or by mere unfolding

In modern times, the opposition to the Aristotelian view of development as genesis and epigenesis and of explanation as dialectical and physical reached its culmination in the work of John Locke whose position was a strict return to the views developed in the introduction to this chapter: development as strict function of time. Locke was essential and instrumental in promulgating the dogma of Time as the mother of Progress and Perfection, because he was the one to relegate the ancient categories of substance, quality and finality to the limbo of mentalism and to consider any form of complexity and organization as merely epiphenomenal. With Locke, everything is the result of the association of simple elements, the atoms of mental life, according to a principle of temporal contiguity and spatial proximity. These elements in themselves are not modified by the association, they remain stable and identical to themselves. Development becomes a purely incremental juxtaposition of these elements. Thus, growth and development are confused with evolution, history and progress. The mind becomes a pure snowdrift of impressions or stimulations agglutinated by chance in a mechanical way, so much so that any mental activity becomes the blind interplay of external forces with the sorry consequence that any theory (including his own) is the accidental collocation of ideas making thinking a vacuous occupation.

In sharp contrast to British empiricism and French mechanicism, the Germans swung the pendulum in the opposite direction. Leibniz is the paramount example of this change of ideas. Where Locke considered the organism as passive and deprived of subjectivity, Leibniz put all the emphasis upon activity and subjectivity. Because of that, Leibniz conceived development as a theological process inherent in the nature of organism considered, as I noted above, as a centre of dynamic activity. In opposition to empiricism for which the mind is totally under the control of what contemporary Anglo-Saxon psychology calls 'stimulus variable', Leibniz asserted that nothing could be in the mind without having already been in the senses except mind itself ('nihil in intellectu quod non prior in sensu nisi intellectus ipse'), which means that all thoughts and actions come from the inner depths of our soul and are not given by the senses. This Latin dictum due to Leibniz was one of Piaget's favourites, because it was very much in line with his own views expressed in different places, but, first of all, in *La naissance de l'intelligence* (1936), in his theory of assimilation. Even Leibniz's famous monadology contributes to a developmental view of cognition and cognitive development. Monads form a 'great chain of beings', to use A. Lovejoy's phrase (1936), not only in the form of Russian dolls called *matrioshka*, embedded in one another in such a way that they form a hierarchy of sizes, but also, and more accurately, like a mirror reflecting a mirror reflecting a scene, or even more precisely like a pool containing little fish in which each fish would contain a pool containing little fish, containing, etc. *ad infinitum* (hence infinitesimal calculus). The living things analogy retains something of the internal dynamic of monadology that the mechanical mirror does not contain.

This succession of monads each reflecting the multiplicity and totality from its own vantage point, i.e. its own developmental stage, can be understood analogically as a landscape as seen variously by a painter, a roamer, a botanist, a geometer or a squire. In this sense, it is the prefiguration of developmental constructivism in psychology. The landscape is in the eye of the beholder. The world is constructed from these differences (hence differential calculus) or multiplicity and their integration (hence integral calculus) into unity. This indeed comes very close to the process of differentiation and integration as an ordering principle of development in Heinz Werner's organismic-developmental theory.

Thus, in a way, Spinoza is Leibniz's only opponent, radically, because Spinoza's philosophy posits that the monad is unique and that substance is one. Consequently, there is no possible interplay between unity and multiplicity, space and matter, mind and body or mechanism and finalism, because Spinoza postulates a complete *coincidence overlapping* between mind and substance, extension and thinking, God and nature which is his psychophysical parallelism. Nowadays, A. Damasio advocates a similar position in his *Looking for Spinoza* (2003). This parallelism is the opposite of Descartes's, because, when Descartes postulated a mere compatibility between matter and mind, Spinoza postulates that both are the two sides of the same coin, the pantheistic manifestation of the eternal divine necessity. Therefore, time becomes the mere medium for the unfolding of this eternal necessity. There is no real nor actual development. No evolution. We are here in a gallery of reflecting mirrors. Hence the influence of Spinoza upon people like N. Chomsky, on the one hand, and Soviet psychology (particularly L. Vygotsky) on the other, because both are victims of the same form of epistemological communism, although they express it in different forms. For Chomsky, it is the invariant structure of the brain. For Soviet psychology as a whole, the locus of mind is society. But the difference is simply due to the difference in contents between the American society, basking in a Protestant ideology of individualism (hence the emphasis on the individual brain), and the Russian one nurtured by the Orthodox tradition for which notions such as communion, community and chorus are central.

By opposition to this, one can see in the developmental psychologies of A. Gesell and D. Rappaport (ego psychology) some after-effects of Leibniz's monadology.

Kant and the epistemological question

As everyone knows, Kant refused to choose between empiricism and rationalism. He could accept neither the reliance upon representations that characterizes empiricism nor the rationalist's assumption that scientific knowledge stems out of innate ideas. Since, contrary to Chomsky or Fodor, he distinguished innate from a priori, he was much more concerned with a slightly different idea but with a similar epistemological scope, that of the relationship between 'thoughts and things', to put it in James Mark Baldwin's famous phrasing of the question. Such a question is interesting in two ways: on the one hand, it does pose the givenness of things at first; on the other hand, it asks the condition for the possibility of knowledge. How can human beings reach valid objective knowledge? This is a reformulation of Aquinas's old question about intelligence: 'adequatio rei et intellectu', the act of adequating things to the intellect.

Kant's answer to this question is well known: on the one hand, the senses provide sensations, i.e. representations; on the other, the intellect provides the categories into which these sensations will take shape. Contents of thoughts are empirical, i.e. given through experience. Forms of intuition are provided by the structure of the mind. This means, at first inspection, a middle-of-the-road solution, a synthesis between empiricism and rationalism. But one should observe that there is here a strong rejection of empiricism by a refusal of psychology. As Kant writes in his *Logik* (1800), resorting to psychology would be

as absurd as drawing ethics from life. The question is not about contingent rules (how we think) but about necessary rules that are to be drawn from the necessary use of understanding that one finds in oneself without any psychology . . . Everything in nature happens according to rules . . . for instance exercising our faculties: such as understanding . . . Understanding is the source for rules in general for thinking. The question is how does understanding proceed to think, which are the rules applied in this process. We cannot think and use our understanding otherwise than according to certain rules.

(Kant, 1972, pp. 332, 334)

Such a view anticipates those of Claparède, Piaget and Popper as well as a good deal of the German psychology of *Regelbewusstsein* (rule awareness), although Kant denied any role to psychology as a scientific form of knowledge in the process. Nevertheless his emphasis on the rule-making activity of the mind in every realm of human action from sensory-motor to post-formal constitutes a rampart against any form of empiristic epistemology in its triple form: a copy-theory of perception in which our sensations mirror the state of the world, an objectivist theory of conception for which abstraction is a direct extraction of certain objective features from the environment and a labelling theory of language by which sounds become words by mere contiguity reinforcement between sounds (names) and objects.

This last approach remains dominant in contemporary psychology which ignores superbly Kant's dictum that there is no such thing as 'immaculate perception' or any truth external to human experience. It is this experience that creates the binomial solidarity between objects and subjects as well as their mutual opposition by means of instruments linking the two together, that is the various forms of knowing that E. Cassirer (1953, 1955, 1957) called 'symbolic forms' and more recently H. Maturana and F. Varela (1980) 'autopoiesis'.

One recognizes here the influence of Giambattista Vico upon Kant's approach in at least three different aspects: 1) the human mind reveals itself in human artefacts; 2) there is a circle of sciences going from logico-mathematical ones considered as the most subjective to biological considered as the most objective (here, of course, the similarity with Piaget is extreme, although Piaget claimed he did not know Vico's oeuvre); 3) there is a developmental sequence in the history and prehistory of mankind.

At this point, the role of J. Herder should also be recognized. Because he worked out his ideas under the influence of Giambattista Vico, Herder, meditating upon the relationships between history and the mentality of the people, came to the conclusion that history is at least one (if not the foremost) form of the actualization of the development of the human mind. In this sense, he influenced G. F. Hegel, J. W. Goethe, E. Durkheim, E. Cassirer and G. H. Mead, all of whom considered that it was the socio-cultural reality that shaped *logically* individual minds, that it is our participation in our civilization that makes us human.

The corollary of their view is indeed that every society and every stage of every society should be considered in itself and for itself independently of any 'must'. This is, in effect, normativity turned against itself in a way, similar to the 1968 slogan on the walls of the Sorbonne: 'it is forbidden to forbid'.

Outside the German-speaking countries, it is rarely mentioned that Goethe had a complete theory of development. This theory was romanticist indeed. It is the opposite of the 'crude English way' (C. Darwin). This is no mechanical descent by elimination of the unfit and survival of the fittest in a gigantic Skinner box enlarged to the dimensions of the universe where we are only trying to depress the right pedal and gain the correct schedule of reinforcement for survival or anything that resembles it.

On offer instead is a view of genesis according to which development is a series of metamorphoses of a primitive original Form (or *Urform*) that gets transformed in all logical ways from the central archetype by constant reconstruction of its structuro-functional plan. Those metamorphoses are basically of two sorts, progressive (true development) or regressive (pathology). Here, the resemblance with Chomsky's generative transformational grammar is as evident as its similarity to Freud's idea of pathology as normality writ large.

Hegel presents a doctrine of evolution and development based on the antithesis between spiritual forces and the world. In this view, the beginning of the world starts with the most extreme alienation of the mind (*Geist*) from itself. Thus there is a kinetic law that can be drawn from this: history is the story of the recovery of the mind. We are faced here with a sort of manicheist perspective in which, via a dialectical mechanism of thesis, antithesis and synthesis infinitely repeating itself along the course of time, the mind regains itself through history to end up in the apotheosis of Reason and Freedom in the end of times. Truly, then, 'the history of the world is the world court' ('Die Weltgeschichte ist das Weltgericht'). This double confusion of time and perfection, and of perfection and reason, is indeed problematic. But, in addition, implicit in this view is the claim that history is progress and that every form of evolution is necessarily progressive. The granting of an eschatological perspective to the history of the universe denies the fact that some historical changes are regressive and not only during a brief dialectical moment, alas. Evolving can be revolving and even revolting. Moreover, this supposes also a criterion of truth that is adaptive in a quasi biological sense. Unfortunately such a criterion, if followed through consistently, leads to Thrasymachos' dictum that 'justice is the interest of the stronger'.

Faced with this ultimate consequence of Hegel's dialectics, K. Marx and the so-called Young Hegelians tried to put Hegel back on his feet, that is, as we all know, to ensure that justice would protect the interest of the weaker. And we know also the dramatic failure this was. All these systems failed because they were based on a success story of their ontology. This is the sorry conclusion of this historical survey. Does that mean that, thanks to the Vienna circle and/or British analytical philosophy which never had any metaphysical temptation, we have, at last, become intelligent and that the great metaphysicians of the past were all fools? I do not think so at all! On the contrary, from the narrow point of view which is ours here, they all contributed to the creation of a strong and vivid trend in developmental psychology, that of genetic rationalism which constitutes the yardstick on which to measure any development in developmental psychology, as we shall now see.

The biological heritage

Besides a philosophical heritage, there is, in developmental psychology, a biological, evolutionist tradition that deserves to be contemplated for its epistemological and methodological consequences.

Darwin and Darwinism

Darwin is at the origin of developmental psychology in two ways. First, as an original contributor to the domain with his papers on the origins of emotion and on 'A portrait of a baby'. Second, as the father of his own brand of transformism that influenced so dramatically the fathers of developmental psychology: G. Stanley Hall, J. M. Baldwin, W. James, G. Romanes and E. Claparède. It needed a Piaget to question Darwin's views on evolution and he was rather lonely in his advocacy of phenocopy or genetic assimilation, although he had the good company of Baldwin and Waddington.

The general function of all these evolutionary epistemologies is the naturalization of the logic of development. Grading mental activity, hierarchizing the various and sundry forms of cognition, is no longer a production of the mind of the beholder, it is truly and really read directly in the great book of Nature. Evidence for this is the fact that grading the order of living entities in terms of their approximation to an ideal standard is now doubled by their temporal order, with the corollary that the later is the better. Recency is fused with efficiency in a very mechanical way towards Perfection as illustrated in this passage from Darwin's *On the origin of species*:

As all the living forms of life are the lineal descendants of those which lived long before the Cambrian epoch, we may feel certain that the ordinary succession by generation, has never once been broken, and that no cataclysm has desolated the whole world. Hence we may look with some confidence to a secure future of great length. And as natural selection works solely by and for the good of each being, all corporeal and mental endowments will tend to progress toward perfection.   (Darwin, 1859, p. 373)

This text is interesting in many different ways. First, it is typical of the nineteenth century's faith in progress. Second, it explicitly mentions the ideal of perfection as the goal of natural selection. Third, the last sentence of Darwin's text above illustrates the Aristotelian origins of his philosophy: remember that Darwin considered Linnaeus and Cuvier as his 'two gods' but as 'mere school-boys to old Aristotle'. Fourth, the mechanicism in the march towards perfection is evident, because this march requires no missing link, no jump, no saltus ('Natura non fecit saltus') in the transmission from one generation to the next. Fifth, the process is totally determined in spite of its using randomness at one point in the course of evolution. Sixth, it supposes a complete invariance in the goals of evolution from the beginning of times up to now, or more exactly up to Darwin's times. What should have drawn the attention, here, is the fact that Evolution, from its origin on, shared the views of nineteenth-century scientists about perfection and progress, which is as naive as it is megalomaniac. More interesting than anything else in evolution is the naturalization process. By making evolution mechanical, Darwin provides a solid foundation for his theory. Once something becomes a natural fact, there is no other way around it. Such is the way things are, as a matter of fact. Normative concepts become natural facts. Two examples in point can be given here: race and maturity. The concept of human races has served (for centuries now) as a warrant for existing social practices: Jews are (too) clever, they should be curbed to give hard-working, honest Aryans a chance; black Africans have small brains, they are just good enough for menial jobs, etc. By naturalization, the reversal of the causation process is allowed. It is no longer the need for cheap labour that excludes black Africans from climbing the social ladder, it is their natural make-up. It has nothing to do with social organization; it is an indisputable fact, not a prejudice.

With the concept of maturity, things are slightly different. The legitimation process works at a different level: it serves to conflate the lawfulness of phenomena with their organic properties. In agriculture, maturity means that a vegetable or fruit is ripe. In social sciences, maturity is the reverse of immaturity and immaturity is a stigma, whereas maturity means a form of behaviour that is irreproachable in the investigator's eyes. Thus the concept of maturity serves more as a pointer to control individuals and groups than as an explanatory principle. The detour through biology serves to mask the distinction between the ideal norms postulated by the concept of maturity and direct observation of facts. Maturity is an 'observable' directly read in the great book of Nature and not an ideal standard, the final norm of a process of development. It becomes at the same time a property of the growing organism and a guiding principle external to the organism itself. Pushed to its limits, it means that universals are phylogenetically determined: phylogeny becomes the logic of development. In this way, it became possible to enter the great tautological circle of Darwinism about the survival of the fittest. Who survives? The fittest! Who is the fittest? The survivor! Thus, the table was laid for logical positivism and its only true statements, because the law of development was, at the same time, the object of observation (immanence) and the τελος or final norm (transcendence). Description and prescription are fused. Hence, a cumulative model of development emerges from this blurring method of using concepts. Development is considered as a sort of Mendeleev table of elements (structuralism) in which new species or new ideas come to occupy one cell of the systematic table at random or, at least, in an unspecified order. Hence, the identification of two guiding principles: indeterminacy accounting for the fortuitous nature of novelty and pre-adaptation because, by rule, there is necessarily a cell ready for each novelty in the system.

Psychologists followed suit on this. We will limit ourselves here to developmental ones and take three examples: G. Stanley Hall, J. M. Baldwin and W. James. G. Stanley Hall took the Haeckelian principle that ontogeny recapitulates phylogeny literally, and considered, for instance, that when children were playing with matches they reinvented fire for their own sake. This naive view of development was quickly discarded in that very direct form but was rapidly adapted under different forms such as collective unconscious, atavism, empire of the genes over behaviour, etc. What is important to remember from Hall is that developmental psychology is the embryology of behaviour and as such becomes an objective science.

William James took seriously Thomas Huxley's (1881) statement that 'the struggle for existence holds as much in the intellectual as in the physical world. A theory is a species of thinking, and its right to exist is coextensive with its power of resisting extinction by its rivals.'

James conceptualized spontaneous variations as some sorts of metamorphoses of the same original form or species. These transformations observe more or less a certain scale of beings similar to Mendeleev's table. Thus, the production of new emotions, ideas or thoughts and feelings happens at random. They are preserved by natural selection. Natural selection, by creating links and bounds among things, put some order (causal, substantive or logical) in the world. Those bounds and links that make the universe deducible (essentially logic and mathematics) are then preserved because they are verified empirically: 'the things of Nature turn out to act as if they *were* of the kind assumed' (James, 1890, vol. II, p. 688, his emphasis).

James's position can be summarized in a nutshell: there is no irreducible element of sense-data as in empiricism, no subjectively guaranteed certainty as in the Cartesian cogito, nor Kantian transcendental deduction of epistemological a priori, no dialectics of opposite as in Hegel or Marx, there is only a ballet of variations caused by chance and preserved by natural and sexual selection. Back to Democritus: 'everything in the world is the product of chance and necessity' (Liard, 1873).

With J. M. Baldwin, things look a bit different, because he was, at the same time, closer to biology than most psychologists via his theory of genetic assimilation anticipating Waddington's and Piaget's phenocopy and further away from strictly biological adaptation by his theory of genetic epistemology.

The phrase 'genetic epistemology' was coined, in 1906, by James Mark Baldwin in his famous book: *Thoughts and things or genetic logic* (Baldwin, 1906, 1908, 1911). For Baldwin, genetic epistemology 'concerns itself with the implications of reality at each of the greater stages of conscious process, from the most primitive to the most derived' (Baldwin, 1911, vol. III, p. 16). Epistemology, for Baldwin, is equivalent to 'instrumental logic' or the science of truth by the control of facts by opposition to 'axiology' or the science of value or worth covering the whole range of 'normative' disciplines. This dichotomy is founded on the fundamental distinction between the two possible controls (according to Baldwin) mediated in the thought content. If the control of fact, then we have epistemology. If the control of the inner sort, then we have axiology, that is to say 'the relative selection and utilization of facts through the mediation of the thought system as means' (Baldwin, 1908, vol. II, p. 383).

What is essential here is what Baldwin called 'genetic modes' according to which nature presents 'genetic series', which are movements of progressive change that are qualitative, irreversible and non-mechanical. These genetic series constantly place in evidence the rise of new and progressive 'genetic modes' or sorts of organization which are each for itself novel, *sui generis* and creative.

'In passing from one genetic mode to another, nature achieves a real evolution; there is an actual production of novelties' (Baldwin, 1911, vol. III, p. 258). The logic of this general movement is stated in the 'axioms' of genetic sciences (Baldwin, 1902) and is interpreted for the movement of mental process in the 'canons of genetic logic' (Baldwin, 1906, vol. I, ch. 1). This movement is externally guided in accordance with the Darwinian principle of natural selection.

The concept of genetic epistemology was not Baldwin's exclusive property. One might mention from Germany, W. Wundt (1880), C. Sigwart (1894–5) and E. Cassirer (1903–20). In the Anglo-Saxon tradition, there were B. Bosanquet (1888) and L. T. Hobhouse (1888, 1912).

Thus, the tacit procedural assumption that 'genetic epistemology' is, or ought to be, identified with Piaget's specific undertaking constitutes a total misapprehension of the domain. On the contrary, the concept of 'genetic epistemology' should be disembarrassed from the unhappy fusion it has undergone, in recent times, with Piaget's specific attempt to orient that discipline along certain lines.

The goal of epistemology is to provide a theory of knowledge in whatever form it occurs. This aim has traditionally been conceived as a matter of logic rather than psychology, of abstract norms rather than concrete facts, as a normative discipline, regulative of inquiry, rather than a positive discipline shaped by the results of empirical investigation. But the demarcation of epistemology from empirical inquiry involves a decision and not a description of 'the way things are'. This decision is not regulated simply by the character of the concept to be defined, but depends also on the soundness of the interest it is designed to serve, so that the proceeding is partly normative. On the other hand, between the conception and the creation of such a logic falls the shadow of a presupposed psychology, because every epistemology is shaped by underlying conceptions of the mind and conduct of which cognition is a product.

This dual characteristic of thinking as both a process and a product was clearly understood by Baldwin and by most of the early genetic epistemologists. Hence, the recurrence in Baldwin's writings of such reversals of terms as 'worths as thoughts' and 'thoughts as worths'. This passage from facts to norms and vice versa is indeed central to any epistemology and especially to genetic epistemologists who agree in recognizing that any form of knowledge is triple: 1) a social system; 2) a group of psychological behaviours; and 3) a system *sui generis* of signs and cognitive activities. But they do not all agree on Piaget's solutions to these two main issues: the relationship of facts to norms cleverly eschewed as 'normative facts' ('faits normatifs') of the consideration of science as the form of knowledge *par excellence*. Cassirer, for instance, would consider Piaget's emphasis upon the scientific forms of knowledge as extremely limitative, and Baldwin as simply preposterous. The 'fusion' of norms and facts under the heading of 'normative facts' would be considered as muddy by most of the genetic epistemologists mentioned here.

The posterity of these diverse evolutionary epistemologies has been as different as possible. Out of Hall's position came most of the nativistic psychologists of development starting with A. Gesell. From James, Claparède got his idea of the needs of the infant and the interests of the child which was very much in line with pragmatism and its conception of truth as the interest of the species or the individual. Piaget is definitely, in spite of strong differences, a spiritual son of Baldwin. They share the central idea of a genetic logic.

In spite of their differences, all these views have in common a solution to the problem of the adaptation. They all deal with the old problem of the 'adequatio rei et intellectu' in which Aquinas saw intelligence and of which James gave the best contemporary expression. Indeed how does the mind fit reality, how are things and thoughts related with each other, to speak the language of Baldwin? How are our actions successful? Our feelings met by similar feelings in others? How can we decide and be right or wrong?

The monist's answer to these questions is too simple to be acceptable: it states that things and thoughts are somehow the same, i.e. thoughts are things in the end. But anyone's impression is nevertheless that things are out there and thoughts in here! There is a clear difference between the two. So one has to come back to the problem of their mutual agreement. When one looks at the problem from the angle of specific examples, one is always given the same examples: diamonds on the skin of pineapples and Fibonacci series or Einstein's relativity theory and Riemann's geometry. As one knows, starting from Euclid's axiom that 'from one point outside a straight line, one can draw one and only parallel', two mathematicians, N. Lobatchevsky (1792–1856) and B. Riemann (1826–66), drew two opposite axioms – Lobatchevsky: 'from one point outside a straight line, one can draw an infinity of parallels', and Riemann: 'from one point outside a straight line, one can draw no parallel at all'. Lobatchevsky's geometry is called hyperbolic and Riemann's elliptic. The first is used by psychologists to explain the nature of perceptual space in vision. The second was used by Einstein for his theory of relativity. Consequently, the so-called 'miraculous' coincidence between mathematical concepts and physical reality is not so miraculous. In fact, there are some mathematical games such as playing with axioms and seeing what comes out of it: Euclidean and non-Euclidean geometries and, among non-Euclidean ones, hyperbolic and elliptic. One fits one series of events, the other another, just as Euclidean geometry fits a third order of events. This has nothing to do with objectivity and reality for two sorts of reasons: one, because, in every instance, the geometry is somehow modified to fit the facts (Einstein 'geometrized' physics and 'physicized' geometry in his theory of relativity) and, two, because the fit is not in reality but in the mind of the thinker. This is the difference between thought and fact. Explaining something is representing in the mind something which is in reality. But this representation is not the duplication of what stands 'out there' at another level. As Virginia Woolf used to say about art representing reality: 'one of the damn things is more than enough!' British empiricists have made a lot of mere contiguity as the explanation of causation. Contiguity, proximity, etc. means nearness but near and far are relative to the observer. They are not out there. They are in the eyes of the beholder as shown in the example of Buffon's *Histoire naturelle* in which the portrait of the dog as an animal species follows that of the donkey 'because this is usually the case in our farms'. Contiguities are made in the mind. They are not observable, because they are a link, an implication, a relationship, a way of understanding, classifying, showing, selecting experience. As such, contiguities are normative. Consequently, the miraculous 'fit' between physics and geometry is neither a miracle of pre-adaptation, nor the outcome of the natural order of the universe (without expressing any opinion about the eternal, developmental or whatever nature of this universe, which would give rise to different epistemologies), it is simply the expression of rule-behaviour or *Regelbewusstsein*, as K. Popper called it in his doctoral dissertation (1928), that is to say looking for invariances or laws. So, even in the most empiristic notion of causality or in a physical theory like relativity inspired by the form of empiricism and determinism represented by E. Mach's epistemology, one finds the opposition between the law and the observable, the fact and the norm, the standard and the variable. Thus, once again, from the point of view of the biological origins of developmental psychology, the notion of a norm is, implicitly at least, present in the process and plays the most important role in explaining evolution.

The psychological paradox

In philosophy, as we have seen, the notion of development is presented in a sort of triumphalistic view of evolution synthetized in H. Bergson's book *L'évolution créatrice* (Creative evolution) in which the role of evolution is to bring about life and life in abundance (moral life even for human beings). History, evolution, progress are goal-directed and they *must* end up in a sort of apotheosis, be it the manifestation of Reason, the second coming of Christ or simply the Messiah at the end of times.

In the biological perspective, the situation is about the same. But there is one important difference: norms are no longer postulated, they are no longer an ideal, there is a fusion between facts and norms.

In a certain way, norms become observable because the law of development is more or less mechanically immanent to the object of observation and, as such, directly readable in the book of Nature. The norms are, at the same time, a propriety of the organisms *and* a guiding principle. This logical paradox will stand at the core of development psychology as it develops at the turn of the twentieth century as we shall now see. In addition, psychology developed as an independent science at a historical moment: the invasion of the rest of the world by bands of white men coming from Europe who felt that their duty was to colonize the rest of the world. This event happened to be significant for the way in which developmental psychology was going to conceptualize its normativity. With the spreading of the (British, French, Portuguese) Empire, the contact with other cultures and civilizations was posing a problem. In order to be an Empire, it was the Empire's burden to impose its value-system on the rest of the world, but, as a matter of fact the Empire was not facing a vacuum. There was something out there, a pre-existing culture. Faced with such a situation, the Portuguese discoverer of the Congo river, Diego Cão (fifteenth century), reacted by attributing to the various Bakongo tribes a social organization similar to that of Portugal with its kingdom (the kingdom of Congo) and its various princes, dukes, earls and barons. In his report, there is no mention of skin colour, for instance, as there is no imperialism in his covenants with the local authorities of the Congo. In the nineteenth century, after a considerable amount of discussion about the existence of a soul for the natives, it was decided that they had one but one more or less like that of women, that is of an inferior quality when compared to the soul of white men. What is relevant to the history of developmental psychology is the presence of a hierarchical order of souls replicating the order of species in Nature. Thus, there were developed civilizations and under-developed ones, the standard being indeed the Empire. On this order of mental development an indissociable trio was established: the savage, the woman and the child who were inferior. The women were inferior because they were juvenile men: high voices, no beard, emotional labil-ity, etc. They were, thus, child-like. The savages had not developed the advanced tools of Western civilization because their make-up was infer-ior. The children combined the disadvantages of women and savages, but, paradoxically, little white boys had the greatest potential of all three groups.

The very fact of linking the trio together resulted in a constant com-parison of the three among themselves and with the standard, generating an epistemological and methodological reflection upon development that was going to end up in the paradox of genetic-structuralism at the end of the twentieth century.

In the course of the twentieth century, behaviourism dominated de-velopmental psychology thanks to the propagation of J. B. Watson's ideas in all sorts of circles preoccupied with the welfare of children. Its only competition was A. Gesell's special form of nativism that did not run in the same direction as the general American Zeitgeist. The American mentality of the late nineteenth century and early twentieth century was cast in a mould that was action-oriented. It was the result of the large influence of a new migrant population upon the earlier population of the Americas. Hence, the discovery by G. S. Hall of a specific age that he called adolescence – that age between childhood and adulthood was typical of the 'anomie' (as E. Durkheim called it) caused by the passage from the rules of the old country to those of the new one for the youngster of the second generation.

The emphasis upon action and change was also characteristic of a new country where everything seems possible. Hence, the 'American dream'. To gain a better idea of the impact of such a mentality upon psychology, compare the image of the animal in German and American schools of psychology. In the United States, psychologists such as Thorndike, Hull, Watson or Skinner observe animals running through mazes, opening boxes, depressing pedals, etc., thus always active. German psychology draws a very different picture of the animal indeed. Consul, the famous chimpanzee studied by Köhler in Tenerife, does not run all the time locking and unlocking secret padlocks as Thorndike's famous chimp does. Consul, after a few trials and errors, sits still in the position of Rodin's 'thinker' and meditates on what to do next, which is have a brilliant insight. American chimps behave more like American humans and German chimps like Germans, as Bertrand Russell cunningly remarked killing two birds with one stone. Reality, not unlike beauty, lies in the eye of the beholder.

In a such a context, the mentality of the child had to obey the American ideology and conform to the American dream of the success story. Gesell's nativism did not fit this image. Consequently it lost ground except in early education where people like to think that there is not much to do anyway with very young children. They have to go through phases: the negative two-year-old, the terrible three-year-old, etc. Development's inexorable unfolding was running too much against the American mainstream. Hence, the success of behaviourism by virtue of which one could shape children to become what one wanted them to be, as fits 'a conquering, killing nation', to put it in Clifford Geertz's phrase (pers. com.).

In the fifties, this behaviouristic shaping reached a limit at the practical level and, at the same time, it was reaching a limit as an explanatory principle. Its reductionism, its antipathy to different domains of research considered as contaminated with mentalism and other mentally transmissible diseases became unbearable to many psychologists who rebelled and started the so-called 'cognitive revolution'. Ventures into the forbidden realm of thinking were again possible. The late H. E. Gruber was instrumental in this revolution in two ways: one, he visited Europe in the early fifties and met with Piaget in Geneva, two, he organized a symposium on cognition with such figures as J. Bruner, U. Neisser, G. Miller, etc. The timing was well chosen because, in 1952, Piaget had submitted to the Rockefeller Foundation (already closely associated with the Genevan School of Psychology) a proposal for support to create his future International Centre for Genetic Epistemology that had been received with great interest by the Foundation. In 1954, Bärbel Inhelder was offered by the Foundation a four-month tour of the USA in order to visit centres of excellence in child psychology and she was sad to discover that very little experimental research was being done there except for child-rearing practices and that the status of developmental psychology consequently was very low in journals such as the *Annual Review of Psychology*. So she became instrumental in the coalescence of a scientific community which would address the same set of issues with similar procedural tools used by most of the cognitive developmental psychologists, thanks to her presentation of the work in progress at the University of Geneva.

At about the same time, in France, C. Lévi-Strauss was working on his *Structural anthropology* (first published in 1958). F. de Saussure's structural linguistics was rediscovered and R. Jakobson had just published *Preliminaries to speech analysis* (1952). All these publications were confirming the return of structuralism in social sciences that was made easy by the additional factor that some of the American psychologists who contributed to the so-called cognitive revolution had been trained by German exiles of *Gestaltpsychologie* which was the first wave of structuralism hitting the USA in 1933–9. Moreover, there existed also a developmental variation upon *Gestalt* represented by the Austrian exile Heinz Werner at Clark University and his organismic-developmental theory.

This was also the period of decolonization with its interrogation about the 'white man's burden' and the place of non-Western cultures in the world of ideas. The outcome of this quandary was that each culture should be examined for itself, in itself and by itself. In addition, this was still the aftermath of the Shoah and its reflection upon civilization and barbarism with the outcome that there were limits to tolerance and that pure relativism, à la Frankfurt School, was impossible, or at least intolerable.

All these factors contributed to the paradox of developmental psychology, because there was, on the one hand, a structuralist stand to be taken: children, women and 'savages' should be treated for and in themselves, and, on the other hand, a developmental one: there are lower *and* higher mental structures, immature and mature behaviour, advances and retardation. Pure relativism was positively untenable: some changes are progressive, others regressive and some evolutions are revolting. Thus, there was a tension between genesis and structure that is at the core of the cognitive developmental revolution in psychology.

The stucturalist approach proposes a self-contained explanatory principle. When Ferdinand de Saussure finds the exact (ten) forms of pronouncing the letter A in Indo-European languages, the explanation is contained in the structure itself. The same is true for Lévi-Strauss's explanation of father/son relationships in Western and non-Western cultures: in Western cultures, father/son relations are stiff, severe, stern and tense, whereas avuncular ones are the opposite. In non-Western cultures, the same argument holds in reverse, the father/son relation is easy and relaxed, and the one with the maternal uncle is not.

Thus, there is one structure with four elements: the father, the mother, the son and the maternal uncle and two relations of which one is uptight and the other not. There is no need of any extra-systemic element in order to explain the phenomena to be explained. The system accounts entirely for itself. The limit of this stand was reached by Lévi-Strauss himself and his book on racism. In the end, in Lévi-Strauss's opinion, a racist is someone who does not adhere to cultural relativism. And this is, in and by itself, a stigma. The problem then becomes one of tolerance. What is the limit of tolerance? Nazism, for instance, demonstrates the impossibility of cultural relativism as well as the difficulty of holding a balance between freedom from parochial, ethnocentric values and total relativism. Where should the line be drawn? If there are no stable standards of the good, the true and the beautiful, if everything depends on the time, place and circumstance it took place in, then we are back to H. Taine's psychology and pure positivism for which what there is what there is, period. Moreover, taken seriously and brought to the limit, such a position leads directly to anarchy: each individual organism is a law unto itself containing its own and matchless standards, making any comparison not only impossible but also scientifically irrelevant. A comparative analysis does presuppose some kind of universal categories that necessarily transcend the system under scrutiny. At first, in conformity with their factual bias, developmental psychologists have tended to objectify their norms. They made development a concept by intuition directly observable in Nature. It was an objective fact like maturity: some behaviours were more advanced than others, certain conducts higher than others, certain acts better than others without any question. This objectivity was rooted in time. But, if later meant better, then time was the mother of perfection and progress was identified with the passive passage of time. Besides the logical difficulty implied by such a view of development and comparison, there is a certain amount of counter-evidence in the form of regression, stagnation and the simple fact that human beings do not perform constantly at the same level. Some human actions are primitive, others advanced. Some are immature, others not. In the same individual, at the same time.

Thus during the twentieth century, developmental psychologists felt the need to move to a notion of development by postulation, that is to say as an a priori stipulation. It followed from this that they had to distinguish from one another: history, evolution, growth, progress and orthogenesis or true development. History is what happened. Evolution is a series of transformations over time. Growth is considered as continuous and quantitative change, whereas history and evolution are not. Progress is a qualitative change. Orthogenesis is a progress from non-differentiation to differentiation and correlative hierarchical integration, as described by Werner and Kaplan (1963).

By so doing, developmental psychologists have transformed development into a pure norm. Development is thus conceived of as a process of ideal ordination of organisms, structures, systems and principles according to a principle of differentiation–integration that accounts for unity and multiplicity, eros and conflict which are the eternal open wounds of the human condition.

These perennial oppositions and contradictions most probably stem out of the very nature of human knowledge with its 'two astonishing characteristics which render it ever liable to conceptual dilemmas, illusory inferences, and erroneous biases: on the one hand human knowledge constructs novelties and ever new human relations; on the other hand, it is irrevocably in the logical framework of (psychologically) necessary implications. Freedom and newness on the one side, logical necessity and universal norm on the other' (Furth, 1986, 26). Any developmental theorizing has to assume this tension in a dialectical fashion. Suppressing one of the two elements of the tension is pure non-sense and has led developmental psychology into the dramatic cul-de-sac in which it has been for more than a century. So far psychologists were very happy to keep the wounds open and to scratch them sometimes, whereas they needed to sew up the two lips of the wounds.

Epilogue

It has not been the purpose of this chapter to advocate any particular concept of development nor to advance any brief for the fact that all developmental psychologists are doing the same thing at the same time, even though psychologists tend to be like fish and swim in schools. The intent of this chapter is to trace back the evolution of the concept of development among different developmental orientations in psychology. This implies the recognition that, in reality, developmental psychologists behave like any other human beings: they can be epistemologically primitive, immature or advanced at the same time, because they function at different levels at the same time. But, inside this complicatedness and in spite of their overwhelming tendency to favour simplicity and parsimony over complexity, positivism and realism over constructivism and rationalism, facts over norms, causes over reasons, there is, in the field, a subjacent move towards normativity that has not yet been fully recognized and that is coming as the return of the repressed and will become conscious in spite of all present disclaimers rejecting norms as mysticism or an illusion without future.

3 Developmental normativity and normative development

Mark H. Bickhard

Development is guided by multiple norms, and further normativities emerge in development. This should be a commonplace observation – after all, it characterizes the core dialectic of developmental processes – but normativity is instead a perplexing and sometimes desperately ignored aspect of development. I will address some reasons why normativity is so perplexing, reasons that begin with Parmenides, and, therefore, that have a rather long history. Within the framework of that historical and conceptual diagnosis of the problem, I explore a model of the emergence of normativity. Finally, I will illustrate with several examples of emergent normativity in learning and development.

These emergent normativities include the normativity of truth and falsity that constitute representation and the – so I argue – related instrumental normativity of motivation, that of success and failure that guide learning, and the positivity and negativity of emotions. Within that outlined framework, I show how higher level motivations, such as curiosity, aesthetic motivation and competence motivation, emerge.

Studies of the mind and person – including psychology, including especially developmental psychology – suffer from a problematic conceptual framework that stems from the pre-Socratics, has dominated Western thought since that time and that makes fundamental theoretical understanding, especially regarding the mind and persons, impossible. I will outline this problematic framework, and show how it renders the normativity of mind and development naturalistically inscrutable. I begin with Parmenides.

Change and substance

Parmenides argued that change cannot occur: For A to change into B, A would have to disappear into nothing, and B would have to emerge out of nothing, and those are impossible (Campbell, 1992). The difficulties with 'nothing' were taken seriously and, in fact, are still with us today: How can you point to nothing? How can you encode nothing? – or What is this thing 'nothing' that 'nothing' refers to?[1]

In fact, Empedocles proposed his metaphysics of earth, air, fire and water as a response to the Parmenidean argument: earth, air, fire and water do *not* change, and thus satisfy (sort of) Parmenides. Only their locations and mixtures change, and the world can be accounted for in terms of these more superficial kinds of change. Similarly, Democritus' atoms do not change, only their locations and relationships.

This substance or atomic form of metaphysics has, in multifarious forms and guises, dominated Western thought since then. But it creates fundamental problems, problems that are most especially focused in attempting to understand minds and persons (Bickhard, 2003b).

Metaphysical perplexity

Substances and atoms 'solved' the Parmenidean problem, solved it so apparently successfully that they have remained the basic framework for metaphysics since then. But they create a hierarchy of metaphysical aporia that have never been solved, and, arguably, cannot be solved within that framework.

The first level of this hierarchy is that substances are, in themselves, inert and passive. Activity and motion – process – require additional forms of explanation. Self motion, in the case of animals, for example, seems clearly to exist, but, at best, it requires special elaboration to try to account for it (Juarrero, 1999). So, stasis is the default, and process requires explanation.

The second level of the problematic hierarchy is that emergence is not possible. Earth, air, fire and water can change position and mixture, but they cannot change themselves and no new, fifth, substance can come into being. It was such emergence that they were designed to avoid in the first place.[2]

---

[1] Frege gave us a means of avoiding some of the problems of these issues (Coffa, 1991; Hylton, 1990), but they have not gone away. We still do not have a consensual naturalistic understanding of encoding (Bickhard, 2003b).

[2] Aristotle, for example, proposed a model in which earth, air, fire and water could change into one another, but these were not the metaphysical foundations for Aristotle, and those foundations did not change (Gill, 1989). Aristotle also, arguably, allowed for a form of emergence (Caston, 1997), but Aristotle was not a pure substance metaphysician, as is mentioned later in the text.

The third level is that substance is actual and factual, a bearer of properties, and that is the extent of the world that can be accounted for within this framework. One issue that this renders aporetic, but that required over two millennia to become explicitly problematic, is that of relations (Brady, 2000; Coffa, 1991; Hylton, 1990; Olson, 1987): properties may in some sense inhere in their bearers, but how do relations attach to their relata?

More deeply, however, the factual world of substance has no natural place for phenomena of intention, of modality, of normativity. A substance metaphysics splits such phenomena into a separate realm that is dirempted from the rest of the world. How to account for such phenomena – phenomena of minds and persons – has remained among the deepest perplexities in Western thought since then.

Metaphysical options

Given this metaphysical split, there are only a few general options available. One can accept the split as fundamental, and posit a metaphysics of two realms as the basic nature of the world. Thus, for example, Aristotle posited both substance and form; Descartes proposed two dedicated substances for the two realms; Kant argued for a noumenal realm and that of the transcendental subject; and the logical positivists proposed that science deals with the world of facts while philosophy is concerned with that of normativity constituted in language and social practices.

A second possibility is to try to account for everything within just the 'mental' side of the split. This yields an idealism or panpsychism. Hegel, Green and Bradley are powerful examples.

The third possibility is to make the opposite election, and try to account for everything within just the substance, factual side of the split. Hobbes, Hume, Mill and Quine exemplify this framework.

These three options exhaust the possibilities, so long as the basic split is assumed. We are currently living in a historical period in which the third orientation – that of materialism in some form or another – is presupposed as background truth.[3] This is so much so that issues about

[3] The logical positivists (and continental philosophers alike) attempted to derive modality, in the form of necessity, from structure, especially logical and mathematical structure, and then to account for normativity using this as a primary resource (Rouse, 2002). This attempt fails, though there are still threads (and puddles) of such orientations throughout contemporary work.

the normativity of, for example, representation, can seem non-scientific, 'mystical'. After all, as Hume showed, normativity is fundamentally distinct from factuality, and cannot be derived from fact.

Emergence?

One might want to try to account for the *emergence* of normativity in the world, but the impossibility of emergence is among the basic 'accomplishments' of substance or atomistic frameworks in their origins and motivations. Furthermore, Hume's argument that norms cannot be derived from facts actually has the broader consequence that nothing new can emerge. Ontological emergence cannot exist. In that respect, Hume's argument codifies the Parmenidean split.

Hume actually didn't provide much of an argument, simply commenting that authors do not account for how normative terms can be derived from factual terms and that it seems 'altogether inconceivable' that they could do so (Hume, 1978; see also Smith, this volume, Chapter 1). The argument that is derived from these points, however, is based on how new terms *can* be validly based on others.

In particular, if the introduction of new terms must be by definitions making use of already available terms, then, so the argument goes, any terms in a valid conclusion can in principle be back-substituted through their definitions, each of which uses only prior terms and those available in the original premises of the argument. We can continue such a substitution of what a term abbreviates for each term until there remain *only* terms that were in the premises. At that point, by assumption, we have only factual terms, no normative terms, and no valid argument could introduce any normative terms if none was available to start with. Of course, with an empiricist conception of knowledge and perception, all initial premises will contain only factual terms, and so normativity cannot be validly introduced.

Notice, however, that the form of the argument, if sound, precludes introducing *anything* new. *No* term that is more than a structure of abbreviations for phrases using only terms in the premises can be validly introduced. That is, among other consequences, there can be no emergence. Facts are dirempted from modality, intentionality and normativity, and no valid argument can put them back together.

Fortunately, Hume's argument is itself unsound. Emergence is possible (Bickhard, 2000b, 2003b). The false assumption is that the only valid way in which to introduce new terms is via abbreviatory definition. If that were correct, then the Hume-inspired argument would be sound. Instead, however, there is implicit definition.

The basic notion of implicit definition is that a set of axioms implicitly defines the class of models that satisfy those axioms. Hume didn't know about implicit definition, but it was powerfully introduced in Hilbert's development of geometry around the turn of the nineteenth into the twentieth century. Schlick, Carnap and others worked with implicit definition, but did not recognize that it rendered Hume's argument unsound. They continued to accept the fundamental split between facts and norms.

Implicit definition blocks the argument because back-translation through the definitions is not possible: implicit definitions do not abbreviate anything constructed out of previously available terms. So new terms can be validly introduced that cannot be reduced to the terms in the premises.

Hume's argument against deriving norms from facts, and, more generally, against any kind of emergence, is unsound. The presumed in-principle barrier to an emergence account of normativity is removed. But that does not provide any model of any such emergence. To defeat the claim that such a model is impossible leaves the task of actually constructing such a model intact.[4]

The emergence of normativity

Normativity, I propose, is derived from a fundamental asymmetry in thermodynamics. In particular, among organizations of process that manifest a temporal stability, we find two fundamentally different kinds. Some process organizations are stable in virtue of their existing in an energy well, such that a change in the organization would require an input of energy to disrupt that organization. So long as sufficient energy for disruption is not encountered, energy well stabilities can remain stable for cosmological time periods – e.g. atoms.

If such energy well organizations are isolated, they simply go to thermodynamic equilibrium and continue in the same organization. There is another class of stable process organizations, however, that are *essentially* far from thermodynamic equilibrium. Such processes react very differently if isolated: they *must* engage in continuous interchange with their environments to maintain their far from equilibrium conditions, and, if isolated, those interchanges cannot proceed. Consequently,

---

[4] Furthermore, Hume's argument 'merely' codifies the split introduced by the substance-particle response to Parmenides' argument. That split cannot be transcended unless such a substance metaphysics is replaced with a process metaphysics (Bickhard, 2000b, 2003b).

the processes go to equilibrium, and the necessarily far from equilibrium processes cease to exist. Stability for such far from equilibrium organizations of process, then, requires environmental interchanges, while stability of energy well organizations of process does not. This is the fundamental asymmetry.

Far from equilibrium processes can be maintained in their far from equilibrium conditions by completely external means – perhaps pumps maintaining a far from equilibrium mixture of chemicals in a vessel of some sort. For my purposes, however, those process organizations that make contributions to their own far from equilibrium stability – that are *self maintaining* – are central. A canonical example is a candle flame: a candle flame melts wax so that it can percolate up the wick, it vaporizes wax in the wick so that it can burn, it induces convection which brings in oxygen and removes waste. A candle flame is self maintaining in multiple respects.

A candle flame, however, cannot do anything different if conditions change. If it is running out of wax, it cannot detect that nor adjust its processes accordingly. It cannot maintain its condition of being self maintaining across variations in conditions. Some system organizations, however, can do that. They are **recursively** *self maintaining* – they maintain the condition of being self maintaining across variations in their relationships with their environments. A canonical example is that of a bacterium that can swim, and continue swimming if it is heading up a sugar gradient, but will tumble if it finds itself swimming down the sugar gradient (Campbell, 1974, 1990). Swimming is self maintaining, but only if it is oriented towards higher sugar concentrations. Otherwise, swimming would detract from the bacterium's self maintenance.

There are two kinds of normativity emergent in the bacterium. One is that of biological function: swimming is functional for the bacterium, if it is oriented up a sugar gradient, in the sense that it makes a contribution to the stability, the continued existence, of the far from equilibrium system (Bickhard, 1993, 2003b; Christensen & Bickhard, 2002). If it is oriented down a sugar gradient, swimming is dysfunctional. And if the bacterium swims up a saccharin gradient, that too is dysfunctional.

The second kind of normativity is the emergence of a primitive kind of truth value. If the processes in the bacterium select swimming as the activity to engage in, there is a functional presupposition that that is the functional thing to do, that swimming will in fact contribute to far from equilibrium stability. That presupposition will be true under some circumstances, such as being oriented up a sugar gradient, and false under others, such as being oriented up a saccharin gradient.

But truth value is the fundamental normative aspect of representation. The bacterium's swimming inherently presupposes that the current conditions are among those that make swimming a functional activity. *We* know that one of those kinds of conditions is orientation up a sugar gradient; the *bacterium* knows nothing of sugar or gradients. Nevertheless, its presuppositions can be true or false, with the conditions for being true being implicit in the chemical and other relationships between the bacterium and its environment. I propose this primitive truth value emergence as the emergence of primitive representation.

More complex representation

Primitive it is, however, and, if a claim that this is foundational to all representation is to be sustained, it must be at least indicated how more complex and more familiar sorts of representation might be accounted for on this base. More complex representation involves resources of differentiation and complexity, already present *in potentio* in this primitive case, that evolution has exploited over time into the possibilities of more familiar sorts of representation.

In the bacterium, detection of a sugar gradient orientation triggers the appropriate interaction. This relation of *triggering* has two aspects that become differentiated in more complex organisms. A frog, for example, may have several interaction potentialities to deal with at one time – perhaps a fly in one location, another fly in another location, a worm and the shadow of a hawk approaching. The frog must select which of these to engage in, and, in order for such selection to be possible, they must all in some functional sense be indicated as possibilities available to be selected. The direct triggering relation has become differentiated into an indication of potentiality and a selection among potentialities indicated.

Both aspects are interesting and important, but, for current purposes, the focus is on the indications. First, note that the indications have the same kinds of functional presuppositions, thus truth values, as the triggerings: if selected, they either interactively flow as indicated, or not – they are being indicated as potentialities of interaction between the organism and the environment, and those indications are either true or false. Second, note that, even when there is no fly in some particular location, the infrastructure is still there in the frog to set up the appropriate indication should the relevant visual scan take place. That is, the conditional relation between engaging in such and such a visual scan and indicating a correspondingly appropriate interactive potentiality is present in the frog even when it is not being used. Such conditional indicative relations of interactive potentiality are crucial to more complex representation.

In particular, in more complex organisms, those conditional indications can branch from each other and iterate. There may be multiple possibilities indicated on the basis of current conditions (branching), and some of the indicated potentialities may be potential only conditional on other intermediate interactions taking place first so as to create the conditions for the next interactive potentialities (iterating). In organisms such as humans, such branching and iterating of conditionals of interactive potentiality create vast webs of indications of interactive potentiality based on other interactive potentialities. It is in special organizations of sub-webs in such overall webs that we find more familiar representations, such as of small manipulable objects.

Consider, for example, a child's toy block. It affords multiple visual scans, manipulations, chewings, droppings on the floor, and so on. Furthermore, each of these possibilities is reachable from any of the others, perhaps with appropriate intermediary interactions. A visual scan of the back of the block, for example, will require an intermediate manipulation of the block to bring that back to the front. Finally, this overall internally reachable organization of interaction potentialities remains invariant under a large class of further interactions. The block can be left in the room when the child leaves, it can be put in the toy box, and so on, and the organization of interaction possibilities remains, so long as the appropriate intermediate interactions are engaged in, such as going back into the room and opening the toy box.

This is 'just' Piaget's model of the representation of small objects, translated into the interactive model (Piaget, 1954). It is possible to steal models from Piaget in this manner because both are models of representation as emergent in action systems. Piaget's model and the interactive model differ in multiple respects (Bickhard, 1988, 1992d; Bickhard & Campbell, 1989), but they are both pragmatist models in the sense of proceeding from a framework of action systems rather than from a framework of passive input processing.

Piaget's model is also relevant to another challenge to the interactive model: perhaps it could account for representation of the physical world, but how can it account for representations of abstractions, such as numbers? What is the world that is interacted with in such cases?

A system interacting with the world might have properties that would themselves be worth representing. A heuristic strategy, for example, might organize interactions with 'try three times before giving up'. Such a strategy would instantiate the property of 'three'. An interactive system cannot represent itself: the relationship is asymmetric. But a second level system interacting with the first could very well represent the property 'three' in the organizations of the first. Such a reflective second level system, in fact, could represent and transform first level organizations and their properties in potentially powerful ways. Furthermore, a second level system would have properties that could be represented from a third level, and so on. These levels constitute levels of epistemic reflective abstraction, close to, though not identical with, the Piagetian notion (Piaget, 2001). They are important for many considerations, including that of development, which must honour the sequencing of such levels in its constructions: it is intrinsically impossible to construct an interactive system at level $N+1$ if there is no system already constructed at level N for the new system to interact with. This is not a causal constraint, from the environment or from the genes: it is intrinsic in the ontology of the levels.

The hierarchy of potential levels is unbounded, though humans generally remain in the lowest few of them. The point of central relevance to the representation discussion, however, is that the interactive model has rich resources for modelling the representation of abstractions. The primitive emergence of truth value in the triggering of interactions in bacteria remains a powerful candidate for the origin of all representation.[5]

Representation and motivation

Any autonomous agent faces the problem of selecting next actions and interactions. In the simple case, the next interaction is simply triggered. The differentiation of the function of indicating potential interactions and that of selecting those indicated begins to distinguish between two aspects of this function of interaction selection, creating distinct infrastructures for indicating and for selecting. They both, however, continue to serve the more general function of interaction selection.

I have explored how representation emerges in the indication of potentialities aspect of interaction selection. An examination of the selecting function shows that it constitutes an early form of motivation: representation and motivation emerge as differentiated aspects of one single underlying function, that of selecting the course of the agent's interactions.

---

[5] I am not elaborating in this chapter the multiple and wide-ranging arguments against alternative models of representation (Bickhard, 1993, 2003b, in preparation). If those are taken into account, then the interactive model is the *only* remaining viable model of representation.

There is one conceptual barrier to understanding this point that I will address briefly. The problem of motivation is often construed as the problem of what makes the system do something rather than nothing, what energizes or stimulates the organism into activity. This cannot be a correct characterization of motivation: living systems are intrinsically far from equilibrium, and intrinsically must be engaged in interactions with their environments in order to survive. Any organism that does nothing dies. So activity is the background for motivation, not that which is to be explained. The problem of motivation has to be what determines what the system will do next, not what makes it do anything at all. And the selections of next interactions are precisely the determination of what the system will do next.

Representing and motivation are differentiated aspects of the same underlying process (Bickhard, 2003a). And, as we shall see, they continue to be tightly interrelated throughout development.

Learning and development

If we assume that representation is a matter of the world impressing itself into an otherwise passive mind or brain, perhaps by transduction or induction, then action and interaction may make *use* of representation, but they are not *necessary* to representation. Representation can be purely a matter of input processing, beginning, for example, with the 'transduction' of light in the retina. The logic of such approaches is essentially not different from the signet ring pressing itself into the wax of the mind of Plato and Aristotle (Plato, 1892; Aristotle, 1908), and the informativeness of the models is also equal – no one has any idea of how light hitting the retina could create a *representation* of that light or of anything else (e.g. Fodor, 1987, 1990a, 1990b, 2003; see Bickhard, 1993; Bickhard & Richie, 1983).

If we assume, on the other hand, that representation is emergent in systems of interaction, then action and interaction are no longer irrelevant to representation, and, further, no one is tempted to think that a competent interaction system could be impressed into an otherwise passive mind or brain. Representation must be constructed, internally constructed, and, barring prescience, those constructions must be tested and checked out, and eliminated if not successful. An action base for the emergence of representation forces an evolutionary epistemological constructivism.

How might this work? The central nervous system of a complex agent is not 'hard-wired' with separate wiring for each of the interactions of which it is capable. That would be enormously wasteful and unnecessary. Instead, the nervous system can function in one manner or mode at one time, and a different manner or mode at a different time. It can look for food at one moment, and consider a problem of arithmetic a moment later, both with the same parts of the nervous system. The difference between differing modes of functioning is akin to the setting up of a computer processing unit register to do an integer add at one moment and a floating point multiply the next: it is the same register, and the same circuitry, but it is set differently in the two cases – the parameters are different. Similarly, in the continuous case of the oscillations in the central nervous system and their mutual and reciprocal modulations, setting different local parameters of ion and transmitter concentrations, for example (or, more realistically, creating temporal trajectories of such local conditions), will induce differing kinds of local processing. This process of setting up local conditions is that of *microgenesis* (Bickhard, 2000a, in preparation; Bickhard & Campbell, 1996).

Microgenesis is, in the first instance, a dynamic continuous 'reprogramming' of local nervous system functioning that greatly expands the capabilities of neural organizations. It has evolved in a co-evolution with faster and more local processes (Bickhard, in preparation). If we assume, however, that the microgenesis for a form of interaction that fails – for which the flow of interaction does not remain within the bounds of what the dynamic parameter trajectories are prepared for – is thereby destabilized, we have, in addition, a primitive form of learning. If successful interacting involves stable microgenesis, while unsuccessful interacting induces destabilization, then failure will induce variations in how the interaction will proceed the next time, and success will increase the probability that it will proceed in the same manner as the currently successful one. As before, we have a simple evolutionary epistemology of interaction construction.[6] The normativity of learning is success in anticipating the course of interaction in microgenetic set-up for that course of interaction.

Learning, then, is a constructive process, a variation and selection constructive process. Learning, however, is not a context-independent process. The constructions of learning are made in the context of and using the resources of previous constructions already made: learning is a *recursive* constructive process. Furthermore, the processes of construction, not just what is constructed, are themselves subject to further

---

[6] More complex processes are required for more sophisticated learning, such as heuristic learning; though, it turns out, they still deeply involve microgenesis (Bickhard, in preparation; Bickhard & Campbell, 1996).

construction, recursive construction. That is, (human) learning is constructive, recursively constructive, and meta-recursively constructive (Campbell & Bickhard, 1992). All such constructions are context sensitive not only on whatever is being interacted with in the moment, but also on the legacy of all previous constructions. Construction, then, is highly dependent on its own past history: it is highly historistic.

One immediate consequence is that some tasks may require constructions that are too difficult unless other simpler constructions are available from previous experience to serve as enabling constraints and resources for the new constructions. Some constructions may *require* certain kinds of prior histories of construction. 'Learning' is the investigation of moment to moment constructions, while 'Development' is the consideration of learning constructions in their historistic framework and with their historistic properties.

For example, if we can block selections for some constructions, allowing attempts to master a task to temporarily work even though they are not competent to the full task, then we may enable a constructive trajectory of more and more competent constructions, culminating in a full task capability, even though the intermediary constructions would be selected out under 'normal' conditions in which the selections were not blocked. This perspective provides a functional notion of the *scaffolding* of learning and development: scaffolds block selection pressures in order to make successful constructive trajectories more likely. This notion converges with standard conceptions of scaffolding as the provision of knowledge (e.g. coordination) that the child may not already have, but goes beyond in that, for example, it makes perfectly good sense, in this view, for an individual to engage in self scaffolding. This is an internal contradiction if scaffolding is constituted in the provision of knowledge, but an individual can block selection pressures for him- or herself, such as by breaking down problems into sub-problems, moving to ideal cases, setting aside one or more problem constraints, making use of some resource that may not be available in general, and so on, without having to already have the knowledge that is to be constructed (Bickhard, 1992a, 1992b, 2001, 2003c).

Another consequence is that, as an individual comes to know more about a domain of knowledge, there will be richer resources available for further learning and development within that domain. This can soon manifest a domain-specific competency – for further learning as well as for interaction – that is itself developed (Campbell & Bickhard, 1992), not something that is innate.

Developmental trajectories will be forced to honour various kinds of constraints. It is difficult, for example, for a construction to proceed that makes use of some resource before the resource is itself available. Such constraints may force various kinds of developmental trajectories, or perhaps some small set of possible such trajectories.

One constraint that is imposed on all development is that of the levels of reflection. No construction can skip levels. All ascent through the levels, if it occurs at all, must be sequential. This imposes a stage-like organization on possible development, except that there are no domain-general structures involved, and (with one exception[7]) no domain-general shifts in the possibilities of construction at a new level. The individual, then, can be in differing levels, or stages, in differing domains of development.

Microgenesis and emotion

An organism as modelled to this point is capable of interaction and of learning, and, if the constructive processes are sufficiently complex, of historistic learning, or development. It is clear that learning increases the ability of an organism to successfully interact with varying environments: if it does not already know how to interact with an environment, then it has a possibility of learning how to interact with it.

There is, however, at least one significant deficiency in an organism capable of interaction and of learning and development. If it encounters a new condition, it can make variation and selection learning attempts, and will inherently do so in the destabilization of the microgenesis of interaction attempts, but it cannot learn or develop general heuristic ways of interacting with various kinds of novel conditions. It cannot learn or develop heuristic kinds of interaction strategies for kinds of microgenetic uncertainty conditions. An interacting and learning organism in a novel situation will be *in* a condition of microgenetic uncertainty, but will be unable to *interact* with that condition.

This could create unfortunate situations, such as engaging in variation and selection trials of various behaviours upon first encountering a large cat in the jungle. Having the capability of generic heuristic means of interacting with uncertainty situations would be advantageous.

There is a relatively simple way in which evolution has provided for this capability. But to model this process, I must first explore a little further how the learning model works and interacts with motivational considerations.

---

[7] An initial maturational enabling of development beyond the first interactive level (Bickhard, 1980, 1992d; Campbell & Bickhard, 1986). This is, however, an enabling of further construction; it is not that further construction itself nor does it guarantee that such construction will occur.

Forms of learning and motivation

Like the organism as a whole, the nervous system is always active, always doing something. The question is what to do next, and what determines what to do next. One kind of determination of what to do next is created by the receipt of an input stream. The nervous system is always engaged in activity, and receiving an input stream will modulate that activity, inducing microgenetic uncertainty unless and until there is successful anticipation of the course of interaction with those kinds of inputs. But interactions can do more than merely passively anticipate input streams, and, in general, will do so. Instead, induced interactions will have *consequences* for those input streams: there will be an *inter*action.

If, for example, a pure tone is received, the stable interaction that will ultimately be settled upon is to create an output flow that anticipates the input flow, and subtracts that input flow to the point of eliminating it. The tone will be habituated. For simple tones, this may ultimately all occur in the first cochlear nucleus; for more complex tones, it may require some small portion of temporal lobe. Note that such habituation requires that the nervous system be organized so that the crucial neural 'subtraction' processes are possible.

Suppose, however, that the input flow crosses modalities. Suppose it begins as a tone, and finishes as a shock, where pain consists of inputs for which no successful interactions are possible, no neural subtraction organizations exist. Under such conditions, any interaction with the input trajectory that yields the pain will be unsuccessful, and will remain unstable. An interaction that will succeed with such an input, however, is one of jumping off of the shock grid. Learning a successful interaction in this case, then, is generally called classical conditioning, but it involves precisely the same microgenetic dynamics as habituation.

Suppose now that an input flow is generated by something that responds to an internal condition, perhaps low blood sugar, and for which no habituation interaction is possible. In this case, the only stable kind of interaction is one that will result in raising the level of blood sugar – eating. Eating, in turn, will depend on multiple additional considerations of context, environment, and so on, so the learning in this case may be unbounded with respect to such contextual considerations. In this case, we have instrumental conditioning.

And so on. The general attractor of successful microgenetic anticipation suffices to model all learning, including those not addressed here, such as incidental learning (Bickhard, 2000a, in preparation). And one way in which this process can be activated is by input flows under various conditions of what kinds of interactions would in fact be potentially successful with those kinds of inputs. So, the interactive, the learning and the motivational aspects of such processes are just aspects, not separate processes.

Interacting with microgenetic uncertainty

Microgenetic uncertainty already is involved in learning, so the problem of being able to interact in general heuristic ways with such conditions depends on the existence of input flows from such uncertainty. Thus, just as input flows generated by low blood sugar can induce appropriate learning and interaction, so also can input flows generated by microgenetic uncertainty induce appropriate learning and interaction.

In these cases, appropriate interaction will depend on the nature, the kind, of the uncertainty situation. These, in general, will vary from basic evolutionarily reliable sorts of conditions and interactions to subtle social and cultural conditions and interactions. Interactions with microgenetic uncertainty situations constitute *emotions* (Bickhard, 2000a).

Emotion is a massive subject, and I can address only a few properties of it here. What is most relevant are some of the interactions between emotion and motivation. First, however, I need to show that this model of emotion is consistent with a basic distinction between positive and negative emotion. All interaction, including emotional interaction, is anticipative. Emotional interactions, to be successful, interact with uncertainty inputs in anticipated ways that maintain the condition of successful anticipation. So, any interaction can involve an anticipation of microgenetic uncertainty, and, therefore, of some appropriate kind of emotion, and this includes emotional interactions themselves.

Note that emotional interactions are interacting both with the original environmental conditions and with the internal condition of microgenetic uncertainty. That internal condition is part of what characterizes the situation for the organism, and helps determine what sort of interaction will be engaged and what sort of further anticipations will be involved.

If the anticipations of an emotional interaction are for eventual success in resolving the uncertainty, then the anticipations will be of an ultimately successful interaction. If the anticipations of an emotional interaction are for further uncertainty about how to deal with the original uncertainty, and then to deal with that double uncertainty situation, and so on, a runaway positive feedback of uncertainty can result. This is canonical of a negative emotional interaction, an anticipation of interactive failure. In this case, possibly a panic attack.

The differentiation between positive and negative emotion, then, turns not directly on the uncertainty input flow, but on the anticipations that are set up by that flow in the kinds of conditions that the organism categorizes itself as being in. Given kinds of environmental conditions, then, might be experienced positively by one organism, perhaps a child, and negatively by another, depending on their learning experiences. If algebra is an opportunity for exploring and eventually resolving various kinds of uncertainties about how to solve this problem, then it may be experienced positively. If, on the other hand, it is an opportunity for yet another confirmation of my incompetence, perhaps even with social shame, then it will be experienced negatively.

Some emergent motivations

At this point, I again take up the point that the organism and the central nervous system are always active. The issue of motivation is what determines what will be engaged in next, not whether or not something will be done rather than nothing. This point holds as well for the emotional aspects of interactions.

If there are sufficiently strong modulations of internal and interactive activity from the body or environment, then those will, in general, constrain further interaction to deal with those sources of input flow. Hunger, for example. If there are no strong 'external' modulators of activity, however, the system will not do nothing. Instead, it will select what to do within the range of kinds of interactions that are anticipated to be successful. This point includes the emotional aspects of interactions.

So, unless otherwise motivated, the organism will tend to select kinds of interactions that induce emotions that are anticipated to be successfully resolved. This means that the organism will tend to select, will be motivated to select, kinds of interactions that will induce uncertainty – so they will involve novelty and some form and degree of lack of full mastery – but of a kind that is anticipated to be resolved successfully – so the anticipation is that the uncertainty will be removed by learning, the lack of full mastery will be made good. That is, there will be a tendency to manifest what we variously call curiosity, mastery motivation, competence motivation or play. One special version of this is aesthetics: situations, music, mathematics, and so on that reliably induce uncertainty, perhaps massive uncertainty, but uncertainty which, it has been learned, can be (potentially) massively resolved.

Such motivations will depend not only on the phenomena being interacted with, but also on what the person brings to the phenomena.

A toddler may enjoy playing with grass, but the available novelties are exhausted relatively quickly. If that toddler, however, grows up to be a botanist, grass may again bring satisfying uncertainties to explore. Avant-garde jazz may not be enjoyable for someone who has not learned how to listen to it, to approach and resolve the kinds of uncertainties in it. Again, mathematics can be a deeply aesthetic field, or a deeply upsetting field. And so on.

In this model, cognition and motivation develop together. New motivations that are crucial to learning and development are themselves emergent in this co-evolution of cognition and motivation. They emerge out of the interplay of cognition, learning and emotion. Motivations like curiosity are not distinct innate modules; they are inherent in human forms of the emotional influences on motivation with respect to cognitive and interactive phenomena. New normativities emerge from the historistic developmental and interactive interplay of already extant normativities.

Values

In a system interacting with its environment, some interactions will be organized around satisfying the conditions detected (or represented) by other interactions. In particular, the detections or representations (detection does not require representation: the hypothalamus may detect low blood sugar, but it doesn't represent it) will function as set-points or goals for other interactions. This can hold for interacting *per se*, as when obtaining an ice cream cone is the goal, but also for learning, as when an input flow is encountered that the organism does not know how to interact with. Such novelty will evoke emotional reactions and learning attempts to try to successfully interact with the situation.

A similar point holds for higher levels of interactive knowing, except that the detections and representations are about lower level process and organizations, not about the external environment. Higher level 'goals' of this sort, whether evoking interactions *per se* or learning or emotions, constitute *values*. In organizing interaction and learning and emotion, values are motivating, inherently so. I would like to address a few properties of values as they function in development.

The unfolding of values

Higher level values can constrain lower level activities and constructions, but lower level organizations impose an interesting constraint on the construction of higher level values. Values will be constructed to interact with, to represent, aspects and properties that are already instantiated, and, thus, available for interaction, in lower levels. That is, the construction of values will *unfold* values that are already implicit in lower level organization and process. This constraint, however, is not a full determination because there may be multiple values that might be unfolded.

Once a higher level value is constructed, however, it serves not only to constrain further lower level activity, it also serves to make explicit some aspect of what was before only implicit. A value may be satisfied by the organization from which it unfolded, but, once explicit, may be found to contradict some other aspect of lower level functioning. Or two higher level values may contradict each other. The value of being the toughest kid on the playground may not fit well with the value of being liked.

Values will always lead development in this sense of being unfolded into explicitness, constraining further activities and constructions, and making implicit conflicts explicit. Values are the leading edge – the leading *normative* edge – of development. They give direction to development, and their conflicts both force further development and, potentially, inhibit it. Values are motivating in both the interactive sense and the learning sense, and their satisfaction, or lack thereof, is an emotional issue – satisfaction is a kind of successful interaction, and failure of satisfaction is failure of interaction.

Self-referential values

There is one special kind of value that I would like to elaborate a little further. Values that refer to the whole person, not just to one or more lower levels, can induce a particular kind of difficulty. A value about how the entire person should be in the world is a value about how the entire person should be spontaneously. But to take such a value as something to be approached instrumentally is to create a self-imposed double bind. It is to give oneself the command to be spontaneous (in a certain way). There is no way to obey such a command – to obey it is to be not spontaneous. So, I cannot decide to be at peace in the world, or to feel kindly towards others, and instrumentally adopt appropriate strategies that succeed in doing so. Any such strategies will be adopted *by* myself, and, thus, will not be the spontaneous actions of my whole self. Instead, my *central* spontaneous activity will be to be concerned about obeying the command of this value, which is not the same as living the value in itself.

On the other hand, it is certainly possible to cultivate the *development* of ways of being in the world, so such a value, even though a trap if taken as something to be approached strictly instrumentally, may well serve as a useful guidance for kinds of activities to seek out and kinds of reflections to engage in. Particular versions of self-referential assumptions about oneself, however, can be especially difficult to deal with in any way, and can constrain the development of rigid pathologies (Bickhard, 1989, in preparation).

Intrinsic motivational values

Finally, I address the development of values that are concerned with the emergent intrinsic motivations mentioned earlier. The emergence of curiosity and aesthetic motivations will, in general, be relatively specific to various domains of interaction. The aesthetics of mathematics is not the same as the aesthetics of photography, and the development of one may not carry over to the other. Such motivations, then, will be learned as values about particular kinds of domains of interaction.

These values can ground continued pursuit of valued domains throughout the lifespan. They found potentially fulfilling and creative involvements with the relevant domains. Such values are among the most important developments of education.

Conclusion

Development is an inherently normative process, involving normativities at multiple levels and of multiple emergent kinds. Representational normativity of truth value is intertwined with motivational normativities. Learning involves normativities of successful interactive anticipations. Emotions arise from interactions with interactive uncertainties in pursuit of more powerful ways to resolve such uncertainties.

Development occurs within the constraint and framework of a hierarchy of interactive representational levels, of levels of interactive knowing. Among the most important aspects of this multi-levelled development is the unfolding of values. Such values lead development. They are the normative leading edge, constraints on further interaction and construction, and the locus of the unfolding of value conflicts.

Among the important kinds of values are those of emergent intrinsic motivations and the appreciations and involvements that they reflect. These can range from music to mathematics to a sense of aesthetic appreciation of one's own life. The scaffolding of the development of such values, and of the development of self-scaffolding skills of such involvements, is among the more important accomplishments of education.

Normativity saturates all of development. There is no possibility of understanding development without understanding the normativities and the normative emergences involved. Yet normativity is today still suffering the consequences of a bad metaphysics, a metaphysical framework that makes issues of normativity seem unscientific, even mystical. But science addresses the world as it is, and the world of development, of mind and person more broadly, is normative through and through. It is normative in its basic ontology. Science must ultimately address these issues of normativity, but will not be able to do so until it has abandoned the Parmenidean, Empedoclean, Aristotelian heritage that sets all matters normative aside and outside of the natural world.

4 Genetic epistemology: naturalistic epistemology vs normative epistemology[1]

Richard F. Kitchener

Introduction: the rise of naturalistic epistemology

The period of the 1960s produced several monumental revolutions in a variety of disciplines. This was true, for example, of the cognitive revolution in which not only did psychology take a cognitive turn, but a new combination of disciplines – *the cognitive sciences* – also emerged. Although psychologists are well aware of both of these revolutions, there was another revolution that occurred in a sister discipline – philosophy – that has escaped the attention of many psychologists. This was an epistemological revolution – the rise of naturalistic epistemology (NE). (For an introductory survey, see Kitcher, 1992; Maffie, 1990.)

This epistemological movement can correctly be called a *revolution* because it claimed to be doing epistemology in a new and nontraditional way, one that broke radically and completely with the past. It had its major defenders, most notably Willard Quine (1969), who christened this heretical movement – naturalistic epistemology; but there were several other contemporaries who were making similar claims, e.g. David Armstrong (1973), Paul Churchland (1979), Alvin Goldman (1986), Larry Laudan (1987), etc.; in fact, many individuals claim that John Dewey was one of the first naturalistic epistemologists, whose ancestry can be traced back to nineteenth-century thinkers (e.g. Helmholtz, Mach) and even earlier (e.g. Hume).

Naturalistic epistemology

Although there is no universal agreement among naturalistic epistemologists about all of the basic tenets of NE, there is substantial consensus. I would like to suggest the following as fundamental principles of NE, widely shared by naturalistic epistemologists.

[1] I wish to thank Les Smith for reading and critically commenting on this manuscript. He continues to disagree with many of the things I say here.

First, NE, unlike traditional philosophical epistemology, claims that *scepticism is a pseudoproblem*. Although epistemological scepticism – roughly the view that knowledge is impossible or doubtful (see the entries in Dancy & Sosa, 1992) – may be a logically tenable position, it is not a position to be taken seriously and that is because it sets out standards of knowledge that are impossible to meet. Because it is widely accepted that we have a paradigm-case of knowledge in the case of science, scepticism is not a serious position to be refuted.

Second, NE rejects the claim that epistemology should be or can be a *first philosophy*, i.e. a purely philosophical endeavour that produces absolutely certain foundations upon which depend all of the disciplines, including the sciences. NE rejects the very notion that the various sciences need to have absolutely certain foundations established by philosophy (or that even such an enterprise is possible).[2] Hence, traditional philosophical epistemology does not stand *above* the sciences as a superior kind of endeavour logically presupposed by the various sciences.

Third, not only is there no 'super-scientific' discipline of epistemology, *epistemology is not an autonomous discipline*. There is no philosophical endeavour called 'epistemology' that is radically separate from the empirical sciences. On the traditional view, epistemology was supposed to be an autonomous endeavour with its own distinctive subject matter, methods and results. But NE denies these claims: epistemology does not have a separate subject matter; there are no distinctive philosophical methods of epistemology; and its results are not unique in any philosophically important way. On a conservative 'separate but equal' view, NE sees the philosophical epistemologist as one who works hand in hand with the empirical sciences, open to the results of the various empirical sciences. But such a conciliatory position assumes that there is something autonomous about philosophical epistemology or at least that there is something to do over and above what there is to do in the empirical sciences. But if one denies this, as naturalistic epistemologists seem to do, there is nothing left for philosophical epistemologies to do. This is a much more radical view, a kind of 'withering away of philosophical epistemology'.

---

[2] It remains an open question whether a particular science, say, physics, should take over this philosophical role and provide the foundations for all of the other sciences. Some would reject this project as being misconceived since foundation talk bespeaks the quest of certainty, which is a will-o'-the-wisp; others would reject it because of the fear of the hegemony of physics and instead would plump for more local and pluralistic endeavours. Most naturalistic epistemologists would seem, however, to be committed to some version of the hegemony of physics.

Fourth, epistemology is a part of science and employs whatever scientific method is employed in the sciences. *The only epistemological method, therefore, is the scientific method.* Needless to say, if such a position is to be defensible, the nature of the scientific method must be viewed in a pretty liberal way, certainly including abstract theory construction, meta-theory and what traditional philosophers have called 'conceptual analysis' (see Kitchener, 1999). Nevertheless, a central component of the scientific method – at least as applied to the non-formal sciences – will be a heavy reliance on empirical observation and experimentation.

As we have seen, NE assumes there is no special endeavour called 'philosophical epistemology'. If epistemology is to become thoroughly naturalistic and to employ the scientific method, then it would seem that all epistemological analyses must (in some sense) be *empirical* in nature, countenancing no non-naturalistic entities, no non-naturalistic cognitive faculties and no non-naturalistic methods. This brings NE into confrontation with three traditional distinctions favoured by epistemologists: the analytic–synthetic distinction, the a priori–a posteriori distinction and the necessary–contingent distinction. (See the entries in Dancy & Sosa, 1992.)

Traditional epistemology can be characterized as being concerned either with *analytic* propositions established by *a priori* means, or *synthetic* propositions established by *a priori* means – both kinds of propositions being *necessary*. On the other hand, the (natural) sciences were traditionally thought to be concerned with *synthetic* propositions established by *a posteriori* methods, the result of which was *contingent* propositions. With the emergence of Quine's (1951) attack on the *analytic–synthetic* distinction, the *a priori–a posteriori* distinction and the *necessary–contingent* distinction, the viability of these dichotomies became questionable and hence the distinction between philosophy and psychology became questionable. If there is no distinction between psychology and epistemology, then why not (Quine asked) simply settle for psychology? NE was thus born: it would be a scientific study of knowledge based upon the empirical results of psychology.

Quine lopped off the first member of each of these pairs, and plumped for the exclusive admission of synthetic, a posteriori and contingent propositions. Although it does not seem required for NE to deny necessary propositions (contrary to Quine), it does seem that one's account of necessity must be some kind of *natural necessity*. Be that as it may, it certainly seems to be the case that NE is committed to denying the *a priori* and the *analytic* pairs of these dichotomies (or at the very least giving a 'naturalistic' interpretation of them). What seems ruled out, therefore, is the assumption that the *a priori* and the *analytic* require special non-naturalistic methods for their investigation. We may take this, therefore, as the fifth postulate of NE: *the denial of non-naturalistic a priori methods and analytic propositions.*

Normativity

Although the above set of assumptions throws into question the alleged radical distinction between philosophy (epistemology) and science (psychology), there is one particular class of propositions that has always held a central place in epistemology and has traditionally served to distinguish epistemology from the sciences: epistemology, it was claimed, is a *normative* discipline, whereas the sciences are *empirical* (factual) disciplines. According to this notion, epistemology, like ethics, aesthetics and the law, was concerned with normative concepts and principles of a certain kind: epistemic concepts – concepts such as *justification, warrant, evidence, evaluation, rationality, objectivity* – and epistemic principles and criteria – whereas the sciences were concerned with pure matters of fact. This was the basis of the traditional *fact–value, is–ought* distinction championed by Hume, Kant, Frege, Weber and many others. (See Smith, this volume, Chapter 1.)

The term 'norm' belongs to a family of terms including: *standard, rule, evaluation, criterion, ought, excellence,* etc. Normative judgments, judgments that employ such terms, indicate not merely how things actually happen to be but how they *ought* to be. They indicate that there was or is an alternative course of action or state of affairs that is better than the actual one. Such normative terms have their natural home in ethics and related disciplines such as aesthetics, political theory, the law and even logic, but they are also present in our day-to-day endeavours. 'You should not have believed that used-car salesman when he told you how great that car was,' we say; 'It's no longer rational to believe the earth is flat'; 'How naive of you to believe your lover will leave his wife for you. You should not have been taken in by him.'

Epistemic norms are those norms relating to knowledge. When we say someone knows something, we are not merely describing his psychological state or behaviour, we are saying this state has a normative dimension to it: his belief was correct (warranted, justified, backed by evidence, etc.). Similarly, in the case of a legal decision, we say that the verdict was justified, and in the case of reasoning, we say his conclusion was reasonable.

Normative concepts function as what we can call *appraiser terms*, terms used to evaluate, assess, grade, etc. The employment of such terms results in a normative judgment, and such judgments require standards of evaluation – norms. Most epistemological arguments turn on the question of appropriate normative criteria, since these determine the legitimacy of the normative judgment.[3] Epistemology was thus likened to ethics in being concerned with several classes of normative goods: epistemic *value* (what things are *good* from the epistemic point of view), epistemic *obligations* (what things it was one's *duty* to believe, what things one *ought* to do in order to attain knowledge, etc.) and epistemic character traits or *virtues* (those traits of a person relevant to the acquisition of knowledge).

On this received view, sciences did not – could not – make such normative claims because they investigated the empirical, factual realm, and it was an accepted view that one could not derive a value statement (an 'ought') from a factual statement (an 'is') for a variety of reasons. Psychology, being an empirical science, was severely restricted to discovering empirical facts, but it could not, on pain of committing the naturalistic fallacy, make normative judgments.

Of all of the alleged distinctions between epistemology and psychology, it was this distinction – the normative versus the empirical – that was the linchpin in the traditional argument that epistemology is radically different from psychology. Although Quine and others did not (initially) bother to question this distinction, clearly it was thought to be a distinction that a NE had to undercut or soften in some way, either by claiming that the distinction was not a radically sharp one – and hence the empirical could be relevant to the normative – or by eliminating the distinction altogether in favour of the hegemony of the empirical. I believe the consensus among epistemologists (including most naturalistic epistemologists) is that the normative cannot be eliminated from epistemology. Hence, NE has the task of showing how the normative can have a place in a NE and how empirical matters of fact could be relevant to the normative dimension. Indeed, we may go so far as to claim that, according to NE, *everything normative can be explained, constituted or accounted for in purely naturalistic ways* either because norms can be *reduced to* natural facts, norms are *identical* to certain kinds of facts, normative concepts can be *defined* in naturalistic terms, norms *supervene* on natural facts, or natural facts can (in some way) *explain* how norms emerge in the course of nature. Many naturalistic epistemologists believe, for example, that norms supervene on facts, that there is no

---

[3] Just consider the necessity of a criterion in order to warrant the verdict 'guilty' in a court of law, a grade of 'F' on a term paper, or the determination of the monetary value of a home. Many normative theorists would argue that criteria of evaluation are always needed, although others would deny this.

property of an epistemic norm not based upon an underlying natural fact. If this is so, then it would appear that one of the tasks of NE is to explain how this is possible. As we will see, this is a crucial part of Piaget's genetic epistemology to explain how it is possible (from a developmental point of view) for norms to emerge from facts.

I will assume that one cannot and should not eliminate epistemic norms from the epistemological enterprise. I will also assume that epistemic norms cannot be reduced (at least in a simplistic way) to brute empirical facts. How then can a NE accommodate epistemic norms? To begin to answer that question, one must have a rough idea of the major philosophical (epistemological) views regarding the nature of these epistemic norms.

Contemporary normative epistemology

Current discussions of normative epistemology among analytic epistemologists take their departure from ethical theory. Since ethical theory can (roughly) be divided into three types – deontology, consequentialism and virtue theory – it is not surprising that one can find (roughly) the same approaches holding sway among normative epistemologists. Recently, a fourth approach to ethics has emerged, one I will argue is preferable to the others.

Epistemic deontology

Deontological theories of epistemic normativity stress the crucial role of one's normative duty and obligation. On this account – different versions of which can be found in Descartes (1984), Locke (1975), Clifford (1999), Chisholm (1977), Ginet (1975) and most recently in Conee & Feldman (2004) – one is justified or warranted in holding a belief only if one has done one's epistemic duty, if one has fulfilled one's epistemic obligations.[4] What is one's epistemic duty? One might say: *believe a proposition if (only if) it is true.* But since one needs to know when a proposition is true, a much more useful account would be to say: *one's epistemic duty is to believe a proposition if (only if) there is adequate evidence supporting it;*[5] *and that one's degree of belief in the proposition should*

---

[4] Some individuals prefer to phrase epistemic deontology as the weaker view that a belief is justified only if it is *permitted*, only if one did not violate one's epistemic duty in forming a belief.

[5] How we formulate this is important. On the first ('if') formulation, if there is adequate evidence supporting a view, then it is one's duty to believe it; on the second ('only if')

be a function of its evidential strength. If, therefore, one believes a proposition for which there is not adequate evidence, the person may be blamed; and if one does not believe a proposition for which there is adequate evidence, the person may be blamed; if one does believe a proposition for which there is adequate evidence, one may be praised; and so forth. In short, at least one epistemic duty consists of seeking an adequate amount of evidence for one's belief.

Three closely related issues confront this kind of *epistemic deontology*: (1) What is an adequate account of 'evidence'? (2) From whose perspective is the evaluation of the epistemic agent made? (3) How free are epistemic agents in forming their beliefs? Suppose, for example, a particular epistemic agent believes a particular experience of his is adequate evidence for his belief in God and, as a result, believes that God exists. Has he satisfied or failed in his epistemic duties? Suppose an epistemic agent has been raised in a seriously impoverished epistemic environment and as a result forms the belief that women are to be denied all basic human rights. Is he to be blamed for his belief? Clearly, how we answer these questions will depend on answering a host of other questions about subjective versus objective justification, doxastic voluntarism versus doxastic involuntarism, an adequate theory of evidence, etc. Unfortunately I have no time to discuss such issues.[6]

Epistemic consequentialism

Ethical consequentialism, as traditionally conceived, is opposed to ethical deontology, and epistemic consequentialism is opposed to epistemic deontology. According to epistemic consequentialism (Alston, 1989; Bonjour, 1985; Goldman, 1986; Laudan, 1987), the most popular form of which is *epistemic utilitarianism*, a belief is justified (warranted, reasonable) if it produces consequences of a certain kind, namely, desirable ones. Such a belief is justified because of its instrumental value, its leading to a certain kind of end-state, which is deemed good or valuable. Such ultimate end-states are typically thought to be intrinsically valuable.[7]

---

formulation, if there is not adequate evidence supporting a view, then it is not one's duty to believe it, and this may be interpreted to mean that you should disbelieve it (rather than being neutral on the issue).

[6] Alston (1989) rejects epistemic deontology because it is committed, he claims, to a false view about the freedom of belief formation, i.e. that we can choose either to believe a proposition or not to believe it (doxastic voluntarism). Plantinga (1993a) rejects it for a similar reason – it is committed to internalism.

[7] This is an example of what could be called, following the model of ethical theory, act epistemic utilitarianism. The other form would be rule epistemic utilitarianism,

These end-states might be valuable from an epistemic point of view or from some other point of view. Let us suppose these valuable end-states are epistemic in nature. What could they be? The standard answer is that the epistemically valuable end-state is *truth* – true belief, true scientific hypothesis, etc. This is not the only possible candidate, however, for this epistemic end-state might also be wisdom, understanding, predictive power, explanation of the data, etc. These have also been suggested as epistemic values, although whether they are intrinsically valuable (good in themselves), or whether, in turn, they are to be conceived instrumentally is an open question. Let us suppose, however, that our epistemic value is truth. Then we have a version of consequentialism – epistemic utilitarianism. On this view, therefore, *a belief is warranted or justified if it produces (results in) epistemic value – truth.*[8]

Aretaic (virtue) epistemology

Recently, a third candidate for a theory of normative epistemology has become popular – a normative theory rooted in Aristotelian ethics (Aristotle, 1984). Aristotelian ethics has traditionally been seen as an account of ethics different both from deontology and from utilitarianism. The basic thesis of such an account is that an action is morally right (or praiseworthy) if it is the outcome of a moral virtue, where a moral virtue is (roughly) an internal character trait of the moral agent. On this account, moral virtues are logically primary and moral acts secondary. Hence, on this account, an action is to be described as noble or courageous because it issues from a noble or courageous person. These moral character traits are excellences of the moral agent.

As the Greeks put it, the eye has virtue (excellence) if it fulfils its function well – sees excellently – and this excellence, in turn, is due to a certain set of natural properties; the same can be said of our other epistemic faculties such as memory, perception, reasoning, etc. By extension, one can speak of a virtuous knower who fulfils her functions – knowing – in an excellent way because of her possession of a set of

---

according to which a belief is justified because it is an instance of a kind K and K-beliefs result in desirable end-states.

[8] A slightly different form of epistemic consequentialism could be called axiological epistemic justification. According to this view (e.g. Alston, 1989), S's believing p is justified only if S's believing p was epistemically good. The epistemic good or value in question could be truth or (better) its being based on adequate evidence. The latter formulation seems to be a version of epistemic utilitarianism since adequate evidence is indicative of truth in a reliabilist or truth-frequency way. However, here it is not the belief itself but the grounds that have epistemically beneficial consequences.

properties, in this case, a set of epistemic dispositions involving certain intellectual functions.

In *aretaic* or *virtue epistemology* (Axtell, 2000; Fairweather & Zagzebski, 2001; Sosa, 1991; Zagzebski, 1996) the epistemic agent is logically primary and her beliefs are logically secondary. Such an epistemic agent can be characterized as possessing certain virtues or excellences – intellectual, cognitive or epistemic virtues. For example, being careful in collecting empirical data is, no doubt, one such epistemic virtue; so is critical, reflective reasoning about the data; similarly with a certain kind of open-mindedness and intellectual courage in entertaining new ideas. Such epistemic agents can, therefore, be characterized normatively in terms of possessing these epistemic traits. We routinely do this, I believe, when we characterize the epistemic nature of great scientists and how they do science.

On this account, therefore, we evaluate epistemic actions in virtue of underlying epistemic virtues and we evaluate the beliefs of such knowers in a similar way; we claim that *a belief is justified if it is the result or outcome of a virtuous faculty possessed by a virtuous epistemic agent* where 'virtuous' is defined in a variety of ways but where all of them contain the core notion of *excellence* – epistemic excellence – and this in turn is understood as an adverb describing the functioning of a faculty or epistemic disposition.[9]

Epistemic contractarianism

Finally, I would like to briefly mention what I take to be a fourth approach to ethical theory and epistemology, one that combines features of the above accounts, but one which is also distinctive in its own right. This is contractarianism, whose most ardent defender is David Gauthier (1986); closely related to this view is contractualism (Rawls, 1971).

According to both of these views, rooted in the social contract tradition of Hobbes, Locke, Rousseau and Kant, a political or moral norm (and, *mutatis mutandis*, an epistemic norm) is legitimate or justified if it is the result of a hypothetical social contract or rational mutual agreement between certain parties. The key difference between these two views – at least for the naturalist – is that contractualism attempts to derive norms from an original position in which moral norms are already presupposed, whereas a contractarian attempts to derive norms from

[9] Another recent approach, a kind of spin-off of virtue epistemology, is Plantinga's *proper function theory* (Plantinga, 1993a, 1993b).

an original position in which no moral norms are presupposed.[10] For the contractarian, norms are derivable from non-moral facts because the original position is one in which persons are assumed to be self-interested (or egoist), interested in maximizing their own utility.[11] It is also assumed that cooperation is a moral norm since it involves sometimes acting against one's immediate self-interest. Hence the task, in short, is to derive cooperation from egoism. For a naturalist, therefore, contractualism would be the more serious contender and hence I will focus on it.

The programme of the contractarian is to show that moral norms can be derived (or generated) from non-moral states of affairs. It is here that game theory and rational choice theory can be used to show how to accomplish this task.

Game theory assumes the standard economic conception of the individual, that individuals are utility maximizers and that their behaviour can be modelled by principles of economic rationality – purely instrumental rationality. According to this account, individuals pursue their interest, preferences or utilities by selecting the most rational means towards achieving this state of affairs. This is a version of consequentialism and it is empirically unobjectionable since instrumental (means-end) rationality can be interpreted in a purely naturalistic way, as involving (basically) causal relations of 'what leads to what'.

The most famous game theoretic situation is the prisoner's dilemma in which individuals rationally pursue courses of action that are in equilibrium but are not Pareto-optimal. It is the consensus of game theorists that one cannot derive moral principles of cooperation from such a self-interested game theoretic situation. However, it can be shown that this can be accomplished if one begins with a slightly different game theoretic situation, e.g. an indefinitely repeated prisoner dilemma situation, or a game involving coordination (Axelrod, 1984; Bicchieri, 1993; Danielson, 1992; Sugden, 1986; Taylor, 1984[12]). Hence, it is possible to show, as Axelrod puts it, 'under what conditions cooperation will emerge in a world of egoists without central authority' (p. viii). As we will see, Piaget addresses this same question and his answer is close to that of game

---

[10] Whether other norms are presupposed, e.g. an epistemic norm of rationality, is a more complicated question, for if so, then moral norms would be derived from epistemic norms, which in turn would have to be purged of normative elements.

[11] Several individuals have argued that maximizing one's own utility is not necessarily a version of egoism since altruism might be one's preference or in one's interest. I will, however, ignore this subtlety and simply assume that the original position is one of egoism (self-interestedness).

[12] It should be pointed out, of course, that there is disagreement between these individuals on the details of this programme.

theorists. Game theorists and Piaget are both concerned, therefore, with 'the emergence of norms' (Ullmann-Margalit, 1977).

Now, this is all very sketchy and promissory in nature and needs of course to be filled in. But if this contractarian approach is correct in its general approach, then it is possible to show how norms emerge from facts. In particular, it would show how, given certain constraints, norms of cooperation can emerge from an initial state of egoism. This is very similar I would argue to what Piaget claims in his theory of social epistemic development.

To fill out the story, of course, would require several more intermediate steps, e.g. showing how individual behaviour becomes habitual (a behavioural regularity), which leads to social conventions with their appropriate external sanctions, which leads to the individual internalizing these behavioural expectations (with their appropriate internal sanctions), etc. All of this would result in the generation of a norm, a norm concerning how one should act or think. (See Opp, 1983, for a more detailed suggestion of this process.)

Of course this contractarian approach is silent about epistemic norms but we can extrapolate what such an account might be. According to *epistemic contractarianism*, therefore, an epistemic norm would be something like the following: a belief (cognition, practice, procedure, institution) is *epistemically justified if it (or the general principle under which it falls) would be agreed to by members of a society under certain specified conditions* (e.g. given their initial desires, social structure, etc.). Note that, on this account, epistemic norms are socially constructed and hence necessarily presuppose a social epistemology rather than an individualistic epistemology. Epistemic norms do not, therefore, historically precede societies but emerge only within the context of the group, their interests and relations, etc. This is in keeping, I would argue, with a broadly functionalistic account in which epistemic norms originally arose only because they served certain kinds of social needs – in this case epistemic needs These epistemic needs involve questions basically of information transfer from one member of a group to others. In such a context, how such information is acquired would be crucial to the well-being of the group and hence, we might expect, social norms about the procedure of acquiring information would play an important part. Hence, originally at least epistemic norms were social in nature; later, individual epistemic needs might arise but they would be parasitic upon and presuppose social epistemic norms.[13]

---

[13] If this sounds like a theme from Wittgenstein's argument about rule-following, I believe it is. But I do not draw from his argument the anti-naturalistic implications that others (e.g. Kripke, 1982) have drawn.

In conclusion, I have mentioned what I take to be the major approaches to constructing a normative epistemology: deontology, consequentialism, virtue theory and contractarianism. Which of these (if any) are compatible with a NE?

Epistemic consequentialism would seem to be the easiest normative approach to handle, for on the standard reading, the connection between a belief and the epistemic end-state is an empirical connection – an example of hypothetical means–end relation. It is an empirical question as to which kind of beliefs lead to truth or verisimilitude, just as it is an empirical question as to which procedures in science lead to which beneficial results. This aspect of epistemic consequentialism, therefore, seems unproblematic. What is the situation with respect to the epistemic end-state sought, typically truth? This is another matter (unless a naturalistic account of truth can be provided, which I believe it can).

I believe it is also correct to say that a NE can handle virtue epistemology (although not quite so easily), for epistemic virtues also result in epistemic goods on this account and this seems likewise to be an empirical connection. What about the epistemic virtues inherent in the epistemic agent? Here, again, I see no reason to conclude that a NE is not compatible with such an epistemic account (although I do not have the time to develop this line of thought).

However, the situation seems different with epistemic deontology, for here it would seem necessary for a NE to show how *obligation, duty, praise, blame*, etc., can be incorporated into a naturalistic account. One suggestion would be to say that one can analyse obligation (or duty) in terms of hypothetical means-end connections in such a way as not to involve any unanalysed normative concepts, in short, that all categorical imperatives can be translated into hypothetical imperatives.

As I have suggested, I favour a contractarian approach. Not only is it a naturalistic approach to constructing a theory of (epistemic) norms, it is (I will suggest) a thoroughly developmental approach, one closely related to Piaget's developmental social epistemology. I believe the concept of supervenience can be useful here.

Supervenience

Currently, many individuals believe that one can be a naturalist (or as they put it a materialist or physicalist) and reject reductionism – this is sometimes called *nonreductionistic materialism*. For these individuals, the key ingredient in this account is the notion of *supervenience*. According to supervenient theorists, a higher order concept, property or principle may be dependent on a lower one without being reducible to it. So, in the case of the mental, one can believe that the mental is supervenient on the physical without being reducible to it; likewise, one can believe moral properties supervene on naturalistic properties without being reducible to them. Adopting this supervenient approach to the epistemic realm, one can claim that epistemic norms supervene on naturalistic properties but are not reducible to them.

Although there are several ways of expressing supervenience, there are several notions that most individuals accept. For example, suppose we have a set of epistemic principles or properties N and a set of naturalistic, say, psychological properties, P. Then one can say that

N supervenes on P only if there can be no change in N without a change in P. (No normative difference without a naturalistic difference.)

Another way of expressing the idea is the following:

If there are two identical instances, x and y, of F, then if x is P, so is y. (There cannot be two instances alike in their naturalistic properties but differing in their normative properties.)

These are two ways of expressing the fact that N is a necessary condition for P. Still a different way of expressing the idea is in terms of a sufficient condition:[14]

N supervenes on P only if P fixes (determines) N.

With respect to epistemic norms, the basic idea of epistemic supervenience is this: if two beliefs or actions have the same naturalistic properties, then they have the same epistemic properties. Again, the naturalistic (psychological) properties determine, fix, are the basis of epistemic normative properties. On this account, therefore, there are epistemic norms (e.g. of a belief being warranted, rational or justified), but such norms are rooted in naturalistic facts, these naturalistic facts constituting the *reasons* they are (judged to be) normative. Hence, there is no elimination or reduction of the normative.

Epistemic supervenience can be formulated in a purely atemporal (logical) way or in a temporal way. If it is expressed in a temporal way, the doctrine of supervenience seems closely related to the doctrine of *emergence*.

Suppose there are three levels, alpha, beta and gamma (alpha earlier than beta earlier than gamma) and three sets of properties belonging to these different levels: A, B and G. Then we can say that beta supervenes

---

[14] Supervenience is expressed by different authors in both of these ways.

on alpha if, for every property B, there is a property A, such that A is a sufficient condition for B (or perhaps a necessary condition) and gamma supervenes on beta if, for every property G, there is a property B, such that B is a sufficient condition for G (or perhaps a necessary condition). If A is a purely naturalistic (empirical) set of properties, and B is (at least partly) normative, then the normative supervenes on the natural; in addition, there is a temporal condition: A occurs before B and B occurs before G. Since level alpha is the purely natural, beta supervenes on the natural, but beta also contains a normative component (e.g. 'is better equilibrated'); likewise with beta and gamma. However, beta has a mixed natural-normative character. But since beta supervenes on the purely natural alpha, by transitivity, gamma may be presumed also to supervene on the purely natural.

In this case, one could say that, at time t, an epistemic normative property N *emerges* from (a set of) naturalistic properties P in the sense that, prior to t, one could not have predicted that N would have appeared. Developmental stages seem to involve the property of emergence since later stages contain (novel) properties not contained in the lower stages and not predictable from the lower stages.

So, let us assume that *epistemic norms emerge from psychological facts* in the sense that there is a sequence of psychological stages $P_1, P_2, \ldots, P_n$, that an epistemic norm is not present in $P_1, P_2, \ldots, P_{n-1}$ but that at P_n an epistemic norm N emerges (supervenes upon P_n). Without denying the existence of N, then, one can say that N is dependent upon on P_n.

Now, one of the things that one wants to do in this case is to explain the supervenient principle: if P_n then N. Why does P_n give rise to N? How is it possible for a psychological fact to generate an epistemic norm? At one point in time, we have nothing but facts and at a later time we have norms. Norms and facts seem so radically different from each other; how could such natural facts generate such norms? Assuming epistemic norms are supervenient on empirical facts, I want to discuss the problem of showing that such supervenience is compatible with a NE by showing how such supervenience can be explained within the context of something like Piaget's Genetic Epistemology.

Piaget's genetic epistemology

The issue of how epistemic norms are related to psychological facts may seem to be merely an academic controversy pursued by philosophers, one with little relevance to the work of developmental psychologists. This might be true if it were not for the fact that many individuals believe that developmental (genetic) psychology is based upon a larger programme of genetic or developmental epistemology.[15] Consider, for example, the historically important research programme of Jean Piaget. If we are to take Piaget at his word (Piaget, 1972a, 1972b), his theory of the psychological development of the individual is an offshoot or empirical application of his larger project of genetic epistemology (GE). GE is not just another term for genetic psychology, it is a theory of *knowledge*. In doing genetic psychology, therefore, one is not, *ipso facto*, doing GE. If this is so, if his lifelong project was the construction of a GE – a claim buttressed by considering that he named his centre The International Centre for Genetic Epistemology – then it is crucial, first, to understand the general programme of GE (as distinct from genetic psychology),[16] then we must see how it is different from genetic psychology. In doing so, it turns out that GE confronts the issue of how it is an epistemology, how epistemic norms are related to psychological facts, and how GE is related to NE and normative epistemology.

Although there are various definitions of GE to be found in Piaget (Kitchener, 1986), the following can be found running throughout most of his accounts (Piaget, 1950, p. 12; 1955, p. 28; 1957, p. 14; 1967a, p. 7):

GE is the theory of the passage from states of lesser (scientific) knowledge to states of more advanced (scientific) knowledge.

The central claim of GE, therefore, is that there is a passage from a state of lesser knowledge to a state of greater knowledge. This occurs basically because of the process of equilibration. Equilibration explains stage transitions (Piaget, 1985, pp. 3, 147): an earlier stage gives rise to a later stage because of the process of equilibration and this means (partly) that a later stage is *better* than the earlier stage – it is more equilibrated. In his major work, *The equilibration of cognitive structures* (Piaget, 1985), he goes on to say that the concept of *optimizing equilibration* ('équilibrations majorantes') is central to this developmental account. Development, he says, 'is a progressive equilibration from a lesser to a higher state of equilibrium' (p. 3). 'Progress', he says, 'is produced by reequilibration

---

[15] Although most contemporary psychologists use the term 'developmental psychology', Piaget typically referred to this field as 'genetic psychology'. Likewise, although Piaget used the term 'genetic epistemology', I believe a more appropriate label is 'developmental epistemology'.

[16] This is routinely forgotten by developmental psychologists who write about Piaget as if he were a genetic psychologist. It is no wonder that confusion immediately follows. Bärbel Inhelder, a psychologist and Piaget's closest collaborator, was quite clear about this point, that Piaget's programme was a GE. See e.g. Inhelder (1981).

that leads to new forms that are better than previous ones. We have called this process "optimizing reequilibration"' (p. 11). We do so, he says, 'in order to express the idea of improvement' (p. 26). The concept of equilibration is clearly a normative concept, not a normative concept of the epistemic subject; it is rather a norm of the psychologist who is studying the epistemic subject. This normative concept is invoked by Piaget the epistemologist to explain why epistemic development occurs over time. Pretty clearly, therefore, Piaget is making normative judgments.

This very point can be made in a slightly different way. Suppose that knowledge is not just belief or cognition – and Piaget admits it is not[17] – then immediately the question arises of what distinguishes *knowledge* from mere *belief* (or cognition). To know something, an individual must not only believe something, this belief must satisfy other conditions, e.g. it must be *justified* or as Piaget puts it, 'valid knowledge' (1967a, pp. x, 6; 1972b, p. 71; 1971b, p. 4). But when one leaves the realm of mere belief and talks about justification (and to what degree), one is making a normative claim: one is evaluating the adequacy or epistemic worth of a belief, and this is not a simply empirical question, it is a normative one.

Clearly, therefore, Piaget stresses the importance of validity as a cornerstone of epistemology in general and GE in particular. But what he understands by this notion is unclear. On the one hand, he sometimes writes as if validity were equivalent to formal-logical validity (1957, 1967b), in which case formal logic would be sufficient to settle questions of normative epistemology. But such a conception is too narrow since it would overlook non-logical validity, the 'validity' or justification of rules, procedures, etc., that go beyond formal-logical validity. Piaget himself recognizes this point by distinguishing formal validity from experimental validity and arguing for the importance of the latter. The latter would constitute normative epistemic rules concerning the acquisition of empirical knowledge. So, GE as a normative epistemology would involve psychological facts plus logical and epistemic norms.

So, it would seem that Piaget believes there is a difference between GE and genetic psychology. If there is a distinction between facts and norms, as he insists there is (1950, p. 29; 1957, p. 56; 1967b, p. 125; 1995, p. 216), then Piaget has a multifaceted problem (and so do other developmental psychologists who are doing GE). Does Piaget intend

---

[17] Although Piaget does not typically use the term 'belief', he does regularly distinguish purely psychological states of cognition from justified states of cognition.

his GE to be a version of NE as opposed to traditional a priori (normative) epistemology? If so, then GE would seem to be conceptually impossible (Hamlyn, 1971). On the other hand, if he intends his programme to be a normative epistemology, then genetic psychology would seem to be irrelevant. If we are to claim that Piaget's GE is truly a GE and that it is also a version of NE, then he faces the problem of showing how the normative nature of epistemology can enter into this account of GE. We seem to be faced with the following choice: claim that there is no GE over and above genetic psychology (and hence that Piaget's self-proclaimed programme makes no sense); claim that GE is a version of normative epistemology (contrary to what Piaget claims, e.g. 1957, p. 16); or claim that GE is a version of NE (and hence show how such a NE can secure a place for epistemic norms). I believe it is the third option that is the correct one.

Pretty clearly, the first option would appear to be out since, in the above definition of GE, there is a clear-cut normative judgment being made, namely, that there is a passage from *less* scientific knowledge to *more advanced* (i.e. *better*) scientific knowledge. But to do so, one needs a criterion of evaluation, and the standard account is that criteria of evaluation cannot be established on purely empirical grounds. How, then, can Piaget make such a normative judgment if he is merely a genetic psychologist? It would seem to be the case that he cannot.

A second possibility that comes to mind would be to argue that the epistemologist does make normative judgments, e.g. 'scientific knowledge has gotten better', but takes as her standard of 'better' our current criterion of evaluation – what we now consider 'better' knowledge to be. One would be saying, therefore, 'assuming current epistemic standards, this stage is better than that stage'. This Piaget calls restricted GE. If one were to attempt to defend the epistemic credentials of this contemporary standard, one would be doing generalized GE. Unfortunately Piaget has little to say concerning this very distinction, but even so, I do not think it will be adequate. To mention just one reason, Piaget himself in several places (e.g. 1957, p. 24; 1962, p. 176) makes the claim that the final epistemic norm of the epistemic subject – the latest 'normative fact' – coincides with the epistemic norms of the epistemologist studying the epistemic subject. This is because the psychologist himself is (or once was) an epistemic subject and presumably has passed through all of the stages his epistemic subject has traversed (unless of course the psychologist has moved into still higher stages not obtained by his epistemic subject – something Piaget does not consider). In short our subjects' norms are our epistemic norms! It does not seem possible for the psychologist to avoid making normative judgments.

Now, the entire thrust of Piaget's lifelong work is to argue that epistemologists must consult the actual empirical facts of psychology; this
would seem to imply that he is not doing ordinary normative epistemology in an a priori philosophical way.[18] It seems pretty clear, I think,
that Piaget did not imagine GE to be a version of traditional philosophical (normative) epistemology. In several places, for example
(1967a, 1972a), he argues against the possibility of what he calls a
super-scientific epistemology, something that is presumably like a first
philosophy. He distinguishes normative epistemology from NE in several of his writings (e.g. 1950) and argues in favour of a NE (although
not, he insists, a version of positivism). In short, I think it is clear that
Piaget is advocating some version of NE, but which version?

Piaget's theory of the normative

Part of the reason that Piaget's account of the place of the normative in
GE is problematic is that he never set out his views – what we can call his
normative theory – in a clear and consistent manner.

There are several strands or motifs running throughout his account of
norms. On the one hand, he (1950, 1962, p. 165, 1995) gives allegiance
to the standard distinction between facts and norms. The genetic psychologist, he frequently asserts, studies norms in the epistemic subject, but
in so doing, the psychologist does not (or should not) make a normative
judgment himself (1950, pp. 29–30; 1962, pp. 167, 172). The norms
in the subject that he studies he calls *normative facts* (1950, p. 30; 1957,
p. 28; 1962, p. 167; 1967b, p. 126), norms that are *believed* (or *felt*) to be
true (or obligatory) by the epistemic subject (e.g. transitivity), and the
determination of these normative facts is a straightforward empirical
matter. I prefer to call these *normative beliefs*.

On the other hand, the genetic psychologist herself might have certain
normative beliefs – sometimes he (1962) calls these *psychological norms* –
but that is another matter and raises the question of how the psychologist can rationally make such claims and defend such norms. Given
Piaget's strictures against confusing facts and norms, it would seem to
be problematic for any psychologist to make such a normative judgment

---

[18] It has been argued (e.g. Hamlyn, 1971) that in so far as Piaget is doing epistemology, he
must be doing normative epistemology. However, I am not convinced by this argument
and have criticized it already. Furthermore, it assumes that the programme of NE is
impossible and I wish to argue for the contrary position. In any case, it does not seem to
be the case that Piaget is doing normative epistemology.

since such a judgment could not be established on empirical grounds alone.

The developmental psychologist can empirically determine not only the normative beliefs of the epistemic subject, he can also study their development over time. Clearly, such normative beliefs are not static but change over time from, say, childhood to adulthood. The genetic psychologist can thus study 'how the subject gives himself' these norms, i.e. why these normative beliefs have changed over time. In fact, Piaget claims this question, How can one explain logical processes psychologically?, to be the fundamental question of GE (1950, p. 22). The basic problem of GE, he says, is 'how does the mind attain the construction of necessary relations, independent of time, since the instruments of thought are only psychological operations subject to evolution and constructing themselves in time?' (1950, pp. 22–3). In one sense, the answer is obvious: normative beliefs change over time because the epistemic subject *believes* or *feels* a later norm is better than an earlier one. Such a matter is, again, a straightforward empirical one – another kind of 'normative belief'. There seems to be no problem in empirically determining, say, how a subject proceeds to construct a normative system, e.g. a logical system. But Piaget's way of putting this point raises problems, for, as he expresses it, the subject constructs a system that is *necessary* and not just 'believed to be necessary'. (Instead of the term 'necessary', one can substitute the term 'normative' and we would have the same problem.) But to make such a claim is to make a normative judgment oneself, just as one would if he asserted that the basic question of GE is how the mind attains the construction of moral relations from non-moral ones, or valid knowledge from mere facts. Necessity is constructed by the subject, but it is constructed from earlier stages of contingency. How, then, can necessity emerge from contingency? How can normativity emerge from facticity?

How do norms develop from facts?

The first distinction that needs to be made is that between Piaget's account of the emergence of *necessity* from *contingency* and his account of the emergence of the *normative* from the *empirical*. Although Piaget often glosses over this distinction and tends to assimilate the two, they need to be kept separate. Necessity is a metaphysical concept, not an epistemic one (although the subject's cognizance of necessity is an epistemological issue). A third distinction would involve the distinction between *analytic* statements and *synthetic* ones: how do analytic judgments (or statements) develop from synthetic judgments (or statements) (see Apostel et al., 1957)? Analyticity is usually thought to be a semantic issue. Since I am interested in epistemic norms, I will ignore the first and third distinctions. (See Smith, 1993, for a discussion of how necessity emerges from contingency.)

Epistemic norms

The question before us is how norms *can* emerge from (supervene on) psychological facts. Our interest is not in moral norms (in a narrow sense) but in epistemic norms. Piaget's normative theory often runs these two together and tends to focus on the general question of how any sense of obligation – social or epistemic – is possible. Likewise, as we have pointed out, he has a tendency to equate the normative in general with logic (1950, 1967a, 1995).

The problem, as we have seen, is a 'how-possibly' question (Kitchener, forthcoming): how is it possible for norms to develop from facts? So, beginning from an initial position in which there is no sense of obligation – the self-interested egoism of the child[19] – there develops via a series of stages a final position in which the individual does have a sense of obligation to others. The puzzling question is not only how this happens but how it can happen.

Game theory

If we take seriously Piaget's claim that the programme of GE is concerned with investigating the developmental question of how epistemic norms develop from psychological facts, with how the epistemic subject proceeds to construct such norms from earlier non-normative states, it seems pretty clear that the picture Piaget (1942) has in mind is the following: initially there are just empirical states (certain kinds of weak cognitive structures) and from these states normative states (stronger cognitive structures) emerge. There is a hierarchy of levels being assumed here, with rhythms giving rise to regulations, which give rise to groupings. With each succeeding level, we have an increase in normativity. We can thus say that, for Piaget, norms are supervenient on facts. The question, I have suggested, is how this can happen.

As I have already suggested, one aspect of a solution to this problem of the emergence of norms (Ullmann-Margalit, 1977) can be found in

---

[19] Of course, Piaget's concept of autism and egocentrism is different from (although related to) egoism as a moral theory.

contemporary game theory. Game theory has a long history and recently has taken some new and interesting turns, e.g. evolutionary game theory. Although there is some disagreement about how to formulate the basic ideas of game theory, the underlying notion is that two (or more) players must construct strategies concerning how to play an opponent. Assuming these players are rational (in the sense of *instrumental rationality*), they must devise strategies of play as a result of interactions with the other player(s). There are various kinds of games (one-shot, sequential, repetitive) involving various kinds of social interaction (e.g. cooperation versus non-cooperation, exchange versus non-exchange). One of the most interesting aspects of game theory is the widespread assumption among many game theorists, that certain kinds of strategies result in certain kinds of payoff structures – *equilibria* – which constitute certain kinds of stable payoff matrices that are both desirable and rational to the players. (There are, of course, various kinds of equilibria in game theory.)[20] In evolutionary game theory, a major interest is how various equilibria change – one might say even *develop* – over time. According to many game theorists, it can be shown that, given certain kinds of initial assumptions about the structure of the strategic interaction between individuals over time, certain kinds of equilibria will eventuate as the outcome. If one assumes that, initially, the players are rational egoists of a certain sort, it can be shown that certain kinds of moral solutions will emerge, viz., cooperation (Axelrod, 1984). The basic idea here is that it is in the individual's self-interest to give up unabashed short-sighted egoism and to cooperate with others. In short, cooperation will emerge from competition. Put in developmental terms, what we have here is the following: beginning with an asocial stage of egoism, it can be shown that the individual passes (and will pass) to a stage of initial conflict with others and finally to a stage of cooperation. As one individual puts it, 'Morality . . . can be generated as a rational constraint from the non-moral premises of rational choice' (Gauthier, 1986, p. 4). It should be pointed out that it is irrelevant whether the infant comes into the world as an egoist or not. The logic of the argument is that one should begin with the weakest assumption and this is that the child comes into the world as a non-moral being. If the child were to begin life with morality already in place (e.g. some people have suggested that sympathy is the basis of morality and children are born with this

---

[20] An equilibrium, according to many thinkers, is a combination of the player's actions such that, once reached, no one player wishes he had acted otherwise given the choice of the others.

sentiment), the argument would be much easier to make but this requires a much stronger initial assumption.

Piaget's social epistemology

Piaget's account of how it is possible for epistemic norms to emerge from (supervene on) psychological facts is a complex account and one that has received little attention (see Smith, 1995). I am not able to sketch his entire account, but I would like to focus on a central aspect of it, one that has received scant attention, and that is that aspect of his account that involves what we can call his social epistemology (Kitchener, 2003).[21] Although it now common to read that Piaget underestimates the social, as far as I can tell, this has never been shown or even discussed in sufficient detail to decide whether it is true or not. Certainly, on the face of it, it ignores all of his sociological theory which is only now receiving attention (e.g. Kitchener, 2000).

There are several key elements in Piaget's social epistemology, including his theory of social relationalism, his theory of exchange value and his social theory of rationality. I would like to focus on a central claim of Piaget:

Epistemic norms emerge from certain kinds of social relation between individuals, those involving cooperation.

Egoism, constraint and cooperation possess different degrees of equilibrium and bring into play his distinction between rhythms, regulations and groupings (Piaget, 1942), which is central to much of Piaget's thinking about the social foundations of rationality and epistemology.

Rhythms, regulations and groupings form three different degrees (or kinds) of equilibria depending on the respective amounts of causality and logical implication present in each: the more logical implication present and causality absent, the more equilibrated the structure. *Rhythms* are purely factual (basically causal) patterns in nature. *Regulations* contain elements both of implication and causality but with less causality than rhythms but more logical implication, e.g. pre-operational intelligence, a purely economic exchange of values. Hence, although they are more equilibrated, they are not fully equilibrated. *Groupings*, by contrast, are fully equilibrated, possessing full implicatory relations such as addition, inversion, identity, association, tautology, etc. and hence no causality. A grouping, therefore, involves a fully normative

---

[21] Although Piaget's social epistemology is a central part of his GE, it has been systematically slighted by most scholars. An attempt to redress this is in Kitchener (2000).

(rational) exchange of values, something not present in an economic exchange of values. A fully implicational structure thus emerges from a fully causal structure because the structures of the former contain properties not found in the latter; in particular, when a grouping is constructed, certain logical properties appear as a result of the closure of the system.

A regulation is an exchange of values with a certain degree of equilibrium but lacking conservation. A grouping is an operatory structure that is fully equilibrated because purely implicational. Corresponding to these two types of equilibrated structures is the difference between the social relation of constraint and cooperation. According to Piaget, constraint is a social relation leading to regulations (and isomorphic to it), but *only cooperation can lead to a grouping.*

Constraint is a form of social relations involving an authority (e.g. parents), who enforces social agreement via sanctions, resulting in respect and conformity. According to Piaget, constraint is not an adequate explanation of the moral or logical order, for if individuals are not equals (i.e. the situation of constraint), there is no reciprocity and reversibility, which are present in cooperation, and hence there is no normative obligation. As Piaget surprisingly puts it (1995, p. 200), autism and constraint are not really different from each other, since both are cases of affirming a proposition without proof!

Social pressure, therefore, and the enforced conformity of family cannot account for the nature of logic. Logic does not arise because of the social conformity to group norms, nor merely from the activity of isolated individuals; instead it arises from the interactions between individuals, an interaction and relation of cooperation between equals. Cooperation is thus essential for the development of logic and rational operations; for it is only in cooperation with others (seen as equals) that reciprocity of viewpoints arises and with this general, disinterested normative rules governing how all parties should reason and act.

Piaget's own particular account of this process involves his theory of sociology, social psychology and social epistemology (Kitchener, 2003), an account in which the important role of constraint (or motivation) changes systematically: egoism (or egocentrism) gives rise to the unilateral respect characteristic of *social constraint*, followed by mutual respect shown to peers, which is characteristic of *social cooperation*. Cooperation is more equilibrated than constraint, which is more equilibrated than egoism. When a stage of cooperation is reached, full-fledged norms – moral and epistemic – can be said to appear. Here we have obligations felt to be necessary by the individual, e.g. the obligation to keep a promise, to tell the truth. It is at this stage, we might add, that it makes sense to suggest the individual feels there is an obligation to collect sufficient evidence before making an epistemic claim or to consider all points of view. It is here that epistemic norms first appear. Norms may be respected at first because of an external authority enforcing such a norm but in time these norms are respected on their own. Hence, according to Piaget, norms first are generated from facts, then are maintained over time and develop in a rational way without the need of external sanctions (e.g. social pressure). Taylor (1984) makes a similar claim. Conventions emerge and persist spontaneously since they are equilibria and everyone conforms to them without external sanction (p. 158). Hence, we can say: *epistemic norms emerge from certain kinds of social relations between individuals, namely, those involving cooperation.*

Piaget can be seen to be working in a nineteenth-century neo-Kantian tradition, manifested most clearly by Ernst Cassirer, of showing how objectivity develops from subjectivity. Subjectivity is given as the initial epistemic starting-point and (scientific) objectivity is given as the final state. The task is to show how it is possible to go from the former to the latter. The set of intervening transitions will involve a complex set of epistemic operations of various kinds, eventuating in scientific objectivity.

Objectivity here is to be understood in an epistemic sense, as a necessary condition for the acquisition, maintenance and revision of knowledge since being objective crucially involves the notions of proof, evidence, warrant, verification, replication, inter-subjective agreement, etc. These, in turn, presuppose a multiplicity of points of views or perspectives – a social epistemology – since the upshot of this epistemic process is our common, public, objective world. It is the relation between these points of view that is crucial for objectivity.

This, at least, is Piaget's answer to this how-possibly neo-Kantian question: objectivity is possible only via the process of decentration – of decentring the epistemic subject from his initial, privileged point of view and showing how this perspective is related to the perspectives of others.[22] Objectivity thus consists, following the views of Poincaré and Einstein, in coordinating all these diverse perspectives and seeing the relations between them. When one has constructed such a system of relational transformations, one has constructed the external world and attained objectivity.

---

[22] This is also the answer of others working in this tradition – Cassirer, Russell and Carnap. See Kitchener (forthcoming).

This is my reading of Piaget's account of decentration, an account to be found in Piaget's earliest works (from 1923 up to 1932) and continuing throughout his career, culminating in his *Sociological studies* (Piaget, 1995). A crucial aspect of Piaget's theory of objectivity – decentration – is thus his social epistemology and a key ingredient in this social epistemology is the claim that the very function of epistemic concepts such as *proof, control, reason,* etc., arises only within a social context. The solitary knower has no motive to defend his claims, in fact no awareness of what such a defence would even mean, until others disagree with him and challenge him in dialogue. But this in turn presupposes the individual is aware of the point of view of others. To do this, the epistemic subject must construct a world in which there are several different points of view and this involves a relational perspective, a set of what can be called Galilean transformations from one frame of reference to another.

Furthermore, this can happen, Piaget insists, only if the others are viewed as equals between which there is mutual respect. For one will attempt to justify a view only to one's peers instead of simply announcing it as true or affirming the view of one's parents. All of this presupposes cooperation between equals, not constraint between parents and children.

We can thus say that not only does Piaget have a normative epistemology, we can also say that he has a normative social epistemology. Following other social epistemologists, we can define normative social epistemology as 'the study of the social dimensions of knowledge' (Goldman, 2001, p. 1), 'the conceptual and normative study of the relevance of social relations, roles, interests, and institutions to knowledge' (Schmitt, 1994, p. 1). In short, *rationality consists in certain forms of social interchange* (see Goldman, 1992).

This, in short, is a sketch of Piaget's social epistemology (Kitchener, 2003). It entails the view that the social is necessary for full epistemic development because the social is necessary for objectivity, and because the social is necessary for normative obligation. Hence a Robinson Crusoe could never have a full or complete sense of the normativity of epistemic rules.[23] On this question, therefore, Durkheim was correct

---

[23] Compare Piaget's comments (1995, p. 43):

Individual action already has, in one sense, a normative aspect, to do with its efficacity and its adaptive equilibrium. But nothing obliges individuals to succeed in what they do, and neither the efficacity of actions nor their balanced regularity constitute obligatory norms . . . the study of mental facts in the child shows that the consciousness of obligation presupposes a relationship of at least two individuals, one who imposes an obligation by giving commands or instructions, and one who is obligated (unilateral respect), or two individuals who reciprocally obligate each other (reciprocal respect).

about the initial stage of epistemic normativity – it is social constraint –
but this is not the final stage, which consists of cooperation and respect
between equals.

Conclusion

Pulling all of this together, we can say that Piaget does have a normative
epistemology recognizing the normative nature of epistemic rules. But
such a normative epistemology is fully compatible with a NE – at least
the version of NE I have briefly sketched above – for norms need not be
established according to the methods of traditional a priori philosophy
(even though Piaget concedes this). Instead, they can be seen to supervene on non-normative naturalistic facts – those initially involving egocentrism. From this initial state of egocentrism, a weak normative stage
supervenes – constraint – and from this weak normative stage, in turn, a
stronger normative stage supervenes – cooperation. In short, epistemic
norms supervene on psychological facts just as groupings supervene on
regulations. But these psychological facts are social-psychological facts
involving forms of interaction: autism – egocentrism – constraint –
cooperation. Contractarianism and game theory, I have suggested, provide a useful conceptual model for how this process might be conceived,
with Piaget's writings on exchange theory dovetailing with this theory
rather nicely. Hence contractarianism may be a theory of normative
epistemology useful for understanding Piaget's normative theory, for
(on this account) we can understand epistemic supervenience – how
norms supervene on facts – and this may be all that a naturalist needs to
ground a NE. Such an approach holds out the promise of showing how
norms emerge from facts, how cooperation can emerge from egocentrism ('why is it rational to be moral?'). On this account, it can be shown
that the very meaning and functions of norms – why they originally
arose – is to facilitate and control cooperation between members of a
social group. Epistemic norms are norms of cooperation of a certain
kind – norms of cooperation in the acquisition and transmission of
information. All of this, I would suggest, is basically consistent with
the major features of GE, a kind of completion of Piaget's project.

5 Norms and normative facts in human development

Leslie Smith

> The chess board is the world, the pieces are the phenomena of the universe, the rules of the game are what we call the Laws of Nature.
>
> (Huxley, 1868)

> Norms are not part of the intrinsic nature of things, which is entirely indifferent to them. They are imposed by the will of intelligent beings [who] can act according to a conception of them.   (Brandom, 1994)

1   Normativity and developmental psychology

Modern psychology is not distinctive because of its investigation of the mind – Aristotle's *De anima* set out to do that two millennia ago – but rather because of its empirical investigation of the mind. This leads to two problems, one about normativity, and the other about development.

Normativity

During the nineteenth century, psychology became the science of the mental world, and was regarded as comparable to physics. The causal relations in these domains are empirically investigable, leading to laws of nature in physics, and to laws of the mind in psychology. These psychological laws were also called laws of thought. Yet this parallel between physical and psychological laws is problematic. The minefield between science and philosophy has well-known and still unresolved flashpoints, including problems about mind–body relationships (Descartes, 1931; Nagel, 1995), about freedom of the will (Kant, 1993; Searle, 2001) and about consciousness in the brain (Aristotle, 1987; Chalmers, 1996).

Normativity is just such a flashpoint. Its importance continues to be acknowledged as fundamental but unresolved. Here speaks a neuroscientist:

the fundamental question in philosophy and science today is the nature and validity of the distinction between the factual – what is – and the normative – what ought to be.   (Changeux, 2000, p. 11)

And here speaks a philosopher:

the idea of norm is inseparable from that of someone capable of subjecting and laying down norms for oneself. Therein lies one of the two key ideas composing autonomy: the self-same subject in relation to a norm.
                    (Ricoeur, 2000, p. 212 – my amended translation)

The world of physics is norm-free. The world of human development is norm-laden. Psychology, then, faces a general question. Can psychology be a causal science just like physics and also be explanatory of normativity?

Development

The general question is especially acute in developmental psychology (DP), the branch of empirical psychology providing accounts of the mind from childhood through the lifespan. Norms exist and they are operative in their regulation of human action and thought. Yet this regulation is normative determination, not the regularity of causal determinism. And therein is a problem. Norms had a beginning in time, neither present at the Big Bang, nor for most of cosmological time. The Earth was formed 4,600 million years ago; mammals emerged 65 million years ago, hominids confined to the last tenth of that (Hawking, 2001). If causality prevailed initially from the formation of the Earth, and normativity emerged at some point later, how did this happen, how can norms be the mere effects of causes? Again, norms have an ontogenesis in the lives of individuals and societies, so what is the developmental mechanism responsible for that?

The existence of a norm is a contingent, empirical fact [in that] norms are 'historical', i.e. that they come into being, exist over a period of time, and then pass away.   (von Wright, 1983a, pp. 68, 186)

Human agents can act on norms, violate them, even cancel old norms and create new norms. Almost all children reject in varying degrees the norms of their elders. Were things otherwise, we would still live in caves as hunters and gatherers. Can DP explain the development of these normative capacities?

Two questions, and both are complex. The analogy between game-rules and natural laws is particularly disastrous (Huxley, 1868). In psychology, it has led to the descriptive interpretation of norms (Smith, this volume, Chapter 1). Yet a better interpretation is to hand. My aim in this chapter is to indicate how a normative interpretation of norms at work in human development can contribute to the development of DP. In doing so, I want to *reculer pour mieux sauter*, to step back so as to make a leap forward.

2   Laws of thought and normativity

The first step is to revisit the 'laws of thought' in the critique due to Gottlob Frege. The second step is to revisit the developmental episte-mology of Jean Piaget. Both steps are theoretical. All the same, they are revealing with regard to the contribution made by normativity to human development. As well, they lead directly to an empirical step forward for DP. The step forward is further elaborated in §3 below, with the rest of this section dealing with its theoretical underpinning.

2.1   *Frege on logic and psychology*

Gottlob Frege was the founder of modern logic contemporary to the rise of empirical psychology (Carl, 1994; Humphrey, 1951). Central to his account was a devastating critique of psychologism, the view that the laws of thought in empirical psychology are normative laws of logic (Dummett, 1981; Kenny, 1995; Kusch, 1995; Sluga, 1980). Frege was exercised by the question: What exactly are these laws of thought? Are they causal or normative laws? His answer merits attention on two counts. One is the decisive influence of Frege's position on twentieth-century philosophy and the social sciences generally (Brandom, 1994; Dummett, 1981; Kitcher, 1992; Macnamara, 1994; Popper, 1979). Another is its particular influence on the young Jean Piaget who regarded logic as a promising model for his account of human development (Smith, 1999a, b, 2002a, b).

According to Frege, logic is the formal science of truth:

Just as 'beautiful' points the way for aesthetics and 'good' for ethics, so do words like 'true' for logic [and] it falls to logic to discern the laws of truth . . . From the laws of truth there follow prescriptions about asserting, thinking, judging, infer-ring. And we may very well speak of laws of thought in this way too. But there is a danger here. (Frege, 1977, p. 1)

In this account, truth is a normative notion. Further, it interacts with human knowledge because knowledge entails the truth of what is known (Frege, 1977, p. 18; Moser, 1999). Yet Frege (1979, p. 2) accepted that human knowledge also has a causal origin investigable in causal psychology. Therein lies the danger about the 'laws of thought' in three respects.

Fatal ambiguity

The term 'the laws of thought' masks what Frege (1964, p. 12) regarded as a 'fatal ambiguity'.[1] For Frege, normative laws are laws about 'what ought to be' and so are fundamentally different from causal laws about 'what is the case'. Under this argument, psychology could be the search for causal laws, or for normative laws, but the term 'laws of thought' amounts to their conflation.

Unknown type of madness

Although human thinking can be successful, human thinking can also be wrong. Error in human thought is ubiquitous. Human minds are fallible, falling well short of maximal rationality.

> The causes, which merely give rise to acts of judgment, do so in accordance with psychological laws; they are just as capable of leading to error as of leading to truth. (Frege, 1979, p. 2)

Error is well known in psychological investigations of misperception, 'false memory', pseudo-concepts and misunderstanding. So human error can be both lawful and psychologically valid. There is no problem if psychology is limited to explaining human error. But a twofold problem does arise if psychology takes on something more. One problem concerns how any person can have true memory, correct concepts, a real understanding in an account based solely on a causal psychology. The other problem is how investigators in psychology can be in a position to regard their causal laws as normative laws of thought. Normatively speaking, the law of contradiction states that if A and B are contradictories, they can be neither true nor false together (Quine, 1972). Causally speaking, the law of contradiction applies differently: A can be accepted by people in one contingency, context or culture, and its contradictory B in another. For Frege, therein lay madness. Presented with reliable findings about people accepting A in one condition and its contradictory B in another, causal investigators

---

[1] Frege's reference to the 'fatal ambiguity' is quoted in this volume (Smith, Chapter 1).

could only acknowledge the fact and say simply: those laws hold for them, these laws hold for us. I should say: we have here a hitherto unknown type of madness.   (Frege, 1964, p. 14)

This reference to *madness* was not lost on Frege's successors. It was generalized by Wittgenstein (1978, p. 95) who realized that this 'madness' is not a single strain, but is rather a multi-faceted syndrome. Major outbreaks of the syndrome are virulent today as the predominance of causality over normativity in human biology (Dawkins, 1999), evolutionary psychology (Cosmides & Tooby, 2004), and neuroscience (Changeux, 2000).

Mental processes as eddies

In logic, a statement such as 'Today is Friday' cannot validly co-occur with its contradictory 'No, it's not', nor with its contrary 'Today is Saturday'. Causal processes are another matter. An eddy is a flow of water in a contrary direction to the main flow, such as a whirlpool in the current of a fast-moving river. Neither rules out the other even though their motions are contrary – eddies and currents co-occur. This generalizes to other physical processes. It generalizes to the brain where contrary neural processes can be activated simultaneously. It generalizes as well to the mind in that

[Any mental representation] contradicts another no more than one eddy in water contradicts another . . . thinking, as it actually takes place is not always in agreement with the laws of logic any more than men's actual behaviour is in agreement with the moral law.   (Frege, 1979, pp. 144–5)

Liability to self-contradiction is a fact of human life, documented in psychology (Peng & Nisbett, 1999), even argued to be rationally defensible (Priest, 1998). Liability is one thing; detection and removal of contradictions is another. Yet the latter is impossible in a causal mind devoid of norms. Norm-free, any mental representation can co-exist with any other, which is exactly what a pair of contraries cannot do, normatively speaking. A model of the mind reducible to causal processes cannot explain the means by which contradictions are identified and resolved.

Two conclusions can be drawn from this argument. One is Frege's own conclusion. His was the modest conclusion, the rejection of psychologism. In any normative discipline, the principle to follow is to separate sharply the psychological from the logical, the subjective from the objective.   (Frege, 1950, p. x – my translation)[2]

In proving theorems in logic, logicians do not have to consult the evidence available in empirical disciplines such as psychology. This conclusion about psychologism is well taken – psychology and logic are distinct disciplines, i.e. these disciplines are exclusive. A second conclusion is stronger than this. Many commentators have drawn the stronger conclusion that this distinction is not merely exclusive, but is exhaustive as well. That is, all disciplines are either formal and normative, or empirical and causal, but none is both. The implication from this stronger conclusion is stark: there can be no discipline dealing with both. This implication has been influential during the twentieth century, contributing to the 'division of labour' consequent upon the forced choice between normative and causal sciences. One manifestation is in the social sciences where norms are interpreted factually as non-entities, statistical averages, social regularities or social controls, i.e. as non-normative (Smith, this volume, Chapter 1). Another manifestation is in philosophy, notably in logical positivism, analytic philosophy and linguistic philosophy. But this stronger conclusion goes beyond Frege's own conclusion under which the relation between normative and causal laws was left open.

My conclusion is to side with Frege, leaving the stronger conclusion behind. Armed with his modest conclusion, the question now arises how the exclusivity of normative and causal disciplines can be respected in a discipline with a focus on the relations between them. This is now taken up.

2.2   *Normativity and psychology revisited*

The physical world and the mental world do not exhaust reality. To see why, two questions should be addressed, one metaphysical, the other epistemological:[3]

---

[2] His German text reads:

es ist das Psychologische von dem Logischen, das Subjective von dem Objectiven scharf zu trennen.   (Frege, 1950, p. x)

The standard English translation was due to the linguistic philosopher J. L. Austin whose own position infiltrated his translation:

always to separate sharply the psychological from the logical, the subjective from the objective.   (Frege, 1950, p. x^e)

The first word *always* is an insertion. A comparable insertion occurs in all three principles, *always* in the first, *never* in the second and third. This insertion is an overgeneralization of Frege's own position.

[3] There are many instructive guides to metaphysics and epistemology (cf. Audi, 1999; Searle, 1999).

(A) What is normativity, really?
(B) How do we come to know norms?

Both Frege and Piaget give distinctive answers to these questions.

Frege on (A)

Frege's answer was a version of realism in that normativity is a property of thoughts. On this view, thoughts such as the Pythagorean theorem are neither physical nor mental.

We cannot regard thinking as a process which generates thoughts. It would be just as wrong to identify a thought with an act of thinking, so that a thought is related to thinking as a leap is to leaping.. . . As I do not create a tree by looking at it or cause a pencil to come into existence by taking hold of it, neither do I generate a thought by thinking.   (Frege, 1979, p. 137)

Rather, thoughts belong to a third realm:

a third world must be recognised. Anything belonging to this world has it in common with representations that it cannot be perceived by the senses, but has it in common with things that it does not need an owner.   (Frege, 1977, p. 17)

On this view, matter and mind exist in two different worlds, neither of which is the world of thought.[4] This version of realism continues to attract sponsors (Bereiter, 2002; Popper, 1979).

Frege on (B)

For Frege, thoughts are understood in terms of the act of grasping.[5]

We are not to regard thinking as the act of producing a thought, but as that of grasping a thought. . . Both grasping a thought and making a judgment are acts of a knowing subject, and are to be assigned to psychology. But both acts involve something that does not belong to psychology, namely the thought.
(Frege, 1979, pp. 206, 253)

This position seems attractive in that thinking and thought seem to be connected. When in July 2005 British journalists asked 'What do you think about the terrorist bombings in London?', some New Yorkers replied, 'Our thoughts are with you.' For Frege, a process of grasping secures this connection.

Yet this position runs into a formidable problem. Grasping a thought is a process comparable to grasping the use of a word. If so, this process is problematic

---

[4] For Frege, the world of thought is a 'third' world non-reducible to the other two. A psychology of representational thought merges this distinction between thinking and thought (cf. Smith, 1998, 1999c). It is thereby open to refutation as an account of human knowledge (Bickhard, 2003; Ricoeur, 2000).
[5] English *grasp*, German *fassen*, French *saisir*.

when we are led to think that the future development must in some way already be present in the act of grasping the use and yet isn't present.

(Wittgenstein, 1958, §197)

Wittgenstein's objection was as follows. In grasping the use of a word, how can any fact about what I do now determine my – or anyone else's – future uses? If the sign at a traffic light in the USA reads: 'Do not walk,' that means that walking is forbidden, i.e. neither I, nor you, nor anyone else is permitted to walk across the road while this sign is on view. If I disregard the sign and do walk, that is the wrong thing to do. But that is a normative matter. How can facts about my word-learning have this normative consequence on action? The difficulty is acute, and has been exploited in a famous argument about addition (Kripke, 1982, pp. 8–9). If right now by '+' you mean 'plus' as in

$$8 + 7 = 15$$

that fact about you is compatible with my meaning this same '+' as 'quus' where this addition has the same answer. But 'plus' does not mean 'quus'. Although the meaning of 'plus' is such that

$$68 + 57 = 125$$

the meaning of 'quus' is such that

$$68 + 57 = 5.$$

You and I use the same numerals and the same signs, and that is a factual matter. Further, you and I use these in the same way in some cases, notably in additions up to 15. But some is not all, and in additions after 15 there is a normative split between us. If you say 'But "+" means "plus", so you are wrong,' I will say 'If "+" means "quus", that is not the case.'[6]

---

[6] The dialogue might run thus:

YOU Are you joking?! 68 + 57 is, and has to be, 125.
ME Not for me. I can see nothing in the expression '68 + 57' to mean, still less necessitate, that. For me, it means 5.

Anyone tempted to 'write off' this dialogue as too clever by half is invited to do two things. One is take on board the moral drawn by Lewis Carroll (1895). The other is take stock of facts about children's number development. Children placed four marbles in container H linked by a ramp to an empty lower container L. They were then asked to drop one marble at a time from H (Piaget & Garcia, 1991, p. 45):

ADULT Stop before the 3rd one falls.
BRI Three of them will be in L.
ADULT And in H, then?
BRI Four.

In short, the objection is a *reductio*. A causal account of word-meaning is such that the same facts about learning a word are compatible with contrary uses in the future. But this is hopeless, leading directly to a tower of Babel (Kripke, 1982, pp. 26, 37). The rational step is to reject this hopeless consequence, and so the premises from which it was drawn. And that is to reject any causal account of word-meaning. Now Frege's account of grasping a thought is vulnerable to a comparable objection. Facts are facts, and no fact entails any specific norm (see Hume's Rule, in Smith, this volume, Chapter 1). Yet when a thought has been grasped successfully, normativity is in the outcome. If you say '68 + 57 isn't 5', you are making a normative judgment. So if the process of grasping a thought is solely causal, it is too weak as an explanation of the normativity in the outcome. In other words, if normativity is in the successful outcome, it will have to be included in the process as well. Exactly that is precluded by Frege's answer to (A): the norms are in his third world. Yet in his answer to (B), the knowing subject is a person in the first world of physics and the second world of psychology. Accessing the third world from the latter pair is problematic.

To summarize the discussion so far. Frege's threefold critique of psychologism led to his demarcation of normative and causal laws. The open question is whether this critique can be respected in a discipline directed on relations between such laws. As a check on this, any such discipline should provide answers to two questions about the metaphysics and epistemology of norms, about what norms are and how we get to know them. Frege's answer to (A) was in terms of the metaphysics of realism. That answer has been argued to be defective as an epistemology in answer to (B). The basis of this defect has been exposed in the Wittgenstein–Kripke account of rule-use. So the options are either to give up the search for a new discipline, or to look elsewhere for it. Taking the latter option leads me to Piaget's answer to (A) and (B).

Piaget on (A)
Piaget's answer was a version of constructivism in that normativity is a property of the coordination of actions.

> There exists a kind of logic of coordinations of action.   (Piaget, 1974, p. 116)

Notice several things here. First, actions are never singletons, so all agents have the task of coordinating their earlier and later actions. The proposal is that coordination has a logical, not merely a causal, component. And logical properties are normative properties. If there is logic of the coordination of actions, normativity follows on. Second, the normative aspect of coordination amounts to a logical, and so normative, framework. Such frameworks are not thereby well formed. A framework could be a hybrid combining distinct principles from different logics; or could be a fragment including merely some parts of a complete system; or could be a pseudo-logic.[7] A structured framework is well formed, but even so may be complete only in limited respects, i.e. partial equilibrium. There could be no final structure, no final end-point to human development (Piaget, 1970a, p. 10; 1971, p. 155; 1986, 314).[8] Third, the logic of the coordination of actions is a 'general logic, both collective and individual' (Piaget, 1995, p. 94). It thereby amounts to an exchange system, enabling rational agreement or disagreement between individuals in societies. Normative frameworks are used by human agents in the causal contexts of biology and culture. So both causality and normativity are co-present. This bi-directional relationship leads to the problem of their coordination.

Norms have a becoming which thereby brings up a problem that extends its roots right down to the sources of action and to the elementary relations between consciousness and organism. [This requires the dissociation of physiology in a consciousness constituted by] systems of implications whose necessity is essentially distinct from the relations of causality pertaining to the explanation of material facts.   (Piaget, 1950, p.30)

Norms develop through time, and they do so interdependently with the causality operative in biology and culture (Smith, 2002b).

So Piaget's answer to (A) is this. Living beings have normative capacities which are reducible neither to a biological inheritance nor to

---

[7] For example:
  • hybrid logic – *obligated conjunction*, i.e. obligation in deontic logic and conjunction in propositional logic (Piaget, 2006);
  • logic fragment – *class membership* without class inclusion (Piaget, 1952; Smith, 1993);
  • pseudo-logic – over-generalization in word-use (Piaget, 1962; Smith, 1998).
[8] In Darwinian biology, both finality and progress are excluded in evolutionary growth (Changeux, 2000). In Piaget's model of the development of human knowledge, finality is excluded, but not progression. This makes sense – the formation of new species is not the same as the formation of new knowledge which never arises *ex nihil* (Piaget, 1971).

cultural transmission.[9] His position was invoked in his first book, *Recherche*.[10] And he maintained this same view throughout in that

[a human agent] is always 'norm-laden'.   (Piaget, 1965, p. 159)[11]

This position has three attractions. It avoids the proliferation of worlds since the causality and normativity of action operate in the actual world, the one world there is (Searle, 1995). It enables normativity to be at work in the actions performed by agents with the capacity to make normative impositions on an otherwise norm-free world (Brandom, 1994, 2000). Even though normativity is not causality, both are co-instantiated in a continuum which leaves open the extent of their dual contributions (Putnam, 2002; Ricoeur, 2000).

Piaget on (B)

On his view, norms are known in their use and development in that any agent

seeks to avoid incoherence and for that reason always tends toward a certain form of equilibrium.   (Piaget, 1985, p. 139)[12]

Incoherence and contradiction are not part of the causal world, nor can they be detected by the causal machinery of brains and mind. By contrast, if human agents have normative capacities, these capacities can be put to work in the recognition and use of norms. For Piaget, norms are at work in the regulation, i.e. coordination, of the sequence of actions co-extensive with the life of their agent. The regulation of actions by an agent amounts to a use of logic, and so is normative. This use may be unrecognized and impaired. But it is normative, and it can be developed by its use. It is a logic of action, not a 'mental logic' (Braine & O'Brien, 1998; Johnson-Laird, 1983). All the same and in virtue of its use in action, this logic can impinge on conscious actions, intentional activities and acts of judgment (Ferrari, Pinard & Runions, 2001). Crucially, its presence in some form throughout all development is attested:

---

[9] Piaget's position eliminates neither biological nor cultural influence – both are in fact necessary (Smith, 2002b). But it does deny the sufficiency of biology (Piaget, 1971, p. 323; cf. Ricoeur, 2000, p. 54) and of culture (Piaget, 1995, p. 227; cf. von Wright, 1983a, p. 39).

[10] *Search* (Piaget, 1918, pp. 155ff.). For a summary see Gruber & Vonèche (1995), for commentary see Smith (2003).

[11] *Un sujet est toujours 'normé'.*

[12] *Le sujet cherche à éviter l'incohérence.*

from the beginning and even among our youngest subjects, a physical fact is recorded only within a logico-mathematical framework, however elementary it may be.   (Piaget, 2001, p. 320)

A logico-mathematical framework is a normative framework. Neither the content nor character of this capacity is fully formed, indeed not formed at all prior to its use by the infant agent. On this version of constructivism, a central question is not how a mind regulated completely by causality bridges the gap to regulation by normativity. Rather, it is how causal regularities and normative regulations are combined in one and the same mind in action.

Piaget's answer to (B) has two advantages and faces one challenge. One advantage is its requirement for the interplay of causality and normativity in all human action and thought, thereby meeting the Wittgenstein–Kripke objection which undermined Frege's answer. Another arises from this same requirement, namely its compatibility with Hume's Rule (Smith, this volume, Chapter 1) in that some normative framework is operative in all human action and thought, from childhood onwards. Under Piaget's model, no normative 'has to' is ever generated from the 'is' of causality alone. But the challenge is severe. Piaget's (1985) mechanism of advance was equilibration, a process marked by serial outcomes with degrees of equilibrium, none complete in being vulnerable to disturbance by later actions in the sequence. His account of this mechanism is widely regarded as inadequate in two respects. It is inadequate as a formal model since 'the mechanism which Piaget depicts is obscure' (Klahr, 1999), and inadequate as a testable model since 'it is incredibly hard to detect how the mechanisms invoked by Piaget can be investigated empirically' (Bryant, 2001). These objections are well taken. But they are open to reply (Smith, 2002b). First, Piaget's model is intelligible, and open to theoretical and empirical elaboration (Piaget, 2001, 2006). Second, half a century ago, Piaget's psychology of development was characterized as a 'psychology of normative facts' (Isaacs, 1951). The insight in this remark has been missed in the objections, and is now taken up.

3   Norms and normative facts

If the first step back was to the work of Frege, the second step was to the work of Piaget. Indeed, Piaget's answer amounts to a problem-shift (Lakatos, 1974). This can be seen in his answer to a third question:

(C) How can normative laws and causal laws be related in one model?

My argument is that Piaget's answer to (C) amounts to an advance. His answer is intelligible (Smith, 2002b, 2003, 2004). And it can be developed by identifying some of the principles which comprise the normative frameworks at work in human action and thought. In §2.1 above, it was accepted that causal and normative laws are exclusive. What was left open was whether they are also exhaustive. Piaget accepted their exclusivity, shown in his rejection of both psychologism and logicism. Just as logic cannot provide a causal explanation, nor can causality provide a normative explanation (Piaget, 1953, 1966). But he rejected their exhaustiveness. According to Piaget, there is a *tertium quid*, a third alternative, which is neither normative logic nor causal psychology. Piaget's *tertium quid* was developmental epistemology (DE).[13] DE is a linking science with a focus on the relations between normative and causal laws which preserves their independent status. DE has a dual focus, combining both norms in epistemology and normative facts in psychology.

If a norm is not a fact, what exactly is a normative fact? Piaget (1950, p. 29; 1965, p. 49) accepted the widely held view that norms are not derived from observation of the actual world, i.e. norms are not facts. Even so, not all facts are causal facts. For Piaget, there are normative facts as well, and these are

facts in experience permitting the observation that a particular agent considers him- or herself to be obligated by a norm, irrespective of its validity from the observer's point of view. (Piaget, 1950, p. 30)

A normative fact is the use made by an individual of a norm. This use is open to observation, and so is empirical. But it is also the use of a norm, and so this normative component is constitutive of the use. Further on this view, normative facts are

imperative rules whose origin is in social interactions of all kinds, and which act causally, in their turn, in the context of individual interactions.
(Piaget, 1995, p. 69)

An individual's use of a norm typically has both a social origin and a social focus. Its logic is imperatival and so modal-deontic. Although this

---

[13] *Epistémologie génétique*: 'genetic epistemology or scientific theory of knowledge based on the analysis of the very development of that knowledge' (Piaget, 1950, vol. I, p. 7). The term *genesis* has a traditional meaning in reference to origins and formation – as too the cognate term *genetic* – meaning *beginning* or *becoming*. Due to advances in twentieth-century biology, this traditional meaning has now been overtaken, resulting in *genetic* as synonymous with *hereditary*. A *developmental epistemology* removes the incipient conflation of the two distinct meanings of *genetic*, and it does so without denying the contribution made by heredity to the growth of knowledge.

use may be causally efficacious, normative facts are not the same as causal facts, otherwise the causality–normativity distinction is conflated (Smith, this volume, Chapter 1). What is left open here is a generalized account with a dual focus on both causal and normative facts. This version of DE requires a joint focus on

the coordination of factual data and normative validities [placed] in correspondence with each other without reducing one to the other.   (Piaget, 1966, p. 153)

This is a liberating claim. Even if knowing is a causal process (Bruner, 1966), it is a normative process as well, and this insight is captured in Isaacs's (1951) elegant summary of Piaget's model. In short, Piaget's answer to (C) is in terms of his DE, which combines causal regularities and normative regulation in one model.

Normative regulation has long been regarded as a central to the human mind. For Aristotle in his *De anima* (1987, §432a), the mind has representational capacities, but also regulatory capacities for the assertion and denial of truth and falsity. For Kant (1997, p. 41), human minds have two regulative capacities, one for gaining true knowledge, the other for the production of free action. For Korsgaard (1996, pp. 46–7), normative judgments are constitutive of moral reasoning. For Ricoeur (2000, pp. 54, 93), normative judgments make a foundational contribution to scientific thought, a contribution ignored in the slide taken in neuroscience in the reduction of human (normative) capabilities to biological (causal) capacities. For Brandom (2000, pp. 79–83), the use of normative capacities is not the illumination of a Cartesian light inside the mind, but is rather the making of Kantian-like commitment whereby humans can engage in thought (taking-true) and in action (making-true). In general, an agent has the capacity to do or to think otherwise. This capacity is normative, and so could not be explained in an exclusively causal model. That is why psychology is not just like physics. A model with a jointly normative and causal focus would have four principles:

3.1   Dual access

All norms have a double accessibility

(α) manifest in a pattern of action or thought of an individual
(β) in virtue of its binding force on that individual

A regularity, including patterns of behaviour or thought, can be investigated under (α) in terms of its causality. Regulation under (β) in terms of its normativity is different. For example: there are two ways to close a gate. One way is causal. If a heavy weight is suitably attached by a chain to a gate, its effect can be to close an open gate – *the weight causes the gate to close*. The other way is normative: if the sign attached to the gate reads PLEASE CLOSE THE GATE, its outcome can be the same. But the process is different due to the norm-laden actions of people – the norm is the directive *you have to close the gate*. Thus the same outcome – the gate is closed – can be due to different aetiologies under (α) and (β). Another example: two taxpayers – a perfect spy admitting 'I pay my taxes, I don't want to blow my cover'; a good citizen declaring 'I pay my taxes, I ought to do this.' Under both, the tax is paid. Yet the origin is different, the spy acts compatibly with a directive, the citizen acts through normative force in good conscience.[14]

The general distinction between (α) and (β) was famously invoked about moral norms by Kant (1993, §72): 'every action which conforms to the law (thereby) does not occur for the sake of the law'. This distinction is more general, in going beyond moral norms. In Brandom's account, sapience – not mere sentience – is the mark of the human recognition or acknowledgment of norms:

our activity institutes norms, imposes normative significances on a natural world that is intrinsically without significance for the guidance and assessment of action. A *normative significance is imposed on a non-normative world.*

(Brandom, 1994, pp. 30, 48 – italics mine)

Normative action transforms the natural world otherwise devoid of meaning. And the gain arising from (β) is significant. Therein lies a creative potential from the use of normative capacities.

Central to the difference between (α) and (β) is the logic of norms. This logic is modal in two ways, a modal-deontic logic about 'what has to be done' (Horty, 2001; von Wright, 1983a), and a modal-alethic logic about 'what has to be' (Cresswell & Hughes, 1996; von Wright, 1983b). Normativity is well defined in these modal logics, and so could be exploited in formal descriptions of normative frameworks.[15]

First, modal logic defines the character of a norm, that is, the manner in which an action occurs (modal-deontic), or the manner in which a thought is true (modal-alethic). Either way, there are three different

---

[14] Historically, *conscience* in English had two meanings – cognitive consciousness and moral conscience. Its French counterpart still does.

[15] Heuristic in DE: 'that structures exist is, therefore, for the investigator to ascertain and to analyse' (Piaget, 1973, p. 46 – my amended translation). In his final works, Piaget accepted that his logic needed 'cleaning up' by recourse to one modal-alethic logic (Piaget & Garcia, 1991). There are, however, other modal-alethic logics, and modal-deontic logics, too. Nor do they exhaust the class.

modes which can be illustrated using the Luther and Spinoza examples in Chapter 1.

LUTHER		
Nailing his theses to the church door	Here I stand, I cannot do otherwise	
My action – but is it?		
Obligatory	Permitted	Forbidden
My action is obligatory		
So that means		
	Its negation is not permitted	Its negation is forbidden

SPINOZA		
Given the numbers 1, 2 and 3, the next proportion is...	1 is to 2 as 3 is to 6	
My thought, what I am thinking – is it?		
Necessary	Possible	Impossible
It's a necessity		
So that means		
	Its negation is not possible	Its negation is impossible

Observational learning reveals which action is performed (Luther), or which thought is judged to be true (Spinoza). But this leads to further questions. OK: but this action – was it obligatory, permitted, or even an act of defiance in being forbidden? Again, the proportion in these numbers – is it a necessity, or a mere possibility, or even an undetected contradiction?

Second, the modal character of a norm is definable only through the other members of the same modal family. Luther regarded his action as obligatory, not as a logical necessity. Spinoza's proposition is necessary, but it is not thereby obligatory. Further, obligation has equivalences in the same deontic family – an obligation is something whose negation is not permitted, that is, whose negation is forbidden. Again, necessity has distinctive equivalences in its alethic family – a necessity has a negation which is not possible, that is, its negation is impossible.

These modal equivalences are subtle. It is not a requirement that all equivalences are recognized by an agent in using a normative capacity. Human agents have much less than maximal rationality, and this rationality undergoes development (Piaget, 1953, 2006). Rather, the claim is that the failure by an agent to display any such modal equivalence renders indeterminate the character of normativity in the action or thought, including whether it is even normative at all (Smith, 2002a, ch. 5). The complete non-realization of any modal equivalence is to miss the modal point. All the intermediaries lie between 'all and none'. The serial realization of some of these equivalences is at the core of human development.

3.2   Norm-use and norm-consciousness

A norm may be used without an agent's awareness, operative in what I do or think without my being recognizant of this. Distinct from this is an agent's awareness that a norm is valid without its being an operative norm – I can recognize that a norm is binding on you, but not on me. This generates four cells corresponding to the presence–absence and the use–consciousness of a norm.[16]

Norm violation: norm is neither operative nor recognized
The violation of a norm may be due to ignorance of its existence, to inadvertence or to distraction.[17] Violation may be innocent, notably during early childhood, as when Jacqueline and Jacques were playing with marbles by arranging them in a pile with a rubber ball on top, exclaiming 'That's the Mummy ball and the baby balls' (Piaget, 1932, p. 25). Creative play with marbles in a social context is not thereby playing marbles in a rule-governed game.

Norm denial: non-operative but recognized norm
Norms may be non-operative due to human failure – an agent recognizes that a norm is in force, and yet disregards it.[18] Other cases can be overt and explicit. After his capture, Saddam Hussein was put on trial in 2004, leading to this dialogue:

Judge	Who are you?
Saddam	I am Saddam Hussein, the President of Iraq. Who are you?
Judge	I have been nominated by the coalition authorities.
Saddam	This means that you are applying the invaders' laws to try me.

[16] The English distinction *use/consciousness* corresponds to its French counterpart *pratique/ conscience* (Piaget, 1932).

[17] Norms can never be singletons, but are instead always related to other norms. For convenience, single norms are here reviewed. Multiple norms are taken up in §3.3.

[18] *Video meliora, proboque, deteriora sequor* (Ovid, *Metamorphoses*) – I see and approve the better, but I do the worse. Or, in the vernacular of a newspaper editor chided by the

Saddam's second reply shows that he did not accept his trial under 'the invaders' laws', i.e. 'their' norms were invalid for him, and so not operative on him.

> *Normative pressure: a norm is operative but is not recognized by an agent*

Norms are normally transmitted from one generation, group, or individual to the next.

> Learning to participate in institutionalized forms of behaviour is connected with a characteristic motivation. I shall call this motivational mechanism normative pressure. (von Wright, 1983a, p. 39)

Effective transmission can secure compliance, norms can be transmitted without the individual realizing this. So an operative norm can be at work, causally activated without the agent's realization of its normative status, without the realization that norms can be under an agent's own control. To make this realization requires an advance, which is to see that

> the reason for conforming to the set of patterns should, on the whole, *not* be the impact of normative pressure. (von Wright, 1983a, p. 39 – his emphasis)

Piaget (1995, pp. 290ff.) made special reference to socialization as normative transmission in this sense. Indeed, securing the advance to autonomy is, in his model, a developmental priority. Reasoning as an act of obedience and obedience as an act of reason are not the same thing (Piaget, 1995, p. 60).

> *Normative autonomy: an operative norm is recognized as such*

A plaque at Rugby School commemorates the exploit in 1823 of William Ellis who disregarded the rules of football/soccer, then prevailing, by taking the ball in his arms to run with it. This action was the origin of rugby football, eventually attaining its own normative rules.[19] Norms from one generation are transmitted across to the next, ensuring constancy. Norms are created by the next generation, thus ensuring novelty and advance. It is this creative potential which Piaget exploited in his

---

owner of Harrods in London, 'I just can't stop myself – it's like when I keep writing leaders supporting dodgy billionaire shopkeepers who want passports. I know it's wrong, but I feel this overwhelming urge to do it' (Morgan, 2005, p. 281).

[19] The point here is valid even if this story is a myth – see www.nationmaster.com/encyclopedia/William-Webb-Ellis. Other paradigm cases include Galileo's rejection of Aristotle's physics (Kuhn, 1977), or Martin Luther King's (1968) commitment to non-racist civil rights.

thought-experiment about children in a society of exact contemporaries, a society which is causally abnormal, but normatively not so. Every individual – especially young individuals – should be introduced to collective notions prevailing in that person's society with a view to rethinking them (Piaget, 1995, p. 57). This amounts to a 'recapturing of individuality and distancing from collective imperatives' (Piaget, 1995, p. 290; for commentary on this thought-experiment, see Smith, 2002b).

3.3   Multiple norms

The obvious way in which multiple norms are present in any context is due to other people, and especially from people in other cultures. More potent still is the presence of multiple norms in the lives of individuals, notably as normative dilemmas. A dilemma may arise in two different ways:

Contrary norms

An agent can be faced with an exclusive choice if two norms point in contrary directions when only one action can be performed (Holbo, 2002). In 1940, the Nazis captured Paris – what was Sartre's student to do (Mason, 1996)? He could stay in Paris so as to care for his elderly widowed mother (OA). Equally, he could go to London to join the Free French Army (OB). But he could not do both at once – in this context, OA and OB were contraries. Suppose OA was chosen. Then OA was assigned a higher value than OB by that agent. That choice did not thereby nullify OB – that action was still obligatory, even though over-ridden by another norm.

Contrary interpretations of the same norm

Some norms are clear even though complex. Norms about car parking are illustrative, for example:

```
FOR THE ATTENTION OF ALL
         CAR DRIVERS

If you park, you agree to pay:
 ▪ first two hours free
 ▪ thereafter £8 for up to 24 hours
```

Other norms are open to divergent interpretations. The captain gives the order (von Wright, 1963, p. 78):

Someone ought to leave the boat.

The boat is about to sink, putting everyone on board at risk, but if one person leaves, the others may be safe. Who is 'bound' by this disjunctive command – the men, the adults, the passengers last on board? Agents in each of these three classes could well ask – why not women, why not youngsters, why not the first on board? The dilemma in such cases arises because incompatible actions – staying on board/leaving the boat – have their basis in divergent interpretations of the same norm.

The occurrence of dilemmas is one reason why norms require a framework for their coordination. The dilemma brings to light a potential problem: is the framework consistent? The consistency of any system can remain undetected, for example if it has been socially transmitted, or if no breakdown has been detected so far. Yet any consistency is provisional, vulnerable to later coordinations by the same agent. Agents can change their minds. Future actions can run counter to their predecessors.

3.4   *Normative reasoning*

This principle runs full circle back to §3.1. Reasoning can be causally learned in line with (α). Reasoning can also be normatively directed in line with (β). Their demarcation has been given too little attention in available research. There are problems to confront, notably due to major ambiguities in the expressions *has to* and *must*. These expressions are in the language used by pre-school children (Byrnes & Duff, 1989; Scholnick & Wing, 1995). An open question is how they are understood by children, and adults too, by comparison with their counterparts in logic. Unfortunately, there is ample room for doubt, if the case study of deontic reasoning is typical of research in causal psychology generally. This contention is elaborated in §4.2 below.

There is a generic methodological issue here. In causal psychology, investigators are reliant on responses in controlled settings without due recourse to participants' reasoning on which these responses are based. Causally speaking, responses alone suffice; normatively speaking, reasons for these responses should be on display – well, they should if these responses are normative facts tied to norms with a basis in reason (Smith, 2002a, ch. 5). In general, norms in action and thought are rational. Reasons can be given for and against them. Unlike causes which are 'there' at work in the physical world, whether we like it or not, norms can be accepted or rejected, elaborated or criticized and evaluated. As well, they can be adapted and changed. Normative reasoning is the royal road to doing this. It is not an easy road, but it is the only road we have.

4   Norms in human development

The normative model in §3 is presented as a theoretical model which has not been empirically tested. Even so, it is testable. With this model in mind, a review of typical evidence is now presented under five categories: incompatible, indeterminate, compatible, plausible and convincing.

4.1   Incompatible evidence

In neuroscience and evolutionary psychology, psychology is an exclusively causal science (Bjorklund & Pellegrini, 2002; Changeux, 2000). The same is true of psychology regarded as nothing but an experimental science. In these positions, normativity is ruled out in one of two ways.[20] One is to derive non-causal normativity from causality. The other is to reduce non-causal normativity to causality.

The objections to both are the same. Normativity as a phenomenon is not in doubt – see the multiple examples in Chapter 1. Frege's critique in Chapter 1, §2 showed that causality is too weak to count as the sole explanation of normativity. So neither derivation nor reduction can be carried through other than by disregarding the normative nature of normativity. Further, both options conflate two interpretations of the term *origin*. This term can mean descent which is causal, and it can mean precedent which is not. Even if *homo sapiens* as a species has a causal descent, that has no bearing on the capacity of human agents to identify norms in action. It is only by the use of a normative capacity that normativity can be identified at all (Ricoeur, 2000). Finally, these options have ruled out normativity as a possible source of variation. The marginalization of normativity as 'mere noise' is a particularly telling omission in an experimental paradigm.

---

[20] Asked about the explanation of normativity in DP at an open discussion in a conference in Berkeley in 2001, one developmentalist replied along the lines, 'We don't do mysticism.'

4.2   Indeterminate evidence

The selection task is regarded as the single, most investigated problem in the psychology of reasoning (Evans, 2002).[21] The design of this task is based on the truth-table for conditionality in truth-functional logic. The main finding is that conditional reasoning is hard with the success rate at below 10 per cent even for adult undergraduates (Evans, 2002; Johnson-Laird, 1999). This finding was interpreted by Wason (1977) to show the explanatory shortcomings of Piaget's model due to its over-reliance on normativity and under-recognition of causality, a contention that Piaget (see Morf, 1957, p. vi) explicitly did not share. During the last couple of decades, the selection task was redesigned in terms of deontic logic (Cheng & Holyoak, 1985; Cosmides, 1989). Central to the redesign is a deontic conditional whose antecedent refers to an action, while its consequent states a pre-condition. A typical finding is a fivefold amelioration in the success rate for which an evolutionary interpretation is given (Fiddick, 2003). The implication is twofold. One is that normativity explains too little – witness the high failure rate on the truth-functional version. The other is that biological causality explains much more – witness the higher success rate on the deontic version.

This conclusion is premature on two counts. First, although normativity is invoked for purposes of rejection in the interpretation of such studies, it has been given scant attention in their methods and findings. The selection task is a paradigm example of a task restricted to the generation of causal facts. The irony is that its design along with the responses scored Correct/Incorrect are thereby normative, and so a normative system is used by the investigator. But this is denied to the participants. The investigators have declined to use their task in the generation of normative facts. Second, the deontic version of this task is riddled with ambiguities about the scope of *must* and about its multiple readings in logic.[22] Taken together, this renders these conclusions about normativity indeterminate.

---

[21] It is often claimed that the selection task was designed by Peter Wason (1966; cf. Evans, 2002). This is to ignore Genevan predecessors, notably a pioneering September/Clocks task due to Albert Morf in 1957 (Smith, 1993, p. 117).

[22] See Appendix.

4.3   Compatible evidence

A series of cognitive acceleration projects were designed on developmental principles to improve the quality of school learning. Using Piagetian reasoning tasks, a diagnostic survey (n=12,000) set a baseline, showing that only one third of youngsters had developed in line with Piaget's model of formal operations (Shayer & Adey, 1981). Using Piagetian and Vygotskian processes in science classrooms under a quasi-experimental design over two years with youngsters in Years 7 and 8 (11–12 years), the aim was to augment the 'one third' to something higher in three core subjects, English, Mathematics and Science, in public examinations (GCSE) taken in Year 11 at 16 years. The outcome was reliable over two interventions (Adey & Shayer, 2002). By reference to same-school control youngsters, the 'good pass' rate in public examinations was 59%, 51%, 53% in the core subjects respectively, i.e. an 'added value' of some 21%. Comparable interventions are ongoing, including counterparts in primary school mathematics (Shayer & Adhami, 2003). One main feature of these projects is the durable transfer of learning due to the three-year time-lag between invention in Years 7–8 and assessment in Year 11. This evidence is compatible with a model of the mind as 'general processor'. Whatever changed in the minds of these learners was not specific to one school subject, nor dependent on its pedagogical context. The mind as 'general processor' is compatible with the normative model presented here.

This evidence is incomplete in two respects. One shortcoming is that normative principles were used as such neither in the teaching nor in the assessment. A particular absence concerns the 'binding force' of norms, operative and recognized norms, and modality. The outcomes of the interventions were stunning; but did they amount to causal regularities or to normative regulations? A second shortcoming is that one strength of the evidence was its basis in public examinations, thereby securing objectivity in assessment. Although norms are instantiated in the classroom learning – rules to be learned, orders given by teachers, permissions requested by learners, normative actions in evaluations (Shayer, 1997, pp. 54–8) – these are not shown to be present in the marking criteria of the examinations. At issue is what a 'good pass' means. Under the distinction in §3.1 above, correct understanding and norm-based understanding are not the same thing.

4.4   Plausible evidence

Two findings from my (Smith, 2002a) study amount to plausible evidence of norms at work in the reasoning of young children. One hundred children from state schools in north-west England took part in the study. There was an equal distribution of boys and girls over the first two years of compulsory schooling in Years 1–2 (5–7 years).

Number conservation: operative but non-recognized norm

This study was an investigation of number conservation, where 10 per cent of the children gave a distinctive answer. They had been shown two spatially coincident lines each with six buttons (white and blue), and the children agreed the equality. Then the lower white line was spatially lengthened:

Initial Display	Transformed Display
⊙⊙⊙⊙⊙⊙	⊙⊙⊙⊙⊙⊙
✿✿✿✿✿✿	✿ ✿ ✿ ✿✿ ✿

Asked now about the equality, these same children replied that there were now 'More Blues', i.e. more in the upper, non-lengthened line. Reasons given by the children were revealing:

• more blues because you've taken two away
• less whites because these two aren't there

According to these children, the action of lengthening the white line had led to the disqualification of the two end buttons. So there were now four buttons left in the white line, six in the blue line. What is interesting in this reasoning is not numerical miscounting, but normative misconception. Two white buttons – moved merely a couple of centimetres and still in full view – were not counted. For these children, they were 'not there', they had been 'taken away'. These children were using their own norm to disqualify from white line membership two end buttons in the white line. An analogy clarifies things. A referee's disqualification of two players from a football match means that they leave the pitch, perhaps remaining on the side-line. As such, they are discounted as players. Similarly, the answer 'More Blues' is a spectacular argument for the non-conservation of number.

An interpretation of this answer is based on children's norms – valid from their point of view, invalid from ours. In accounts of moral reasoning, some children are credited with a principle of equal action: 'everyone should get the same treatment under any circumstances' (Damon, 1977, p. 75; Turiel, 1983, pp. 158–9). By parity of argument, these children can be credited with a comparable principle in number reasoning: two lines in an array should have all properties in common under all circumstances. Such principles are normative with a regulatory force, enabling these children to make sense of their observational learning.

Number reasoning: operative and recognized norm

This study was an investigation of reasoning by mathematical induction. In one version of the task, the children were shown two boxes, A and B, such that A contained one button but B was empty. After agreeing this, the children then repeatedly made equal additions to each box in three different contexts: open to observation; not open to observation; hypothetical addition. In this latter context, one question was about the addition of a 'great number':

LES	How about if you put a great number in that one and a great number in that one. Would there be the same in each, or more there [pointing], or more here [pointing]?
JOHN	That would be right up to the cover in the sky and that would be right up to God, so then they would still have to be more.
LES	What's the cover in the sky?
JOHN	It's on top of where God lives.

This analogical reply is testimony to children's creative reason. John believed that God lives in heaven on top of which is a cover. By adding a 'great number', the contents of one box would reach as high as God in heaven. But due to the head start, the other would be even higher in reaching up to the cover over heaven. So there would be more in the latter than the former. This superb reasoning matched a quintet of norms in an AEIOU framework (Smith, 2002a, 2003):

> *autonomous*: John's was a free mental act with an individual characterization, and it was distinctively his own.
>
> *entailment*: The normative relation of necessity was explicitly expressed as 'would still have to be more', not merely 'would still be more'.
>
> *intersubjective*: John's inference was 'common ground' between different thinkers, i.e. this self-same inference was made by others.
>
> *objective*: This reply about 'more' in one container than the other was sound (true, correct), and stated in a truth-preserving argument.

> *universal*: This conclusion was a universalization, amounting in
> this context to John's knowing what is always the case,
> whether or not open to transfer to other contexts.

In short, John had recognized a norm operative in his own reasoning,
expressing this in a distinctive way.

It will be objected: such evidence is not causally plausible since insufficient controls were taken. My reply is twofold. Causally speaking, this is
the normal state of things – witness the serial changes in any research
paradigm. In fact, this task is in a novel paradigm which has received no
attention, despite its origin nearly half a century ago in a Genevan study
(Smith, 2002a, p. 22). Normatively speaking, this evidence amounts to a
decisive step in crossing the normative Rubicon.

4.5   Convincing evidence

To my knowledge, the best study is a classic study of children playing
marbles (Piaget, 1932). Marbles is a rule-governed game to be classified
as normative in von Wright's taxonomy (Smith, this volume, Chapter 1).
Piaget's study was empirical and directed on normative facts. At issue in
the study was, first, children's *pratique* or use of rules, and then their
consciousness or reflective understanding of their character as rules (see
fn. 16). And explicit in their reasoning were modal notions. In short,
manifest in this study were most of the principles in the normative model
sketched in the last section.

Rules of the game: pratique

At issue was how the rules were used as the children were playing the
game. The study was designed in sharp contrast to the design of deontic
versions of the selection task in two key respects. One is the adoption of a
first-person perspective – its focus was on the children's own norms at
work in their activity in playing marbles. This contrasts with a third-
person perspective in most other studies. The other difference is that the
modal character of children's understanding was made explicit, thereby
avoiding some of the confounds in deontic versions of the selection task
(see Appendix).

First, note that very young children can play creatively without regard
for norm-laden rules – see §3.2 above when Jacqueline playing with
marbles explained 'I'm making a little nest' (Piaget, 1932, p. 25). Her
play was creative, but blind to the rules of playing the game of marbles.
Second, during mid-childhood, rules can be recognized but also conflated with other rules, manifest as invalid applications. Here are some
examples:

IF A PERSON WINS A MARBLE, THE MARBLE HAS TO BE STRUCK

Playing with Piaget led to this exchange with Baum:

PIAGET Who has won?
BAUM The one who has hit a marble, well, he has won.
PIAGET Well! Who has won?
BAUM I have, then you.

Baum has correctly stated the rule, and then conflated it with another rule about turn-taking. Later, when Piaget had four marbles and Baum had two:

PIAGET [Now] who has won?
BAUM I have, then you.

Later when Piaget has none and Baum has two:

PIAGET Who has won?
BAUM I have [and] you've lost.

So here the rule about winning is correctly applied (Piaget, 1932, p. 28). Another case: Mae is playing with Wid and dislodges four marbles (p. 30):

MAE I can play four times now.
WID [This is against the rules, yet he is complicit.]

Third, in late childhood, rules are recognized and validly applied. Several rules are on offer (pp. 34, 40):

BEN You must play from where you are.
NUS When you play, everyone must play the same.
GROS When there's one boy who has won too much, the others say 'Coujac' and he is bound to play another game.

Notice that modal notions – *must, can, bound to* – are explicit, and used correctly, in these answers.

IF A PLAYER'S MARBLE LANDS IN THE SQUARE, IT HAS TO BE DISLODGED BY HIS OPPONENT

This rule was explicitly invoked during the game (p. 35):

PIAGET [His shooter lands and remains in the square.]
BEN You are dished. You can't play again until I get you out.

Another rule covered accidents (p. 36):

PIAGET [His marble slips out of his hand.]
ROSS You say 'Laché'. If you don't say that, you can't have another turn. It's the rules.

Notice that modal notions were again used explicitly and correctly in these conditionals, namely that the consequent cannot – not merely does not – follow. Generic rules were also stated, for example how to play particular games such as 'Piquette' as opposed to 'Roulette' (p. 34):

NUS When you play Piquette, everyone must play the same.

Play the same is not a prescription for uniformity, but rather for all to play by – and so be bound by – the same rules.

Rules of the game: consciousness
Two questions were interesting, one about creating a new rule, the other about changing an existing rule:

COULD A NEW WAY OF PLAYING BE FOUND?

During mid-childhood, the answer was No (pp. 47, 50 – amended translations mine):

FAL I don't know how to play any other way.
PHA You couldn't play any other way.
GEO I think you can but I don't know how.

All the same, these answers are revealing. Modal notions – *any other way, couldn't, can* – were explicit. Less clear was whether these were interpreted by these children alethically – something was or was not possible – or deontically – something was or was not permitted. The exchange with Ben was especially instructive (p. 55):

BEN I couldn't invent one straightaway like that.
PIAGET [Pressing Ben to devise one]
BEN Let's say that you're not caught when you are in the square.
PIAGET Then we could play that way?
BEN Oh, no, because it would be cheating.

Ben first denied that he could devise a new rule; then, when pressed, he showed that he could do. This is nice reminder that agents' beliefs about their own capacities are fallible and can be false. Yet his 'creation' was unstable in amounting to a pseudo-rule, shown by Ben's relapse into regarding play in accordance with his rule as cheating, i.e. a violation of what he regarded as a 'real' rule.

COULD AN EXISTING RULE BE CHANGED?

A more advanced view in reply to this question was offered in late childhood (pp. 58, 59):

ROSS If they do it often, it will become a real rule . . . So as not to be always quarrelling you must have rules, and then you have to play as is necessary.

GROS Oh yes. Some want to, and some don't. If the boys play that way [changing something] you ought to play like they do.

Modal notions were explicitly used in these answers, in the case of Ross alethically (*il faut jouer comme it faut*), in the case of Gros deontically (*on est obligé de jouer comme eux*).

Several objections might arise:

a. *This study was non-experimental, paying insufficient regard to causality.* Yes, but its replication could address this, provided a dual focus on both causality and normativity is planned. The key point is that this study does focus on normativity in action.

b. *It was reliant on a questionable 'clinical method'.* This is false. The method was critical, methodologically necessary, and tenable (Smith, 2002a, ch. 5).

c. *The level of rationality was not maximal, none of the normative abilities reviewed were 'fully in' and some were scarcely 'first-in'* (cf. Flavell, Miller & Miller, 1993). True enough: but are not adults' norms open to the same objection? It is sufficient that the norm used is a valid norm in adult thought, not that it excludes further revision. These children had made a start on the long, normative voyage.

d. *The study did not deal with moral norms, so it was non-normative.* This is false. Moral norms are merely one of many types of norms (Smith, this volume, Chapter 1). This study really was a study of normativity in human development.

Summary

The normative model in §3 above has yet to be fully investigated and tested. But it is empirically investigable. On the basis of the available evidence reviewed above, it shows promise.

5   Conclusion

My starting-point in §1 was two questions, one for psychology in general and the other for developmental psychology (DP) in particular, about normativity and development:

- Can psychology be a causal science just like physics and also be explanatory of normativity?
- Can DP explain the development of these normative capacities?

My argument is that the answer 'Yes' can be given to both questions, provided that a dual focus is maintained on both causality and normativity. Under this argument, psychology cannot be just like physics, the causal science of the physical world. Although the physical world is norm-free, human action and thought are norm-laden. Since causality and normativity are not the same thing, this has the consequence that the causal world is only one part of reality. This means that psychology can take two roads. One is to remain an exclusively causal science, thereby leaving normativity out of account. The other is to remain a causal science constrained by an inclusive focus on normativity. In my view, the former leaves out too much, roughly everything distinctive about the human mind. My reasons for taking the second road were given in §2. This led from Frege's argument against psychologism to Piaget's argument for a developmental epistemology (DE). I interpreted Frege's argument as showing two things, one that normative and causal laws are distinct, the other that their distinctness is compatible with a discipline covering the relations between both. Under this argument, Piaget's version of DE combined both theoretical and empirical parts. Crucially as well, normativity was in both parts. In §3, a crucial step was to combine the premise that norms are not facts with another, that not all facts are causal. In particular, normative facts are facts open to empirical investigation without being reducible to, nor derivable from, causal facts. My particular proposal was that DP can contribute to the explanation of normativity, provided its focus is augmented to cover both normative facts and causal facts. This led to four principles in a normative model concerning dual access to norms through both causality and normativity, the use and consciousness of norms, multiple norms manifest in dilemmas and contrary interpretations of norms, and normative reasoning as modal reasoning. Although this model has not been tested fully, it is empirically investigable. In §4, this model was evaluated in terms of five types of evidence taken from available studies in five categories: incompatible, indeterminate, compatible, plausible and convincing. The provisional conclusion was drawn that this normative model shows signs of promise.

Piaget's developmental epistemology (DE) has been foundational in this argument. In the twenty-first century, the main aim for cognitive science has become how to combine philosophical insights with psychological evidence (Goldman, 2001; cf. Kitcher, 1992). Exactly that was the aim of Piaget's DE as a linking science between normative epistemology (NE) and empirical sciences such as DP (Smith, 2003, 2004). DE is distinctive on three counts. First, DE is similar to NE in that both are normative theories. DE is distinctive in virtue of its theory-based focus on the bi-directional relationships between norms and normative facts, whereas NE has an exclusive concern with norms alone. Second, DE is similar to DP in that both are empirical theories. DE is distinctive in virtue of its focus on causal laws constrained by normative laws and theories, i.e. the focus on the latter drives the former. By contrast, DP may deal with these laws, severally or jointly, without assigning primacy to either. Third, both NE and DP make a necessary contribution to DE, i.e. neither can be disregarded. Under this argument for DE, NE pays too high a price for its exclusive focus on norms in normative theory due to its vulnerability to empirical disqualification (Smith, 1993, §3). Under the same argument, DP pays too high a price by remaining an exclusively or even predominantly causal science just because its standard problems about human action and thought have an explicitly normative dimension, hitherto insufficiently investigated (Smith, 2002a, ch. 5). Alternatively, DP can augment its problem-stock whereby the investigation of normative facts drives the search for their causal correlates, along with comparable changes to methods, findings and models.

In short, I side with Piaget (1970b), when asked about the future of psychology: 'With optimism. We see new problems every day.'

APPENDIX

In these psychological studies of deontic reasoning, hybrid conditionals are used:

- if the letter is sealed, it must carry a 20 cent stamp (Cheng & Holyoak, 1985);
- Sally, if you play outside, you must put your coat on (Harris & Núñez, 1996);
- if you drink tanka, then you must give your wife a gift (Fiddick, 2004).

These conditionals are hybrids. They are comprised of a descriptive proposition as antecedent and a consequent stated in terms of *must*. Since they are hybrids, this is a sure sign that any buyer should beware.

a. These conditionals are designed as deontic conditionals. In deontic logic, an obligation has a modal property about 'has to'. But there is a difference between an obligation directed on a proposition about

'what has to be', and an obligation directed on an action about 'what
has to be done' (Horty, 2001; von Wright, 1983a). These are not the
same thing since propositions have a truth-value, unlike actions
which are neither true nor false. In von Wright's (1963 – see Smith,
this volume, Chapter 1) taxonomy, ideal rules are cases of the former:

if it is your birthday tomorrow, it must not rain

and directives of the latter,

if the dog barks, you must not run

A key difference concerns what an agent bound by these obligations should or should not do. This is explicit in the latter, which is
personal, but not in the former, which is impersonal, and in any case
your birthday may mean nothing to me. Related to this is the primacy
of first-person perspectives in the case of action, and the difference
between an operative/conscious norm in §3.2 above. There are no
controls for these differences in the psychological studies. Crucially,
it is likely that the propositional reading is assumed and this means
that the action reading has been totally bypassed.

b. Taking the propositional reading, the scope of *must* can vary in these
conditionals. There are two alternatives, and neither is straightforward in deontic logic (von Wright, 1985). Using the symbol O for
must as a deontic 'ought', a typical conditional used in psychological
studies concerns a rule for young children:

if you play outside, then you must wear a coat

Now the use of 'must' in this conditional is ambiguous. It could
amount to

$$p \to Oq$$

that is, 'if p, then it has to be q'. Alternatively, it could amount to

$$O(p \to q)$$

that is, 'it has to be that if p then q'. These are different, and are
further analysed in (**c**). It is sufficient right now to notice that in the
former, the scope of O is restricted to the consequent. That is, only
the consequent is obligatory. The difficulty is that the conditional
then runs foul of Hume's Rule in combining a factual antecedent
and obligatory consequent. This leads to trivialization through its
generalization, for example:

if you read this paragraph, you must pay me £1 million

A rogue consequent, surely, that has emerged from nowhere. You can't seriously accept this hypothetical imperative! Alternatively, take the latter, where the scope of O is the whole conditional. That is, the conditional as a whole is obligatory. Two difficulties arise. First, it is problematic what this conditional means without invoking some further deontic norm. Wearing a coat outside is not binding on a dog, presumably devoid of normative understanding, whereas it could be binding on a human agent on a variety of grounds. Yet these grounds are variable, including the causality of normative pressure (von Wright, 1983a; cf. 'my mother makes me do this, but really I don't see why') and valid normativity (von Wright, 1983a; cf. 'I am only a child and so I should take care'). The former is not a normative necessity, the latter is. Second, even if it is intelligible, this conditional alone does not allow the detachment of an obligatory consequent. Obligation binding over the conditional is not distributed over its constituent parts. The detachment of the consequent

I must wear a coat

is invalid in modal-deontic logic. What is missing here are background norms. Yet these are not given, neither by the investigator, nor by the participants.

c. The conditionals used in this deontic research can be interpreted in three ways. They could be interpreted as necessary conditionship, or as alethic necessity. Both are logical but neither is deontic obligation. An open question is which interpretation it is.

MUST AS NECESSARY CONDITIONSHIP IN PROPOSITIONAL LOGIC

One thing, and one thing only, is at issue in propositional logic, namely the truth value of any proposition. Conditionals occupy a central place in this logic, and they are well defined, and the logic is extensional (Sainsbury, 1991). So at issue is the truth value of the propositions in a conditional 'if p then q':

$$p \rightarrow q = \mathrm{df} \neg (p \,\&\, \neg q)$$

that is, an antecedent is conditionally related to its consequent just in case it is false that p is true and q false. For example, in this conditional:

If Cassius is lean, then Cassius is hungry (Quine, 1972)

a consequent is stated as a necessary condition of its antecedent. It can be read as:

If Cassius is lean, Cassius must be hungry.

This use of *must* is truth-functional. It simply refers to the truth values of the propositions. This conditional is itself false just in case the antecedent is true and the consequent is false. So the truth of the consequent is a pre-condition of the truth of the antecedent, i.e. it is a necessary condition. However, even if this is in fact the case, things could have been otherwise – Cassius could have been anorexic, lean due to his metabolism, a thin man even after a banquet.

MUST IN MODAL-ALETHIC LOGIC

Modal-alethic logic is intensional. At issue is the modality of any proposition, that is, the mode or manner in which something is true/false. Necessity is well defined in modal-alethic logic (Cresswell & Hughes, 1996; von Wright, 1983b). Taking p as a necessity:

$$p = df \; \neg \Diamond \neg p$$

a proposition is necessary just in case its negation is not possible; that is, the truth of a necessity could not be otherwise. An alethic conditional can be read in two ways comparable to the ambiguity in modal-deontic logic above:

$$(p \rightarrow q) = df \; \neg \, (p \, \& \, \neg \Diamond q)$$
$$(p \rightarrow q) = df \; \neg \, \Diamond (p \, \& \, \neg q)$$

Neither reading fits this deontic research. A contingent truth is true, but is not a necessary truth. Suppose it is true that:

If I have seven pounds and five pounds, then that makes twelve pounds altogether

All the same, it is not necessarily true. Rather, it is a contingent fact which could be otherwise, less in the event of theft, more in the event of a donation. A necessary truth is different, it could not be otherwise. If $7 + 5 = 12$, this is not only true, and so not false; more than that, it could not be false, it could not be otherwise. A conditional in mathematics can be read as:

If the addition is 7 and 5, then the sum must be 12

Learners make mistakes, learners can all too easily give other answers. But that is exactly to miss the point by conflating norms with causes. This sum is and has to be 12. Its necessity is independent of what any learner thinks, even if this thinking is in well-known causal conditions.

MUST IN MODAL-DEONTIC LOGIC

Modal-deontic logic is intensional, dealing with the mode or manner in which an action is performed. Taking A as an action:

$$OA = df \neg P \neg A$$

an action is obligatory (O) just in case its negation is not permitted (P); that is, an obligated action is not permitted otherwise. A deontic conditional can be read in two ways:

$$(p \rightarrow Oq) = df \neg (p \& \neg Pq)$$
$$O(p \rightarrow q) = df \neg P(p \& \neg q)$$

Which reading fits this deontic research is unclear. Any proposition, whether necessary or contingent, has a truth value. By contrast, actions are neither true nor false. Of course, any action can be described in a proposition referring to it, but that is another matter (von Wright, 1963). All the same, necessity applies to some actions:

If the gate is open, you have to close it
If the dog barks, you must not run

In these hypothetical imperatives, necessity is explicit in that a factual condition is stated in the antecedent with an obligatory (*must*) or forbidden (*must not*) action in the consequent. Deontic conditionals are well defined (Horty, 2001; von Wright, 1983a). Deontic conditionals are intermediaries between the two previous classes. The action in the consequent is more than a necessary condition in view of its modal character, but less than an alethic necessity in that an obligation may be violated (see fn. 18). Even if an alethic necessity is, and has to be, exceptionless, deontic obligations can be both valid and disregarded.

The upshot for this psychological research on deontic reasoning is this. It is not clear whether the participants in these studies

- conflate some/all of these three interpretations of *must*;
- invoke either the first or second interpretation, but not the third;
- invoke the third interpretation on the basis of an incomplete and limited understanding of the complexities of deontic logic.

In short, the interpretation of the evidence in these studies is indeterminate.

.

Part II

Norms in moral and social development

6 Contextualizing moral judgment: challenges of interrelating the normative (ought judgments) and the descriptive (knowledge of facts), the cognitive and the affective[1]

Lutz H. Eckensberger

Contextualization of moral judgments

Piaget did not only apply the biological metaphor of an equilibrated system to cognitive development but also used it very early (Piaget, 1918) to define morality as an equilibrium between the person and the society. He even reformulated the categorical imperative in these terms when he wrote: 'Act in a way [so] that you can realize an absolute equilibrium of living organisms – the collective as well as the individual' (after Kesselring, 1981, p. 196). This conceptualization already shows that from the very beginning he tried to contextualize morality, thus by necessity also referring to facts. Even later (Piaget, 1932) he retained this view by interpreting moral development as part of personality development. By doing so, he also linked moral judgments to the development of affects (Piaget, 1981). He contextualized the empirical analysis (methods) of moral judgments from the very beginning as well, by looking at children's everyday activities, which entail rule systems, like rules of games. He also constructed an impressive number of small scenarios that represent moral issues (like lying, distributive justice, immanent justice, responsibility, collective guilt etc.), which were intentionally rooted in the life context of children. So in Piaget's approach

[1] The research was supported by the German Research Foundation and by the Volkswagen Foundation. Over the years many co-workers contributed creatively to the conceptualization, data gathering and analysis. I want to thank Heide Reinshagen and Peter Burgard for their cooperation in formulating the action theory reconstruction of moral development; Ulrike Sieloff, Elizabeth Kasper, Anita Nieder, Siegrid Schirk and Helma Halter particularly for working on the first step of contextualization; and Heiko Breit, Thomas Döring and Annette Huppert for cooperating in the construction of everyday morality. Finally I want to thank Ingrid Plath for translating and improving the present version by critical comments.

there was a close and intrinsic relationship between facts (knowledge of rules, understanding the facts of the scenarios, understanding and acceptance of the situation) and norms (what is right or wrong, what is worse etc.).

Basically, Kohlberg (e.g. 1973) was more Kantian. Kant (1966) wanted to keep morality free from empirical facts, and Kohlberg attempted the same, by constructing *hypothetical* moral dilemmas, which were intentionally *decontextualized*, whether he succeeded in doing so or not.

In the following a series of empirical research projects (1980–2003) on moral judgments will be summarized from the perspective of the relationship between facts and norms. Because the theory we developed is partly rooted in Piaget's theory, the projects are Piagetian in their theoretical and methodical orientation, although they began with Kohlberg's theory and went beyond Piaget's approach to a certain extent. We deviated from Kohlberg in at least three ways: (a) We replaced Kohlberg's 'role taking' criterion of the structure of moral judgments by using several action elements (goals, means, ends, results and consequences) and their conflict potential as a criterion for defining the structure of moral judgments and arguments (Eckensberger & Reinshagen, 1980); (b) After having defined what can be called a deep structure of the development of moral judgment, we turned to real-life contexts step by step so as to analyse ecological issues (building a coal-fuelled power plant, water consumption, following conventional or 'green' farming methods). In a way we thus recontextualized moral judgments. We did so by adapting and developing an action theory perspective which theoretically allows the integration of cognition and affect, of subject and context (culture); (c) We also developed different methods, based on the concept of a 'potentially self-reflective subject'. They are therefore not standardized, but, rather, flexible in the sense that the subject's perspective is taken seriously. They also include biographical interviews.

One can object that these data are outdated, particularly because contextualized research is historically dated. But they are not. Gigerenzer once argued that 'Data without a theory are like babies without parents: Their life expectancy is short' (Gigerenzer, 1998, 202). However, the opposite is also true: data live longer if they are collected and interpreted within the framework of a theory. This is exactly what we did.

The central thesis is that the relation between facts and norms can be discussed productively, if one turns to contextualized analyses of moral judgments. And it is particularly advantageous to do so in an action theory framework and from a developmental perspective, because this relationship is shaped through development, which in turn helps to clarify it.

Before the main results of these studies can be summarized, the theoretical approach of action theory has to be explicated, because the data as well as the data collection can be understood only within this framework. We used it over the years (a) to define the (decontextualized) deep structure of moral judgment; (b) to develop a unique method; and (c) to contextualize moral judgments.

A sketch of action theory

We consider action theory as *the theory of choice*, when an approach is required that allows one to integrate the situation and the person, as in environmental psychology and cultural psychology in general or when morality as a prescriptive social cognition is involved. As will be seen, it also allows for the integration, or at least a systematization, of many other relevant psychological processes, like cognition, affects, control theories and coping strategies, risk taking as well as references to the self (identity) etc.

The intrinsic interrelationship between context and action is explicitly underlined by Rosnow & Georgoudi (1986) when they state, 'an act or event cannot be said to have an identity apart from the context that constitutes it; neither can a context be said to exist independently of the act or event to which it refers' (p. 6).

This perspective implies that neither a taxonomy of subjects nor one of situations is envisaged; instead, as Michael Cole (1998) also proposes, a taxonomy based on 'domains of activities' or a 'typology of actions in action contexts' (Eckensberger, 1990) is constructed. This construction, however, requires a specific theory which particularly focuses on actions.

Our work began with Boesch's (1991) action theory, but also made use of some concepts from cultural psychology (Cole, 1998; Valsiner, 1987), Russian activity theory (Leontiev, 1977) and some distinctions proposed in analytical philosophy (von Wright, 1971; Habermas, 1981).

In principle, action theory can be presented from at least four angles: (a) a *paradigmatic* angle, which focuses on the general status of the interrelationship between the acting agency, the action and culture; (b) a *structural* angle, where the analytical relations between goals, means and ends are elaborated; (c) an *integrative* angle, which interrelates cognition and affects, behaviour and cognition, behaviour and control, action and agency; and (d) an *actual genetic* (dynamic) angle, where the emergence, course and completion/termination of an action are analysed. In the present context the second and third angles will

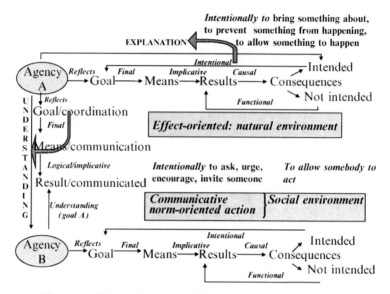

Figure 6.1. Two action types: effect-oriented and norm-oriented actions.

primarily be considered. (For a more detailed treatment of the paradigmatic aspect see Eckensberger, 2003; for the dynamics of action see Boesch, 1991; Eckensberger & Emminghaus, 1982.)

From a paradigmatic perspective we claim that a human being is a 'potentially self-reflective' agency. Therefore *intentionality* of action is a core concept for understanding the individual (Eckensberger & Meacham, 1984), while at the same time also allowing the conceptualization of culture as an intentional world (Shweder, 1990). Without going into details here, it has to be underlined that we neither believe that every action is 'rationally planned' and conscious nor do we assume that the members of a culture are consciously aware of culture and cultural rules as the 'reification of action'.

The structure of actions

In following Habermas (e.g. 1981), we distinguish at least two basic types of actions (Figure 6.1): first, the **instrumental action** which is **effect-oriented** and pertains to the **material, physical (natural) world**. Second, **the social (communicative) action** which is oriented towards **empathy** and **understanding** and relates to the **social world**. From an attribution theory point of view, the natural and the social

environment are in fact *formed by* attributing causal or intentional structures to the world. If a car does not start in the morning, one can look
at the causes, by checking the engine, one then treats the car as part of
the technical world, which is governed by causality and natural laws. If,
however, one starts talking to the car, somehow treating it *as if* it
had the bad intention of not wanting to work, one treats it as part of
the social world, which is governed by intentions and cultural rules.
While one can intentionally bring something about or prevent something
from happening or allow something to happen in the natural world,
one cannot do the same in the social world. Here one can ask persons
to act, one may even urge them to act, but one needs their agreement
(intention) to do what one asks for. One can also compel somebody not
to act (not allow the act), but even this is not causal in its consequences:
he or she has to follow the demand intentionally.[2]

The hierarchical structure of actions

We propose an analytical distinction *between three different 'levels' or
orientations of action* which apply to *instrumental* as well as *social* actions,
and which, in addition, relate psychological concepts to cultural ones
(Figure 6.2). The descriptions of these orientations are extremely con-
densed for the present purpose (for more elaborated versions see
Eckensberger, 1995, 1996, 2003).

We suggest placing the action between the subject (agency) and the
context (culture). Thus, two action-fields are created: the 'external' and
'internal action-field'. They overlap and are interconnected by the
action, which is part of both, and which therefore acts as a bridge (or a
pivot) between them: the 'internal action-field' encompasses the subjective meaning people attribute to a situation and the 'external action-field'
or cultural factors include existing shared cultural concepts such as
shared interpretational patterns, scripts and expectancies.

Primary actions: world-oriented actions

An action is 'chosen' from possible alternatives and can be reflected on
in principle. It is executed and its execution leads primarily to changes in

---

[2] Of course, there are more domains to be distinguished, like technology, logic, aesthetics
and economy in the non-social realm and personal concerns, morality, conventions and
religion in the social realm. They all imply standards (technical functionality, consistency, harmony, efficiency, identity, justice/care, social functioning and salvation) and
emerge by overcoming barriers (problems, contradictions, disharmony, loss/waste, ego
crisis, conflicts and existential threat). Their elaboration is beyond the scope of this
chapter (cf. Eckensberger, 1996).

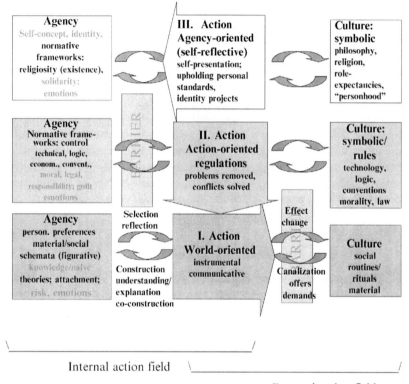

Figure 6.2. A hierarchy of action levels.

the external situation/action-field. However, this choice is not 'free' in the sense of being arbitrary, but predetermined to a great extent by the cultural context which channels or 'canalizes' the choices (during onto-genesis). The cultural context enables, forbids or even taboos possibil-ities of action. In this sense, culture is also the 'medium' (Cole, 1998) in which the subjects grow up. At the same time the subject reconstructs the effects (s)he produces (in case of instrumental actions) or agree-ments which (s)he reaches (in case of communicative actions), or (s)he at least has to explain or understand them as constructive acts. Following Boesch (1991) we call these processes *primary structurations,*[3]

[3] Boesch (1991) proposes a process of secondary structuration which deals with the affective and symbolic aspects of action which is not elaborated here, because it is not relevant to the discussion of the relation between facts and norms.

their 'results' in the subject *objectivation* and resulting changes in the culture *objectification*.

So, basic motives, figurative schemata (knowledge structures of varying complexity), scripts and personal concerns play a crucial role when these primary actions are being executed and evaluated. We claim, however, that even at this first level the subject's 'world' *comes into being* through action and interpretation. These patterns of interpretation originate in and are refined during ontogenesis. The interpretation of primary actions is also accompanied by so-called primary affects/emotions: joy, anger, disgust, sadness and fear.

Secondary actions: action-oriented actions

For the subsequent discussion it is central that various obstacles and barriers almost inevitably occur in the course of primary actions. These lead not only to different forms of coping (cf. Lazarus & Launier, 1978), but also to the emergence of regulations and reflections that are essential for all changes in development (cf. Piaget, 1970, 2001). One can almost regard them as the condition for or motor of development. Following Janet (Schwartz, 1951) we call these regulations *secondary actions* because, on the one hand, they are – just as primary actions – future-oriented and possess a basic teleological structure (they are goal-oriented as they are intended to re-establish and adapt primary actions, and they imply decisions and evaluations of outcomes), so basically they also have the structure of actions. On the other hand, however, they are not oriented towards the world but towards primary actions. Hence, we call these secondary actions *action-oriented*.

In our conceptualization of the relationship between the objective world (ontology) and the subjective understanding of the world (epistemology) we claim that the barriers, which lead to the schemata mentioned above, are not 'objectively given', but basically come into being through interpretations. They achieve their specific quality primarily via interpretation, and more or less 'adequate' ways of overcoming barriers can be differentiated. Basically two types of barriers are important once more: some are technical or instrumental in quality, and these can be called problems. The others have a social quality, which means they are conflicts. So, secondary actions are regulations and reflections of primary actions. A first differentiation of these regulations can be made on the basis of interpreting a barrier as a problem or conflict, because just as interpretations of the social world and the natural world can be more or less 'adequate', overcoming the two types of barriers can be more or less 'adequate' as well. In the case of an (instrumental) problem, the barrier has to be (technically) removed; in the case of a conflict, however, it has to be socially 'resolved'. In light of the action types, distinguished above, it is evident that these are rather different approaches.

It is important to note that in the course of an action every definition of a barrier or obstacle implies some *standard* about how an action is usually carried out, or should be carried out. We call these phenomena *action-guiding frameworks* or *normative rule systems* for actions. These standards differ and they can be technical or social too. These standards are not only pre-conditions for defining barriers as barriers but also imply different 'ways of overcoming' the obstacle that can be more or less 'adequate'. For instance, barriers that are interpreted *causally* (materially/physically) are viewed as *problems* that have to be *removed*. However, barriers interpreted as *social phenomena* (because someone created them intentionally) are considered *conflicts* that have to be *resolved* (for details see Eckensberger, 1996). Many kinds of regulations are possible, but they all depend on whether the obstacle is interpreted as being basically technical, logical, economic, aesthetic, conventional, legal or moral, to name just the most important standards for actions (see fn. 2).

These standards are not just used to evaluate courses of action, but are themselves developed during ontogenesis by experiences in a specific cultural context, in which different expectations, customs, ethical principles or belief systems set the stage. Concepts derived from Piaget's (1970) theory are regarded as developmental principles or processes (assimilation/accommodation, decentration, reflective abstraction) that lead to a qualitative transformation of these standards during development. But these Piagetian principles have to be complemented by a cultural-content dimension, and this becomes increasingly important as the concept of standard gains complexity in the course of development – as research on Piaget's and Kohlberg's theory shows (Dasen & Heron, 1981; Eckensberger & Zimba, 1997). Thus there is an urgent need to complement Piagetian developmental concepts with more content-oriented concepts of development, based on the tradition of socialization processes.

Finally, it is worth mentioning that the different interpretations of barriers also imply different types of emotions: we distinguish manifold 'shades' of affects that emerge as reactions to differently interpreted barriers or experiences (cf. Eckensberger & Emminghaus, 1982). For example, when a barrier is interpreted causally as a physical or material incident (a problem), we speak about a 'frustrating emotion' – *anger* or *rage*. However, we speak about *wrath* in the case of a social barrier (a conflict), and of *guilt* and *shame* if the subject regards him- or herself as responsible for the barrier. It is less important that our terms reflect everyday language exactly; rather, the central point is to distinguish various emotional reactions to frustrations by different emotional concepts, depending on the barrier's interpreted source or origin.

Of course, in many cases one cannot presume that the subject acting alone is involved in these regulative processes. The social world certainly also initiates co-regulations (support, help), which in turn influence the emotional evaluation of the success or failure of a regulation (e.g. if one succeeds, one feels pride or triumph, one feels grateful towards others or appreciates their help, etc., cf. Valsiner, 1987).

Hence, all regulations aim at controlling or, generally speaking, at coordinating actions – to continue or give up an action, to reinterpret the situation, etc. Apart from this, they differ – just like in the case of the primary actions – in the affordances and possibilities a culture provides, as well as in the prohibitions and taboos – the existing 'normative rule systems'. These are, among other things, knowledge systems, but also morals and laws as outcomes of 'time-tested' ways of solving conflicts in a culture.

Tertiary actions: actor-oriented actions

It is only consistent to presume, especially when postulating that humans are '*potentially* self-reflective beings', that impediments to or disturbances of secondary actions inevitably compel the person to reflect or rather to self-reflection (see Piaget, 1977). One asks questions like, 'What goals do I really have?', 'How important is a particular action outcome for me? What does some moral insight mean to me?' 'Is it important for me to "uphold" my personal convictions or character?', which finally raises the question, 'Who am I?' or 'What is the meaning of my existence?' Once again, primarily the barriers of actions (in this case of secondary actions) contain the developmental potential of such questions. At the level of tertiary actions the process of primary structuration leads to role expectations or stereotypes oriented towards others (personhood) in a culture or society, and on the other hand to the development of the subject's identity and self-presentation to the external world. These identity structures also possess an action-guiding potential. They can be considered identity stages, as for example outlined by Robert Kegan (1982), Erikson (1959) and others, and this implies that subjects constantly reconstruct and renew their understanding of their *relationship* to the social world, and thus the relation between autonomy (independence) and attachment (interdependence) in the social world. Essentially, the subject reconstructs the balance between being entitled to personal needs and fulfilling those of others. The relation of the subject to the natural/material world (aspects of culture) is, however, also located here.

One barrier is of utmost importance at the third level, and this is in fact the other side of the coin of self-reflection: the knowledge of one's death or existence on earth. It is religion (on the cultural side) that provides the possibility of an existence beyond death (although this may differ in various religions), thereby 'outwitting' death.[4] Religiosity is what individuals believe. As pointed out by Oser & Gmünder (1984) or Fowler (1981), religious structures are of an existential (religious) nature and can be described as stages that represent man's relation to the 'ultimate' (see also Eckensberger, 1996). This is actually an interpretation scheme in its own right; it usually implies an entire theory of the structure of the world (relations among humans, animals, plants) and its development (created and governed by one or more ultimate being(s)). It also entails rules of conduct (what is right or wrong, or a sin). Some kinds of 'regulation' are even prescribed or afforded by a religion, such as purifying rituals, prayers etc.

So 'agency' is characterized by four relations: it is (1) *reflexively* tied to one's own environment-oriented actions; (2) oriented to the social world by *understanding* the actions of others; (3) *self-reflexively* related to itself (the *Innenwelt* or 'inner world'); and (4) related *contemplatively* to some transcendental or ultimate phenomenon.

Norms and facts in action contexts

In the following, eleven quite different aspects of the relationship between norms and facts will be dealt with.

Analytical relations between norms and facts

It may seem almost trivial, but the distinction between the two action types itself already implies that norms and facts are not independent analytically. Even the classical distinction between different types of causes proposed by Aristotle (final, efficient, formal and material) can be localized in the simple action scheme of an instrumental action (Figure 6.3).

---

[4] Wittgenstein's (1972, §6.4311) notion that death is not an event of life, because we do not live to experience death, seems to contradict this basic idea. But it does not, because he then 'outwits death' himself, by saying that 'if we take eternity to mean not infinite temporal duration but timelessness, then eternal life belongs to those who live in the present'. To finally reach a state of timelessness of course is an idea that is close to Buddhism and Hinduism.

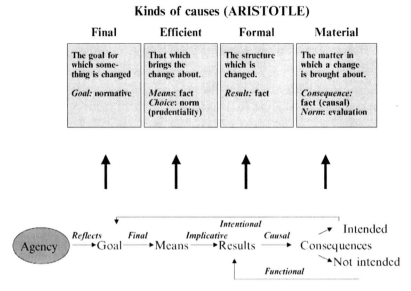

Figure 6.3. Action elements and their relation to Aristotelian causes.

Von Wright (1971) already proposed defining causality (fact) by a similar scheme, when he wrote: 'p is a cause relative to q if and only if by doing p we could bring about q or by suppressing p we could remove q or prevent it from happening. In the first case the cause factor is a sufficient, in the second case the cause factor is a necessary condition to the effect factors' (p. 72). Thus, the pre-condition for defining a cause (fact) is a goal (a normative category).[5] Hence we can conclude:

> 1. Analytically, to define (material) causality (facts), norms (goals) are a necessary pre-condition.

In case of the communicative action, things are even more trivial:

> 2. Analytically, in communicative (norm-oriented) actions, facts and norms are implied by definition.

---

[5] It may seem strange to interpret goals as being normative. Yet this is not the case. The reason is that goals are counterfactual and they imply some kind of a standard which has to be reached. Otherwise one could not fail to achieve a goal.

*Empirical relations of norms and facts in decontextualized moral
judgments: defining the deep structure of moral judgments by goal
taking instead of role taking*

As mentioned, deviating from Kohlberg, we used action elements rather
than perspective taking to define the structure of moral arguments and
justifications (Eckensberger & Reinshagen, 1980). Later, we discovered
that in analytical philosophy a similar logic is applied to the concept of
understanding, when Meggle (1993) elaborates 'to understand a person
means to understand his/her actions'. In the meantime this paradigm
is also increasingly being used in the context of social cognition,
where theory of mind refers precisely to understanding others' actions
(Eckensberger & Plath, in press).

In short, we analysed the *verbal material* (first Kohlberg's manuals then
original interviews) with respect to three features:

a. What *parts of actions* are referred to by the subject: goals, means,
   results or consequences, or even whole actions?
b. Where in the action is the *conflict located*? Is it a goal conflict, a
   conflict about the applicability of means, or are the results mutually
   conflicting?
c. What *standard* is used to solve the conflict? (In Figure 6.4 only the
   standards used at a particular stage are indicated.)

We eventually distinguished *eleven stages* which are combined into *four
levels*. At every stage, subjects (a) have a specific understanding of
actions (at first it is understood intuitively, fairly externally, then it
focuses upon consequences, and later it is coordinated); and (b) follow
a particular standard (first it is an intuitive, one-sided respect, later
mutual respect). These standards, however, do not come about *causally*,
but *emerge* as a result of specific experiences, which are either inciting
conditions or impediments, which, however, lead to a reflection of the
standard, and also to an increase in the complexity of the subject's
reconstruction in terms of actions. It is assumed that the basic process
through which the new structure (standard) is formed is what Piaget
(2001) called 'reflective abstraction'. So the same stage (standard) is at
first operational (structure) and is later reflected upon (thus becoming
a content).

---

3.   Ontogenetically, standards (norms) emerge psychologically from conflicting facts (experiences and action schemata) by reflective abstractions.
Figure 6.4 summarizes the standards, which are at the core of the eleven
stages that can be distinguished during ontogenesis.

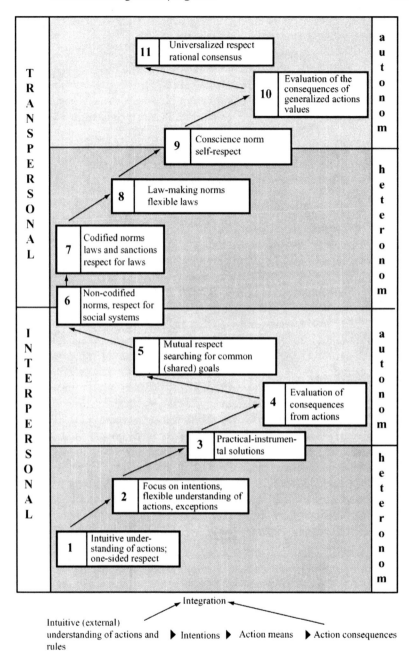

Figure 6.4. Moral stage development based on an action theory reconstruction of Kohlberg's stage theory (cf. Eckensberger, 1986).

From this theoretical perspective the overall transformation of moral judgments occurs along two dimensions:

Two spheres of interpretation

First, two 'social spheres' are reconstructed by the subject.[6] In the first sphere, which we call the *personal* or *interpersonal sphere*, the agencies or conflicting parties are viewed as concrete, more or less real people or subjects.

A second sphere, which developmentally follows the first, is called the *transpersonal sphere*. Here, acting or conflicting parties are primarily understood *in terms of roles* or *functions* or even *general positions* (abstract principles).

From heteronomy to autonomy

We have good reasons to argue that the second dimension in the transformation of moral judgments can still be summarized best as a move from heteronomous (external behaviours, rules, simple interests of people) to autonomous moral judgment (mutual respect), as proposed by Piaget as early as 1932.

But according to our analysis, this movement from heteronomy to autonomy is first developed within the interpersonal sphere and is then repeated within the second 'transpersonal' sphere of interpretation of social reality. This becomes obvious when looking at the standards (now called norms) that the subject applies when discussing a moral conflict.

Table 6.1 summarizes the four levels that we derived from the eleven stages and additionally indicates the relation between facts and norms at each level. One can see that at the first level norms themselves are interpreted as facts (they have an invariant objective status), at the second level norms are reconstructed as norms, and imply mutual respect. At the third level the notion that facts should dominate decisions clearly exists, normative questions are secondary. It is only at the last level that objective facts are barely accepted, and norms are considered necessary to evaluate facts.

---

4. Ontogenetically, the relation between norms (decontextualized moral judgments) and facts varies, beginning with a rather naive interpretation of norms as facts and ending with the opposite being true: the existence of facts as objective entities is called into question, facts serve interests and are dominated by norms.

---

[6] This distinction is also borrowed from Piaget (1995).

Table 6.1 *Summary of moral levels*

Sphere of interpretation	Interpersonal		Transpersonal	
Moral orientation	Heteronomous	Autonomous	Heteronomous	Autonomous
Action concept	intuitive, external, flexible understanding and acceptance of others' intentions	additional evaluation of action-consequences/ shared goals	laws as means to secure morality (flexible rules/ exceptions)	consequences of upholding self-respect; consequences of values, recognize principles as goals
Respect	one-sided respect	mutual respect	respecting social and legal systems	universalized respect (respecting humankind *per se*)
Appreciation of rules	intuitive acceptance of rules	shared rules	rights and exceptions	morality and rights are complementary
Facts/norms	norms as given facts	norms reconstructed as norms	facts dominate, norms as institutionalized facts	facts as such hardly exist, norms dominate and evaluate facts

Facts and norms in contextualized moral judgments

Environmental issues as a domain for contextualizing moral judgments

Particularly since the mid-seventies, conflicts between ecological and economic value-orientations have been considered one of the most salient intrasocietal conflicts in the Western world, at least in Europe (Engelhardt, 1975). Our main interest was to analyse the *role moral arguments play in these orientations,* and we looked upon the specific conflicts regarding the construction of a coal-fuelled power plant in our region as a good example of this more general conflict.

Decisions about changes in the environment (building a new street, building a power plant, using water, farming the land) not only require technical expertise (knowledge about facts) but also usually imply moral (normative) problems: often, benefits and costs are not distributed justly. Benefits (gains) which a ***group/person x*** may accrue from some environmentally oriented action could result in costs (losses) for another ***group/person y***. *This simple truth was the reason for studying this set of problems from a moral perspective.*

Sample

We interviewed 100 persons[7] from different groups, who had *different relations to the power plant on an economic or ecological basis.* The first group of our total sample comprised four sub-samples of fifteen subjects such that each was differently affected by the power plant. This sampling procedure was aimed at *achieving representativity of the problem* – the conflict between economic and ecological orientations. It did not aim at being representative of the region. The economic and/or ecological relations of the sub-samples to the power plant varied systematically: some people were economically dependent on the power plant but not ecologically affected, others were ecologically affected but not economically dependent, still others were neutral and yet others were affected in both respects. Additionally we included persons who were actively involved in the decision-making process of the construction (as politicians/manager, trade union members, citizens' initiative against the power plant and environmentalists) as well as persons who were simply confronted with the plant but did not actively do anything in favour of it or against it. Technically, this last group counts as a control group.

Data collection and analysis

Several steps of contextualization were taken and are summarized here with respect to the question of whether they concerned norms and/or facts. Normative statements were investigated via two steps of contextualization based on the developmental theory of moral judgment. Three relations of norms to facts in the sense of situational content were analysed: (a) descriptive knowledge of the situation; (b) the subjective interest in knowledge; and (c) the relevance of facts in a biographical context. In addition, two kinds of relations between norms and facts in the sense of psychological processes, which allow normative and knowledge-based judgments to occur, were investigated: general coping and defence processes as well as affect control.

a. **The normative: hypothetical dilemma.** To obtain classical estimations of moral judgments as well the **hypothetical** Heinz-dilemma was used.

b. **The normative and the factual: contextualized dilemma.** The first step in contextualization (morality and additional variables)

---

[7] This was the sample of the first most comprehensive study which concerned the evaluation of building a power plant or not. It will be used as the basis for the following discussion. Additional samples were studied with reference to water usage and the risks involved in different approaches to farming.

entailed the construction of a *fictitious dilemma*. This dilemma type aims at information about a 'real case' or domain (in this case building the power plant), but is fictitious in the sense that a highly unlikely situation was construed (building the power plant depended on just one person who had to vote in favour or against it), yet simultaneously has features of a real dilemma (conditions of the regional situation). The subjects were presented only with the *most simple core of a conflict*, and it was up to them to ask for more information. Before this information was given, subjects had to explain why they were interested in the aspects of the situation they had inquired about. It was assumed that a subject, when confronted with a dilemma core, would interpret a situation with more interest and accuracy than if an entire dilemma story were told.

c. *The normative and the factual: biographical interviews.* The second step of *contextualization* entailed *biographical interviews* about the *subjects' experiences* with the process of building a power plant. As these interviews also focused on the basic problem of *unemployment* and *ecological crisis* in general, *they gave the individual subjects a great degree of freedom.* Hence the material was *not* exclusively or even primarily loaded with moral content (as in the case of moral-dilemma interviews), rather it represented a 'narrative' about idiographically relevant experiences. The analysis of this material called for a much broader theoretical framework than the stage theory of moral judgments offers. Therefore a combination of the *four levels of moral judgment* (structures in the theory of moral development) and the *three action levels* were used as an analytical framework.[8] By doing so, we ended up with what we call **types of everyday morality** which – because they are grounded in theory – provide more than just descriptions, they also allow for generalizations.

---

[8] This type of data is of course not unique to our work. The issue of biographical material highly loaded with affective dimensions was, for instance, also discussed by Day & Tappan (1996) and (controversially) by Lourenço (1996). These papers (which did not exist at the time of our data analysis) focus exactly on the problem we were concerned with, namely

- *to take the unique biographical, relativistic and situational content of the material as seriously as possible,*
- *and yet at the same time to look for a common underlying systematic structure, i.e. how to move from narratives to meta-narratives.*

To put it in Lourenço's terms: we did not want to gain free entrance into Plato's Academy in Athens, but tried to respect his motto written above the Academy: 'Let no one ignorant of geometry enter here.'

d. ***The factual: objective measure of descriptive knowledge about the situation.*** The next step entailed measuring the *knowledge* about the situation (about facts) using a specific test (Kasper et al., 1987). It has five subtests: energy politics, economy, law, technology and environment. It has been validated by experts and was found to differentiate between students of relevant faculties (law, economics, biology). Most of its items are moderately difficult.

e. ***The factual: subjective descriptive knowledge as a basis for moral judgment.*** The number and kinds of fact-related questions subjects asked in the contextualized/fictitious dilemma core situation were analysed (see above).

f. ***The factual: affective psychological processes that enable moral actions.*** *Coping/defence processes* as expressed in the fictitious dilemmas were estimated using a text-analytical method of scoring (Sieloff et al., 1988), which is basically rooted in Norma Haan's (1977) theory of coping and defence processes: discrimination, detachment, means-end symbolization, delayed response, sensitivity, regression and selective awareness. However, only a specific selection of the text-analytical questions were used to calculate the score. The extent of coping and defence was rated independently on five-point scales. In other words, coping was not defined as the absence of defence and vice versa.

g. ***The factual: affective psychological processes that accompany biographical interviews.*** Immediately after the interviews the interviewers rated the control of affects on graphical five-point scales (five scales represented successful affect control; five represented failure in affect control). The scales were intercorrelated and factor analysed. A strong first bipolar factor was extracted, with control of affects and failure of control as its respective poles. Means of the high loading variables will be given in the result section.

Empirical results on the relation between norms and facts in contextualized moral judgments

A note about the effects of contextualizing of moral judgments

As mentioned, we used three estimates for the moral competency of the subjects: the hypothetical Heinz-dilemma, the fictitious contextualized dilemma and the biographical interviews, which also served the purpose of constructing 'types of everyday morality' (see below). These estimates involve increases in contextual information as well as in ego-relevance. Before additional relations between facts and norms are discussed, a note on the general effect of contextualizing moral judgments is neces-sary. No details about differences across the three estimates of moral judgment (hypothetical to fictitious dilemmas and to biographical inter-view) will be given here. The main trends can, however, be summarized as follows (Eckensberger, Breit & Döring, 1996).

Generally, one third of the subjects' level of moral competency remained stable across all three estimates. If one looks at the distribution of levels within the three estimates, then the *Heinz-dilemma* generally produced more autonomous than heteronomous judgments (53 : 33), one quarter argued at the autonomous transpersonal level, which – compared to Kohlberg's data – is a considerable amount. In the *fictitious dilemma* the two middle levels clearly dominate (28 : 30) and the highest frequency of subjects is classified at the heteronomous transpersonal level (30). Regarding *everyday types* of moral judgments subjects are scored most frequently at the interpersonal autonomous level (42), the smallest number of subjects attaining the highest, the autonomous transpersonal level (11). So without analysing the upward and down-ward movements in any detail, one can cautiously summarize that the fictitious dilemma, which aims specifically at analysing *situational facts*, tends to elicit arguments that represent the heteronomous transpersonal level. However, the everyday types of moral judgments tend towards argumentation at the autonomous interpersonal level, which we think results from the biographically based origin of these types.

---

5. Methods of data gathering, which focus differentially on the purity of moral arguments, facts and personal relevance, mediate moral judgments. Hypothetical (decontextualized) dilemmas seem to facilitate *counterfactual* arguments and lead to more mature moral judgments. Fictitious dilemmas (that focus more specifically on *factual conditions* of decision-making) trigger more heteronomous-transpersonal arguments. Finally, biographical methods, which focus primarily on the *affective relevance* of a moral problem, trigger relatively more interpersonal autonomous judgments.

Independent estimates of factual knowledge (knowledge test) and
levels of moral judgment (hypothetical dilemma)

Building a power plant represents a situation that involves rather com-plex implicit facts. Building and not building the plant is embedded in economic as well as in ecological conditions, but legal, regional know-ledge and history also play a central role. Building or not building the power plant therefore entails extremely complex chains of consequences. The test of 'objective knowledge' should thus allow a more detailed analysis of how moral levels (norms) and facts (knowledge) are inter-related. The results can be summarized as follows (Eckensberger, Breit & Döring, 1997):

1. First, it is interesting that the direction of the decision (being against or in favour of the power plant) is completely unrelated to the amount of general knowledge about the issue. Supporters (n = 51) and opponents (n = 41)[9] achieve exactly the same mean scores in overall knowledge. This phenomenon is also a well-known finding in other fields. This result is important, because it points to the relevance of normative (moral) orientations in explaining why people make one decision rather than another. In fact the number of opponents increases progressively per moral level; whereas most supporters argued at the first three levels, only three were classified at the autonomous transpersonal level.

2. On the other hand, the distribution of knowledge varies. If one looks at the level of knowledge across the moral level of supporters/opponents then the opponents' (n = 41) knowledge is more or less balanced across all four levels (rho = .04, n.s.), whereas the supporters' (n = 51) knowledge increases systematically across the levels of moral judgment (rho = .40, p < 0.01). Opponents achieve the highest knowledge scores at the transpersonal-heteronomous (system) level, though interestingly their knowledge decreases at the highest level of moral judgment, whereas the highest score of the supporters is attained at this transpersonal-autonomous level.

6.   In conclusion, factual knowledge interacts in an interesting manner with normative/prescriptive orientations. It does not fully relate to a normative decision: the highest moral level is not necessarily also combined with the highest level of knowledge.

Moral judgment and personal interests in facts that support the decision

To change the perspective, the analysis in what follows does not proceed from facts to normative judgments, but from normative judgments to facts. In order to do so, the number of questions asked by persons classified at different levels were analysed (in the reconstruction phase of the fictitious dilemma). It is interesting, however, that a small number

[9] The n does not add up to 100 because of some missing data in the test scores.

of subjects (n = 6) could not be classified as being for or against the power plant but remained ambivalent about the decision in the fictitious dilemma (Eckensberger, Breit & Döring, 1997). But regardless of the decision made, it was generally assumed that those who argue at higher levels also explore facts more carefully.

1. In fact, taking all subjects together, the number of questions asked (the interest in facts) increases with the level of moral judgment. But unexpected differences show up once more.
2. Again, this trend is more salient for the supporters. A rather progressive increase in the number of questions they ask is evident across the levels of moral judgments. This is not so for the opponents: in this case the heteronomous-transpersonal subjects ask most questions. Those at the highest level, however, ask a lower number of questions.
3. If one takes a closer look at the 'balance' of knowledge (between what can be done, and what the consequences for ecology and workplaces would be) then it turns out that in fact (a) most persons classified at transpersonal levels reconstruct the dilemma optimally, while (b) deficiency regarding the means mostly occurs at the interpersonal level. (c) Deficiency of knowledge regarding means and in one chain of consequences is more or less equally distributed across all levels. (d) A few subjects with *deficiencies in all aspects, however, still argue at the two transpersonal levels*, which means that it is possible in principle to develop arguments at higher levels although the facts of the dilemma are not adequately reconstructed.

---

7. Although there is a trend towards a relationship between the level of moral judgment and the amount of interest in knowledge as well as between moral judgment levels and balance of knowledge, detailed interest in facts is neither a necessary nor a sufficient condition for arguing at the highest moral level as long as a medium level of knowledge is given. Also an expressed lack of knowledge of facts does not prevent moral arguments at transpersonal levels.

Coping and defence processes as factual enabling conditions for moral judgment performance

Several approaches were used to analyse these data (Sieloff et al., 1988). To make sure that the relation of coping (according to Haan, 1977 the accurate reconstruction of the situation) and the level of moral judgment (according to our theory, the complexity of action elements considered) was not empirically trivial simply because it was analytically true, only a selected number of text-analytical questions regarding coping/defence processes were included in the analysis (Eckensberger, 1993). Once more only general trends will be presented here. First, it is worth noting that there is no relationship between coping or defence and being in favour of or against the power plant. Second, there is also no relationship at all between coping or defence and the amount of knowledge. However, the relationship between moral levels and coping or defence processes presents a rather clear picture.

1. Basically, coping is more pronounced at all levels than defence (highly significant). Hence, generally, more accurate reconstructions of the situation exist.
2. There is a general increase in coping across the levels of moral judgment ($r = .44^*$) and a general decrease ($r = -.32^*$) in defence. So, generally, the higher the moral level of argumentation, the more accurate the reconstruction of the situation.
3. Yet there is an interaction term in the sense that apart from these trends, autonomous judgments are related to more coping and less defence than heteronomous judgments (in both social spheres).

---

8.   Coping and defence processes seem to modify the performance in moral competence. Coping improves, defence impairs the performance at higher stages, but particularly autonomous judgments.

A summary of four everyday types of moral judgments

In the biographical interview the dilemma structure is abandoned and subjects have to reconstruct the situation to which they apply moral norms on the basis of their own experiences and not on the basis of a given dilemma structure. In other words, moral judgments are integrated with non-moral judgments. In order to retain the *structure* of the moral judgments and to define the *biographical relevance of the situation* as well, the *three action levels* (see above) were combined with the *four levels of moral judgment* (see above), first analytically and then empirically. By doing so, the three action levels were basically looked at from a moral developmental point of view. Table 6.2 summarizes the results of this effort, which were called 'types of everyday morality' or 'types of environmental moral judgments'.

The table can be read in columns (types) or rows (attributes of types) and a first empirical relationship between norms and facts can be summarized as follows.

Table 6.2 *Four types of contextualized everyday moral judgments*

MORALITY / ACTION LEVELS	Interpersonal		Transpersonal	
	Heteronomous	Autonomous	Heteronomous	Autonomous
Identity	based on similarity	relationships, tradition	functional roles	good life (virtues)
Solidarity III	shared interests	preservation of group standards	experts, power structure	world of potential moral patients
Affects	not articulated	not articulated	not articulated	**hope**
Control	external, conformity,	co-control	technological realizability	reflection of interests/ goals
Responsibility II	delegation of power	individual responsibility for the group	legal responsibility of 'expert-power'	moral responsibility of all people
Affects	not articulated	**indignation/ guilt**	'objectivity' (not articulated)	not articulated
Perception of facts	important, individual	dependent upon group-interests	objectivity	reflection of limitations of knowledge
Risk I	individual, to lose property/ advantages	to lose one's reputation, lifestyle, group-related	to lose wealth or the power of society	loss of justice for all
Efficiency	maximization of benefits, adaptation	exchange, reciprocity	functionality of the system (market, technology)	self-commitment
Affects	rage/wrath	not articulated	not articulated	not articulated

A moral dimension occurs at all three action levels. In primary actions, morality appears in the concept of *risk*, in *secondary actions* it is primarily tapped by the concept of *responsibility*, and in *tertiary actions* by the concept of *solidarity*, i.e. it is the subject's moral relation to the group, which is relevant.

All other aspects of the action levels (affects, efficiency, facts, control of actions and identity) are also *transformed across the four types by the moral framework* involved, which means that normative orientations clearly interact with quite different aspects of actions. But here only the 'perception of facts', interpretations of risk and affects will be referred to.

1. *Affects* are explicitly referred to only by three types (the heteronomous-interpersonal type mentions rage/wrath; the autonomous-interpersonal type refers to guilt and indignation, and the autonomous-transpersonal type speaks of hope which may even be *counterfactual*). The heteronomous-transpersonal type *refuses* to accept the relevance of affects in decision-making.

2. It is of particular importance that the *interpretation of facts* is clearly shaped by contextualized everyday moral types (Breit & Eckensberger, 2004; Eckensberger, Breit & Döring, 1999a).

   At the **interpersonal-heteronomous** level the reconstruction and evaluation of facts is based on individual advantages and disadvantages. The egocentric perspective prevails. If the power plant is useful to the subject's welfare, he or she stresses the positive aspects of its construction. If, on the other hand, the subject is concerned about the destruction of nature, he or she points to the negative consequences. There is no explicit distinction between natural and social facts because the social order is considered a direct consequence of external life conditions.

   At the **interpersonal-autonomous** level the subject takes into account other points of view. If he or she profited economically from the plant, then the subject would admit that people living close to the plant and gaining no economic advantages from its construction could see things differently. Compared to the previous stage, natural or respectively objective facts are not regarded as that important. The social position of an individual is acknowledged, his or her role in a lifeworld shared in common with others determines the factual evaluation processes. Not external constraints, but human *will* rooted in relationships and social interaction influences how a situation is evaluated.

   At the **transpersonal-heteronomous** level, the subject reorganizes his or her arguments in the external action field and reconsiders the significance of objective facts. But there is an important difference to the first level: the subject does not evaluate the situation from an individual perspective any longer, but rather from a societal one. He or she takes into account that interactive processes create an important basis for societal action. A situation is understood not only to be the result of an unchangeable external human condition (level I) or of human intentions and relations (level II), but also the consequence of *latent* functions of nature, society, its institutions and the non-intended effects of human actions. These functions can be analysed by purposive rationality, on the basis of which one can solve problems intelligently and effectively. In the case of the power plant, supporters and opponents of the construction deal with issues such as unemployment, data on environmental destruction, laws and technological possibilities.

At the **transpersonal-autonomous** level the subject reflects on human beings' construction of meaning and reality. He or she also believes that purposive rationality is a result of socio-historical processes initiated by human action, and not a way of understanding objective reality. Facts, as well as formal and scientific ways of reconstructing them, lose their untouchable transcendency and once more become consequences of human intentions and relations. The main difference to the second level is that the subject goes beyond the limits of individual will and face-to-face relations. Facts are considered to result from socio-historically rooted interpretations and expectations as well as societal goals and norms. The concrete conflict between economic and ecological interests can be solved, if the socio-historical limitations of problem-solving are recognized and new forms of thinking and living are developed.

---

9. Facts are interpreted differently in different moral argumentations: whereas facts are taken as given and represent important individual property for the heteronomous-interpersonal type, the interpersonal autonomous type regards the meaning of facts as not objectively given, but dependent upon group-interests. Consistent with playing down the importance of affects, the heteronomous-transpersonal type considers facts as the most important parameter in decision-making, facts are understood as 'objectivity of facts'. This interpretation is exactly what the autonomous-transpersonal type doubts: he or she particularly reflects on the limitations of 'true' or 'objective knowledge'.

---

3. *Risk* is a concept which by definition is an amalgamation of norms and facts, because risks refer to causal processes (facts) and to standards of some kind (norms) which are threatened. Given the four levels of everyday morality, it is not surprising that the understanding of risk also varies in terms of 'risks for what or for whom', which allows for a more detailed understanding not only of this amalgamation of norms and facts, but also of risks themselves (Eckensberger, Döring & Breit, 2001).

---

10. The heteronomous-interpersonal type understands risk as risk for the individual, as a possible loss of property or some other advantages. For the autonomous-interpersonal type risk means something different, namely

the loss of reputation and of a particular group's lifestyle. The heteronomous-transpersonal type interprets risk primarily as threat to one's wealth, and society's possible loss of power. The autonomous-transpersonal type finally interprets risk in terms of a loss of justice for all people.

Affective psychological processes that accompany biographical interviews: control of affects in contextualized everyday types of moral judgments

As mentioned, the ratings on graphical scales representing different aspects of affect control were intercorrelated and factor analysed. Means of the variables loading highly on a strong bipolar first factor are used to represent either high affect control or low affect control. These scores are distributed almost symmetrically across the four contextualized types of morality (Eckensberger, Breit & Döring, 1999b).

1. Although overall *global affect* control (being proper, congruent, flexible and relaxed) is rather successfully achieved by all subjects (it was rated in the upper half of the scale), it is the ethical 'orientation' (heteronomy vs autonomy) that determines the differences between the groups. It is particularly strong (significant) at the autonomous levels, both groups of heteronomous morality were rated as having lower affect control, with a non-significant tendency to rate the *interpersonal heteronomous orientation* as having the lowest control.

2. A similar (although inverted) picture occurs with overall *global failure of affect* control (as being excessive, selective, exhibiting high bodily tension). Again the overall failure of control is rather low for all subjects (it is below the mean of the scale), yet again the heteronomous orientations were both rated as stronger in failure, and the interpersonal heteronomous orientation was strongest in failure of control once more.

   Two items did not load on the one strong first factor. One refers specifically to the successful control of moral affects, and the other to an over-adaptation (social desirability) of the subjects. In a way, the results also mirror each other, but not completely.

3. The *control of moral affects* (the subject demonstrates moral engagement, (s)he expresses moral affects like empathy, sympathy, respect, indignation, guilt, shame appropriately) shows exactly what one would expect, if one speculates why adults express heteronomous-interpersonal judgments at all: *only this type* has a rather low level of moral affect control, all others deal adequately with these affects including the heteronomous-transpersonal type.

4. In the case of ***over-adaptation*** (social desirability) two aspects are important: first it is the interpersonal-heteronomous type again that deviates. This time they show the most expressed failure of affective control in terms of being extremely polite, adaptive etc. The lowest scores in this case were found in the transpersonal-heteronomous group (statistical tendency). This in a way is incongruent with the claims expressed by this group that affects should not play any role in decision-making.

***

11. Dealing with affects (psychological facts) also interacts with moral judgment performance. (1) Although generally global affect control is high and failure to control is low, it is particularly the ethical orientation (heteronomy vs autonomy) which is systematically related to affect control/failure. Heteronomous judgments are lower in control and higher in failure. (2) Dealing with 'moral affects' is particularly low in heteronomous-interpersonal judgments, whereas emotional over-adaptation (social desirability) is particularly low in subjects who argue on a heteronomous-transpersonal level.

***

Discussion

The central claim is that contextualization of moral judgments allows one to discuss the relation of norms and facts in a particularly fruitful way. The relation of norms (moral judgments) to facts was dealt with at several levels, and this was done from an action theory perspective, which is considered to be especially appropriate when moral judgments are contextualized.

First, several arguments were developed to demonstrate that *analytically* norms and facts are intrinsically interrelated, when an action theory perspective is taken. In an action, goals imply standards and therefore they are normative, and effects of actions refer to facts. This is even more pronounced in communicative actions, which are by definition norm-oriented.

Moral judgments were *empirically* estimated using three levels of contextualization (decontextualized dilemma, fictitious dilemma and biographical interviews). Facts were also dealt with at different levels and by different methods: facts as content of the context were empirically defined by a test that measured context knowledge, by information-seeking behaviour (number of questions asked in the fictitious dilemma) and by the interpretation of the meaning of facts (in the biographic interview). But facts also were understood as psychological processes, which can influence or moderate moral judgment performance: coping or defence processes were estimated, and affect control was rated. By and large, there are trends in the data that demonstrate an empirical relationship between moral judgment levels and amount of knowledge on facts relevant to the problem or information-seeking processes. But the picture is much more complex in detail: it is clearer for one direction of decision-making in the case of fictitious dilemma. Second, the highest level of judgments is not necessarily correlated with the greatest amount of knowledge. Third, it seems that knowledge is particularly pronounced in those subjects who take a system perspective (heteronomous-transpersonal level) and largely rely on facts in their judgments. The same trends are true for information-seeking and balanced knowledge. Balanced knowledge about what can be done or what causal chains are set in motion is neither a sufficient nor a necessary condition for transpersonal moral judgments.

Coping processes seem to allow for higher judgments more easily; this is more pronounced in autonomous judgments. Defence processes generally seem to reduce moral judgments slightly; this is more pronounced in heteronomous judgments. A similar picture is true for processes of affect control. Here, however, particularly, the group lowest in moral judgment (whose existence in adults is in fact astonishing) lacks control of moral affects. And again the system-oriented group, which basically negates the relevance of affects in moral issues (biographical interview), is also rated lowest in affective 'over-adaptation' or social desirability.

All these data demonstrate that it is probably an illusion to define moral judgments empirically as a 'pure structure'; in fact they interact with knowledge as well as with ego-relevance and the affective processes involved. But it is also evident, particularly in the interview data, that moral levels structure the interpretation of facts.

7   The development of obligations and responsibilities in cultural context

Monika Keller

The normative framework

Humans can be characterized by a disposition to act, to believe and to feel in ways that are guided by norms and correspondingly by a disposition to experience certain feelings when norms are violated. Norms are fundamental to social life and the capacity to accept norms is a universal human biological and social adaptation. Norms serve the function of coordinating actions, beliefs and feelings. Broadly we can distinguish norms of rationality and moral norms (Keller & Reuss, 1984; see also Smith, this volume, Chapter 1). In line with this distinction, different domains of norms have been distinguished in a developmental context:

- prudential norms referring to goal-oriented instrumental action (Fiddick, 2004);
- conventional social norms referring to arbitrary behavioural regulations such as eating, dress or traffic rules (Smetana, 1982; Turiel, 1983);
- moral norms referring to standards of interaction concerning others' welfare (Kohlberg, 1984; Turiel, 1983);
- legal norms as a mixture of conventional and moral norms that can be enforced with legal sanctions (Cosmides & Tooby, 1992; Kohlberg, 1984).

Norms provide socially constituted reasons for actions. In terms of rationality they define what makes sense to do in view of an actor's goals in a certain situation or what is adequate in view of (conventional) social rules. In terms of morality they define what is blameworthy and wrong or permissible and praiseworthy in light of superordinate moral principles of fairness or justice, care or solidarity (Frankena, 1973), or in terms of a norm of reciprocity (Gouldner, 1960). In general, norms provide justified reasons for actions. Not following or violating norms leads to certain feelings, such as feelings of regret in case of prudential norms or feelings of shame and guilt in the case of violating moral norms.

In the context of our research we are interested in two types of moral norms: moral duties and interpersonal responsibilities. Moral duties, such as promise-keeping or truth-telling, have been seen as based on universal moral principles such as the justice principle (Kohlberg, 1984; Rawls, 1971). Moral duties are seen to be obligatory for everybody and regulate actions that we owe to everybody equally. Interpersonal responsibilities are based on principles of care and beneficence (Gilligan, 1982; Hoffman, 2000). They regulate sympathetic concern, empathy and altruism that from a moral point of view we do not owe to everybody equally. For example, expectations about behaviour in close relationships (Youniss, 1980) in particular involve special responsibilities of empathy and care that result from the long-term relationship, special feelings between the actors and the experience of reciprocity in the relationship.

Cognitive and affective aspects of normative action

Both moral and interpersonal norms serve the function of coordinating behaviour. The normative fact of having given a promise or standing in a long-term affective relationship constitutes a good and justified reason for self to act in accordance. By implication, the person to whom a promise has been given will expect the intended action or, similarly, a close friend will expect certain future behaviour. Norms imply coordinated expectations about behaviour and feelings and define what we (rightly) expect from each other in specific situations. Concerning cognition, this implies in the actor the development of a theory of action with the ability to coordinate the perspectives of self and others. Concerning affect, it implies a motivational disposition to experience certain feelings in case of norm violations. These feelings are correlated in self and other (Gibbard, 1992): when self as a norm violator has a reason to feel guilty, ashamed or embarrassed, other as a victim of violation has a reason to be angry and resentful or punish the norm violator and demand excuses and restitution. In the following I will discuss these cognitive and affective aspects from a developmental point of view.

The development of understanding of moral and interpersonal norms

In Kohlberg's (1976, 1984) theory of moral development the understanding of moral norms has been assessed in the context of reasoning about hypothetical dilemmas in which different moral obligations are in conflict. The most prominent example is the 'Heinz-dilemma' in which two legal norms, the right to life and the right to property, are in conflict. The questions of what is the morally right decision for Heinz, to steal a medication in order to save the life of his wife or to respect the property rights of a pharmacist, have to be considered under various contextual conditions. Based on the answers to these questions from samples of persons at different ages, including a longitudinal study, Kohlberg defined different stages of moral reasoning as transformations of the understanding of fairness (Kohlberg, 1984; Colby & Kohlberg, 1987). Moral reasoning stages are increasingly more differentiated and comprehensive in terms of a person's understanding of the social perspectives of the actors involved and in terms of the understanding of the normative (justice) demands of the situation. Kohlberg has distinguished three levels, each with two sub-stages. At the first sub-stage of preconventional morality the person is focused on the perspective of the self. The evaluation of what is right is motivated by selfish interests, obedience to authority and fear of sanctions from authority in the case of norm violation. At the second sub-stage the perspectives of self and other can be coordinated. What is morally right is defined as a pragmatic reciprocity, but the interests of the self are predominant concerns. At stage 3 of the conventional level the self is understood as part of relationships, and empathy and care for others become dominant moral concerns. At the fourth stage, self and relationships are understood as parts of society, and the societal implications of norms and norm violation are in focus. At the postconventional level, conflicting claims are judged in the light of social contracts, universal human rights and responsibilities.

Over time, Kohlberg's theoretical position has given rise to considerable criticism. This concerned the exclusive focus on the principle of justice as the defining criterion of morality, the theoretical definition of the stages and the assumption of structural homogeneity, the assumptions about the relationship between moral understanding and moral action and the role of emotion (see Keller, 1996). Gilligan (1982) has designed a theory of moral development based on the principles of care and responsibility. Similar to Kohlberg's conception, in her developmental model early forms of morality were also seen to be selfish. However, research on empathy and altruism (Eisenberg, 1982; Hoffman, 2000) has provided increasing evidence that the conception of preconventional moral reasoning with the predominant focus on self-interest is inadequately defined because empathy and sympathy play a role already in children's moral reasoning. In Kohlberg's theory, altruism and empathy are the main concerns of the conventional stage 3. They have neither precursors at the preconventional level nor can they be adequately defined at the higher levels of moral reasoning. This issue has been discussed in particular in cross-cultural research including people from Asian cultures (Boyes & Walker, 1988; Eckensberger & Zimba, 1997). Furthermore, even young children distinguish different types of norms and understand the validity of moral rules independent of authority rules, sanctions or self-interest (Gibbs & Widaman, 1982; Keller & Edelstein, 1993; Keller, Eckensberger & von Rosen, 1989; Nucci & Lee, 1993; Turiel, 1983).

However, research has also documented that self-oriented reasoning decreases in the course of development, when the person becomes increasingly aware of interpersonal concerns (Eisenberg, 1982). Similarly, Keller, Eckensberger & von Rosen (1989) documented both self-oriented and fairness/empathy types of reasons in children's arguments in a Kohlberg-dilemma. Keller (1996) could also show that empathic reasons increased in particular in early adolescence substantively. Thus, children seem to have a more differentiated moral reasoning than originally assumed and both fairness and interpersonal responsibility are part of moral reasoning.

Moral reasoning, moral action and feelings

Moral consistency

Concerning the relationship between *moral reasoning* and *action*, researchers assumed that the experience of necessity to act according to one's moral knowledge and to establish consistency between moral judgment and action has a developmental component (Keller & Edelstein, 1993; Kohlberg, 1984). It is only in adolescence that a moral self is established that accepts obligations as binding (Blasi, 1980, 2004). In line with these developmental assumptions it could be shown that young children even in the case of knowledge about obligations and responsibilities were guided by self-interest in decision-making in a morally relevant situation (Gerson & Damon, 1978). Keller & Edelstein (1993) documented that in particular adolescents established consistency between moral judgment and action choice in a morally relevant friendship-dilemma. Younger children frequently revealed a split between their action choice and what they judged as right in this dilemma-situation. However, later cross-cultural work by Keller and her colleagues revealed that this developmental assumption was true only for Western children whereas a Chinese sample did not show such inconsistency (this will be discussed below). Thus, factors other than the developmental have to be taken into account in the relationship between moral judgment and action.

Moral feelings

Another line of research has explored feelings that an actor experiences after the violation of a moral rule. In the post- Kohlbergian area, feelings have been seen as an important indicator of moral development. From a cognitive perspective they indicate that a person has knowledge about a moral norm. From the perspective of motivation they indicate that a person is concerned about the norm violation. Feelings in the case of a norm violation have been classified into two types: feelings of fear based on external sanctions and feelings of guilt and shame based on inner sanctions of a moral self. Only the latter have been seen as genuinely moral.

According to Kohlberg's theory, moral feelings are a relatively late achievement of stage-3 moral development in adolescence. More recent research with younger children has evidenced moral feelings much earlier in development. In cognitive-developmental research, children were presented with situations of moral rule violations of a child protagonist and were asked whether this violation was right and how the protagonist felt in this situation. Research supported the assumption that, already, young children emphasized the validity of moral norms such as not hurting somebody or not stealing independent of authority rules or sanctions. However, when children were asked how the hypothetical violator would feel after a rule violation only older children attributed ambivalent or negative feelings while five-year-olds mostly attributed positive feelings to the violator (Nunner-Winkler & Sodian, 1988). This finding was particularly surprising in view of the fact that even the youngest children were aware of the negative emotional consequences of the rule violation for the victim (Arsenio & Lover, 1995). Nunner-Winkler (1993) interpreted this 'happy victimizer effect' to indicate different developmental trajectories for moral knowledge and moral motivation. She concluded that knowledge about some fundamental moral norms such as not hurting somebody or not stealing is developed early and is universal, whereas moral motivation – as indicated by the awareness of moral feelings of the violator – is lagging behind the development of moral knowledge.

In a study using the same type of rule violations as in the previous studies, Chinese children surprisingly did not show any age changes in the attribution of emotions to a hypothetical violator (Keller et al., 1996). This was true even for the nine-year-old children. However, when the question was posed how the children themselves would feel if they had committed this violation, even the younger children attributed negative feelings to the self. We interpreted this finding such that the Chinese children differentiated between the hypothetical violator as a (bad) person committing a morally bad action and themselves as a (morally good) person who would not commit such a violation. This explanation was supported by the fact that the Chinese children frequently spontaneously rejected the rule violation and commented on it negatively. Keller et al. (2003) confirmed this self–other differentiation in a cross-cultural study comparing German and Portuguese children. They found a developmental change for both other and self, but negative (moral) feelings were significantly more frequently attributed if the child was asked to imagine the feelings if self had performed the action. Furthermore, we could show that children distinguished how a rule violator would feel and how he or she should feel. Interestingly, all children knew that a rule violator should feel bad after a rule violation. Thus, prescriptive moral knowledge about rule violations seems to be different from descriptive social knowledge. In two further studies, Keller et al. (2004b) interconnected deontic-reasoning about contract violation (Cosmides & Tooby, 1992) with the attribution of emotions to violator and victim of contract violations. This study again supported the finding that even the youngest children attributed negative feelings to the victim of a contract violation. In contradistinction, the feelings attributed to the violator were dependent on the context of the contract violation. In a situation of mother–child contract violation, children across ages attributed positive feelings more frequently than negative feelings. On the other hand, in a symmetrical peer relationship, feelings attributed to the violator showed the previously found age-related changes. In addition, the intentionality involved in the situation seemed to be important. In the mother–child situation the child as rule violator undeservingly received a benefit, while in the peer situation the child as violator intentionally appropriated an undeserved benefit. In this study the two factors of relationship and type of contract violation could not be disentangled. Unfortunately, this result could not be replicated in a follow-up study in which Barrett et al. (submitted) experimentally controlled the effects of relationship (peer–parent and biologically related–non-related) with the same type of contract violation. In this study, older children attributed negative feelings increasingly more frequently to the violator under all conditions. These findings support a more complex picture of emotion attributions than previously assumed. A recent study by Krettenauer & Eichler (2005) with adolescents also showed that the attribution of moral feelings may be more context-specific than assumed, with different types of tasks producing different trajectories for the emergence of moral emotions.

In general, these findings support the notion that moral reasoning about norms and feelings is a multifaceted phenomenon. Even young children have different types of concerns available when they reason about the validity of moral norms, when they make choices in morally relevant conflicts and when they attribute feelings in case of norm violations. Thus, the type of situation or the type of relationship must be taken into account as an important factor. Which aspects of a situation achieve predominance in moral decision-making and which feelings are elicited depend on development, the context of the situation and also on cultural influences. The following empirical study on obligations and responsibilities in close relationships takes such a broader framework into account when exploring the topics discussed above. In this study we address moral reasoning and moral emotions in the context of close relationships in a cross-cultural framework.

Close relationships: a cross-cultural framework

Children construct the meaning of moral obligations, such as promise-keeping and truth-telling, and of interpersonal responsibilities, such as concerns with the well-being of another person, in close relationships with parents and peers. The morally relevant expectations that govern people's interactions originate in self–other relationships and can be seen as products of the developmental transformations of the self–other relationship. Therefore, the understanding of relationships is intricately connected with the system of moral rules and it appears plausible to investigate the developmental origins of moral rule systems and a moral self within particular, intimate and affectively meaningful relationships (Keller, 1996; Keller & Edelstein, 1993). In agreement with Piaget (1965), peer relations are seen as particularly well suited to explore the moral meaning of close symmetrical relationships. Among those, friendship has a most important status (Bukowski & Sippola, 1996; Keller & Edelstein, 1990; Selman, 1980; Youniss, 1980). Friendship implies caring for the good of the friend, and gives rise to mutual expectations about how one ought to act and feel in order to maintain closeness in the relationship. Thus, the fact of being close friends provides normative reasons for actions and feelings. It involves sympathy and concern for another person and in particular in adolescence a deep mutual emotional sharing (Blum, 1980; Damon, 1977; Selman, 1980; Youniss, 1980).

Rather little is known about the development of friendship understanding across different cultures (Krappmann, 1996). In Western cultures, close friendship is important across the lifespan. In China, friendship seems to be the only relationship of equality (Goodwin & So-Kum Tang, 1996). On the other hand, the pattern of intimate friendship that is so characteristic of Western societies seems to have been less characteristic in China. According to Berndt (1993), family ties and peer relations in general are emphasized more strongly than intimate friendship. Although the Chinese seem to incorporate group structure in the self-definition (as has also been described for Japanese culture), it is a question whether close friendship has the same developmental significance for Chinese adolescents as has been documented for adolescents in Western cultures.

Cross-cultural research on moral development has shown important differences between people from Western and Eastern cultures that have implications for the understanding of relationships. Indians were more concerned with issues of care and gave greater priority to interpersonal responsibilities, whereas US Americans were more concerned with issues of justice, individual rights and personal choice (Bersoff & Miller, 1993; Shweder, Mahapatra & Miller, 1987). Furthermore, Indians perceived interpersonal responsibilities as duties, while US Americans saw them as more voluntary. Similarly, in reasoning about moral dilemmas, Chinese people frequently mentioned issues of interpersonal welfare and mutual benevolence which, in more elaborate forms, could not be adequately captured in Kohlberg's theory (e.g. Boyes & Walker, 1988; Ma, 1988).

These cultural differences have been explained as a distinction between individualistic and collectivistic orientations (Triandis, 1990). People in Western cultures have been described as valuing independence and individualism, compared with social identity and group responsibility in Eastern cultures (Markus & Kitayama, 1991). Recently, various researchers have criticized this view, saying that cultures cannot be differentiated along one dimension (Turiel, 1998; Turiel, this volume, Chapter 8), because they are complex systems that contain features of both individualism and collectivism. This is particularly true for modernizing societies.

Theoretical framework and expectations of the empirical studies

People do not consider moral obligations as strictly obligatory under all circumstances. They take the particular conditions of the situation into account when weighing different claims against each other. They also vary in their sensitivity for the moral aspects of a conflict situation, both developmentally and differentially. When they interpret the meaning of a situation and make a decision they may not spontaneously take into account the moral aspects of a situation, but may be concerned with other – selfish or pragmatic – aspects (Nisan, 2004). Such a broader interpretive framework directs attention from moral competence – the focus of the Kohlberg tradition – to moral motivation (Edelstein & Noam, 1982; Nunner-Winkler, 1993) and the moral self (Blasi, 1980, 2004). In our research we raise the question of the concerns that people take into account in their moral decision-making dependent on development, context and culture.

We argue that descriptive (social) and prescriptive (moral) reasoning are interconnected in the developing understanding of relationships and moral rules (Keller, 1996; Keller & Edelstein, 1991; Keller & Reuss, 1984). Interpersonal and moral awareness and the commitment to moral norms are based on processes of perspective differentiation and coordination through which people come to understand social reality in terms of psychological facts (what is the case) and in the light of normative standards of morality (what is right or what ought to be the case). We have described this understanding in the framework of a naive theory of action. In the course of development the categories or components of a naive theory of action are differentiated and coordinated and gain different meaning in the solution of action dilemmas. Descriptive social knowledge refers to the understanding of actions, people and relationships in terms of motives and justifications, consequences and strategies to maintain relationships. Prescriptive knowledge refers to the understanding that certain actions, goals or means to pursue them are allowed or prohibited, responsible or irresponsible in the light of moral norms and interpersonal responsibilities. The violation of such normative standards gives rise to fear of external (e.g. punishment from others) or internal sanctions (e.g. guilt/shame). Moral awareness of such violations requires acts of compensation, such as justifications or excuses, in order to rebalance the relationship. Comparing children and adolescents from Western (Iceland) and Chinese culture, we expected that the intensive interpersonal and moral orientation of Chinese people (Bond, 1996) sensitizes them to the normative aspects of social relationships and action dilemmas. Moral inconsistency should be avoided and the violation of responsibilities should lead to the anticipation of guilt feelings more frequently in younger Chinese children compared to Icelandic children. We also assumed that the Icelandic children would be focused more on selfish/hedonistic concerns and on contractual aspects of a situation, such as promise-keeping. For the Chinese children we expected that empathy and altruistic responsibilities towards a friend and a stranger would be more dominant because of general concerns about group relationships and social harmony. Given the importance of close friendship in Western cultures we expected that the close friendship would be more important for the Icelandic than for the Chinese children. For both groups we assumed however that close friendship would gain developmentally increasing salience.

Reasoning about relationships and norms: a comparison of Icelandic and Chinese children and adolescents

Children and adolescents from Reykjavik, Iceland (n=120) and from different rural ecologies (n=60), male and female, were assessed longitudinally at the ages of seven, nine, twelve and fifteen years (Keller, 1996). They were compared with a cross-sectional sample of ninety same-aged children and adolescents in Bejing, China from three different ecologies, with partial longitudinal assessment of this sample. People were individually interviewed about various aspects of family, close friendship and promise-keeping in these relationships (see Keller, 1996; Keller et al., 2005). In the following I will focus on the friendship context. This includes (1) the general understanding of close friendship (e.g. what is most important in close friendship; why is it important to have a close friend) and the norm of promise-keeping (e.g. why is it important to keep a promise; what happens if a person does not keep a promise given), and (2) situation-specific reasoning about a morally relevant dilemma in a close friendship (Keller, 1984; Selman, 1980). In the dilemma the protagonist had to decide whether to keep a promise to a long-time best friend or to accept an interesting invitation from a child who is new in class and has no friends. The old friend did not seem to like this new child.

In the interview the different components of the naive theory of action had to be reconstructed in the following issues: definition of the problem, action choice and moral judgment; descriptive and prescriptive reasoning about choice and alternative in terms of motives and moral justifications; the consequences of the choice for self and others, in particular feelings of self and other in case of violation of obligations and responsibilities; and the strategies to compensate for consequences of such a violation (Keller, 1984, 1996). The developmental levels of socio-moral reasoning were scored independently for the different issues. Reliability in age groups and cultures varied between 85 per cent and 95 per cent inter-rater consistency (see Keller, 1996, 2004a).

Cognitive-developmental analyses

Table 7.1 shows the developmental levels of perspective-differentiation and coordination in the general understanding of close friendship and the norm of promise-keeping.

Table 7.1 *Developmental levels of general understanding of close friendship and promise-keeping*

Perspective	Promise	Friendship
Level 1: Subjective-differentiated	One must keep it; one is punished if one breaks it; it is not nice to break it.	Playing; playing nicely/playing often; taking turns; sharing toys; liking to play.
Level 2: Self-reflexive-coordinated	It is unfair to betray; one should not be a traitor; *Self:* Would feel bad; *Other:* Is disappointed; breaks up relationship; thinks about self as a traitor.	Knowing each other long; sharing secrets; helping each other; keeping promises; not betraying.
Level 3: Generalized norm of reciprocity	*Self:* Being a trustworthy person; having a guilty conscience; *Other:* Would not trust self any more.	Being a trustworthy, reliable, dependable friend; sharing intimate, inner problems.

These developmental sequences are similar but not identical to those described in moral and friendship development. Concerning close friendship, children are first oriented towards mutual actions such as playing. At the next level, mutual feelings and a time dimension emerge. At the third level, generalized norms of reciprocity such as trust and reliability and interpersonal intimacy are the focus. Concerning promise-keeping, at the first level, external sanctions, rigid rule-orientation and stereotypic evaluations are emphasized. The last two aspects indicate a moral awareness that is not dependent on authority and sanction. At the second level, a coordination of perspectives of self and other emerges. Promise-keeping is seen as necessary to maintain relationships, and violating the obligation of promise-keeping leads to negative feelings of self (e.g. feeling bad) and the empathic awareness of others' negative feelings. Perspectives of self and other are coordinated such that it is understood that other will evaluate self negatively in this case. At the third level, trustworthiness of the person and mutual trust in the relationship are key concepts. Inner sanctions in terms of conscience regulate the actions of a moral self. This developmental sequence is not fully congruent with Kohlberg's definition of preconventional morality, in which morality is defined by external criteria such as fear of sanctions and obedience to authority at the first stage and instrumental exchange reciprocity at the second stage. Rather, our data support the assumption of a genuine moral understanding that is rooted in the positive

Table 7.2 *Developmental levels in situation-specific reasoning about the dilemma*

Perspective	Reasons for action choices and moral evaluation	Consequences of choice for other and self (feelings)
Level 1: Subjective-differentiated	*Friend**: wanting/liking to play, friend would not play any more, would be an enemy; *New child**: interesting invitation, was invited, new child is alone.	*Other as victim:* feels bad, not good; *Self as violator:* feels good (because she likes to play with the friend/ because the movie is fun).
Level 2: Self-reflexive-coordinated	*Friend:* has promised, not be a traitor; knowing each other long; always meeting this day; friend would be unhappy, insulted; *New child:* unique opportunity; last showing of the movie; new child has no friends; wanting to be friends with new child; helping new child.	*Other as victim:* feels unhappy; left out, disappointed; *Self as violator:* feels bad (because he or she is betraying friend, thinks about friend/thinks about new child who is left out); feels good: it is good/right to keep the promise/meet the friend; friend can/will understand.
Level 3: Generalized norm of reciprocity	*Friend:* wanting to be a reliable and trustworthy friend, not destroy the intimate relationship, not hurt friend's feelings; *New child:* friend would understand decision, having a guilty conscience about leaving out new child who has no friends.	*Other as victim:* hurt feelings over breach of trust/intimacy; *Self as violator:* guilty conscience over breach of trust/of intimacy with friend; Positive feelings: feeling good/right because of the intimate friendship, one has been trustworthy.

Note:
*reasons of protagonist/self for option 'friend' or 'new child'

motivation to maintain relationships. This understanding is gradually transformed by the ability to foresee the consequences of one's own actions for self and others and their (long-term) relationship and the awareness of a necessity to regulate actions in view of normative standards in order to maintain a close relationship, in particular close friendship (Keller & Edelstein, 1993).

Table 7.2 shows the developmental levels of situation-specific reasoning about the two action choices (visiting friend as promised or going with the new child) in the dilemma in terms of practical (descriptive) and moral reasoning (motives and justifications) and reasoning about the consequences of violation of norms.

The description of the levels shows that children use the categories of the naive theory of action in both general and situation-specific and descriptive and prescriptive reasoning. We also see that certain forms of motives and evaluations are connected with specific forms of conse-quences. When the normative dimension of the promise or of friendship is understood, negative feelings are seen as consequences of violating friendship responsibilities or altruistic obligations, and positive feelings arise when priority is given to responsibilities, in particular to close friendship. Thus, when children begin to understand that the friend feels bad as a consequence of the meeting with the new child (under-standing the unintended consequences of choice for the other) negative feelings are attributed to the protagonist/self (coordination of perspec-tives of other and self in terms of emotions). As we will show below, these positive feelings do not emerge in the Chinese children. What is also not presented here is that children change their action strat-egies when they understand the normative implications of their actions. Given the previous example of stage 2 reasoning they would try to make their friend understand the norm violation by reference to either the special situation (such a good movie, last showing) or the neediness of the other child (he or she is alone and has no friends). But another possibility is to hide the norm violation by constructing an alternative obligation, for example with an explicit lie such as that one had to go downtown with the mother. In this case guilt feelings might emerge as a moral consequence.

The empirical analysis of the longitudinal Icelandic data revealed that the separately coded issues are highly interrelated and form hierarchic-ally ordered developmental levels (see Keller, 1996). The same sequence holds for the Chinese cross-sectional and also the longitudinal data. The seven-year-olds in general score at stages 1 and 2, the nine-year-olds score mostly at stage 2, the twelve-year-olds at stages 2 and 3, and the fifteen-year-olds at stage 3. This is consistent with other cognitive-developmental data (Selman, 1980). Thus, the results support the as-sumption that the sequence of developmental levels which describes the cognitive organization in terms of an increasing differentiation and coordination of perspectives and awareness of the normative content of relationships and social situation is the same in both cultures. However, in spite of this similarity in socio-cognitive development a content ana-lysis of the arguments illuminates that the motivational concerns of children and adolescents in the two cultures are rather different.

Content analysis

Content analyses of arguments about the dilemma included (a) the direction of people's choices (new child versus friend) in the context of practical and moral reasoning (What will the protagonist do/is this the right choice?) and (b) reasons offered for the options in practical and moral reasoning. The more differentiated reasons shown in Tables 7.1 and 7.2 were categorized in terms of four types of content that represent theoretically relevant and most frequent reasons for the two options. Two categories referring to the option 'new child' indicate *self-interest* (hedonism: hedonistic offers made by the new child) and *altruistic responsibility* (altruism: helping/being with somebody who is new in class). Two categories referring to the option 'old friend' indicate *moral duty* (promise: given to the friend) and *friendship responsibility* (friendship: concerns of friend). Inter-rater agreement for scoring content categories was above 90 per cent for all categories in the different age groups from the two cultures.

The main findings discussed below are based on statistically significant effects of log-linear analyses (see Keller et al., 1998 for a detailed description of the statistical methods and results).

Figure 7.1 shows the distribution of types of the four types of reasons for the options 'friend' or 'new child' in practical (what the protagonist will do) and moral reasoning (whether this is the right decision).

One salient cultural difference concerns the category of hedonistic self-interests as reasons for the option 'new child' in the practical decision. Across all four age groups the Icelandic children used this category much more frequently than the Chinese. As moral reason the category was used very infrequently in both cultures. In contradistinction, the category of altruistic reasoning was emphasized more strongly by the Chinese children, in both practical and moral reasoning. Closer inspection of this type of argument revealed an interesting developmental phenomenon. The youngest children frequently mentioned a catalogue of rules for elementary school children that make it a duty to help somebody who is new in class (Döbert, 1989). Thus, interpersonal responsibilities in the youngest children seem to be based, at least partly, on obedience to rules and authorities. This corresponds to moral heteronomy as defined by Piaget and Kohlberg. In contradistinction, in Western cultures care and responsibility have been seen as originating from empathy (Eisenberg, 1982). Such empathy-based altruism is observed in older Chinese children who referred to others' state and feelings and to generalized norms of helping a person who needs to be integrated into the group. Overall, these findings are consistent with the cross-cultural findings discussed above, with people from Asian cultures being more concerned with interpersonal responsibilities while selfish concerns are more important for the Western children.

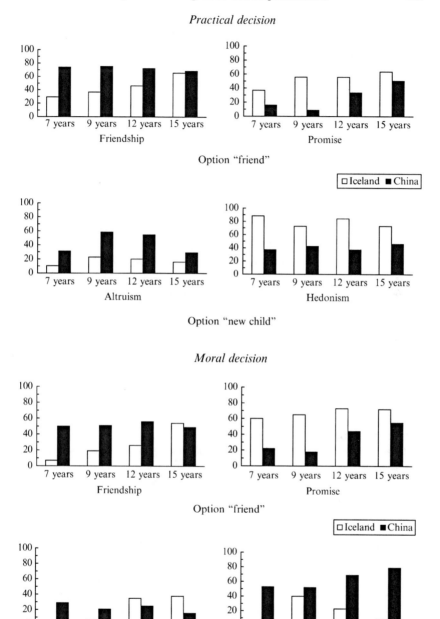

Figure 7.1. Frequencies (%) of content categories for practical and moral decision.

The other two types of reasons for the option 'friend' were used equally frequently in practical and moral reasoning. However, cultural differences in both content categories changed over time and were stronger in the younger children than in adolescents. In agreement with the cross-cultural differences in the literature mentioned above, the Icelandic children were more frequently oriented towards the contractual aspect of promise-keeping, whereas the Chinese children more frequently referred to friendship responsibilities. Whereas in the Chinese sample the reference to the promise increased over time, in the Icelandic sample the reference to close friendship increased developmentally in the same way. Most interestingly, in adolescence no difference obtained in the use of the two categories. These results support the difference between a contractual and an interpersonal orientation that has been shown in previous research. However, different from this research there are developmental changes in these cultural differences.

Overall the results reveal an interaction of development and culture. They show that some cultural differences remain stable across time (self-interest versus altruistic responsibility) while others change over development (moral duty versus interpersonal responsibility).This reveals a more complex picture of cultural differences across development than previously shown in the literature.

Moral consistency and moral feelings

In the following we will compare practical and moral decision-making in order to see whether children establish consistency between moral judgment and action (see Figure 7.2).

The Icelandic children revealed an increasing developmental trend to opt for the close friend and to judge this choice as morally right. In particular the youngest Icelandic children revealed moral inconsistency by opting for the new child and evaluating this choice as morally not right. The Chinese gave priority to the close friend only in adolescence (nearly 90 per cent) and judged this decision to be right. In the three younger Chinese age groups an almost equal split between the two offers obtained, but nearly always the preferred option was judged as morally right. Thus, the Chinese children almost never revealed a split between practical choice and moral judgment but they changed both the direction of choice and moral judgment in the course of development. This developmental trend supports the assumption that in both cultures adolescents feel closely connected with the friend. Consistent with the literature, responsibilities towards a close friend seem to be of central value particularly for adolescents (Bukowski & Sippola, 1996;

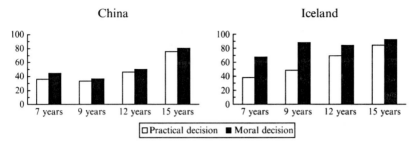

Figure 7.2. Direction of practical and moral decision for 'friend' in Iceland and China

Keller & Edelstein, 1990). This may have to do with universal biological changes and the developmental task to achieve independence from parents in adolescence. Frequent conflicts with parents – which seem to happen not only in Western cultures – make peer relationships specifically important. But it should be kept in mind that this developmental convergence originates from different values in the two cultures. For the Chinese, friendship becomes a predominant value only over time. For the Icelandic children, close friendship is a dominant moral value from the youngest age onwards. But the developmental task apparently is to give this value motivational priority against selfish interests and thus to establish consistency between moral judgment and practical choice. Keller & Edelstein (1993) had taken the findings from the Icelandic children as support of the assumption that moral consistency was a developmental phenomenon and that a moral self was established in adolescence. Because the Chinese did not show this developmental effect, Keller (2004a) concluded that a developmental theory of the moral self built on consistency between action choice and moral judgment could not be validated in cross-cultural research with Chinese children and adolescents. This questions also socialization theories that assume a universal developmental transformation from a selfish to a social disposition that is also inherent in Kohlberg's theory.

Moral feelings
Concerning the feelings attributed to the protagonist/self in the case of violating moral obligations or interpersonal responsibilities, the findings from previous research with Western children also could not be validated. Even the youngest Chinese children expected that whatever choice the protagonist/self made would result in negative feelings about this choice. Across development the Chinese seemed to experience intensive

moral conflict because they interpreted the situation as a conflict of obligations of altruism and friendship. The Icelanders seemed to interpret the situation across development as a conflict between self-interest and close friendship (Keller, 2004a; Keller & Edelstein, 1993) and with increasing age established consistency between moral judgment and action.

This conclusion was also supported by the analysis of the feelings attributed to the protagonist/self as a consequence of choice. Feelings were classified as positive (e.g. feeling good or happy) or negative (e.g. bad, unhappy, mixed feelings). Negative feelings were taken to indicate moral concerns when they resulted from empathy with the other person. The Chinese consistently argued that the protagonist would feel bad, independent of the direction of the choice. In contrast, the Icelandic children attributed negative feelings only when they opted for the new child (a choice that was mostly motivated by selfish interests and evaluated as not right). The older children attributed positive moral feelings when they opted for the friend (e.g. feeling good because this was the right thing to do), while the younger children frequently mentioned regret over the lost opportunity (e.g. feeling bad at the friend's house because it would have been more fun to see the movie) (Keller et al., 1996). We interpreted this finding such that close friendship is a more dominant value with the Icelandic youth than it is for the Chinese. Even when Chinese adolescents gave priority to close friendship in adolescence, they still felt that the protagonist had failed his or her responsibility towards the new child. This again indicates that the Chinese experience interpersonal obligations stronger than Icelanders. They never were 'happy victimizers' but always 'unhappy moralists' (Oser, 2005), living up to the expectations of others.

Conclusion

This chapter has discussed different aspects of normative development. Some of these aspects have been addressed in previous research, but mostly as separate research topics and not in an integrated theoretical framework. In this framework I have discussed the criteria that children and adolescents use when they justify obligations and responsibilities, both in a general and in a situation-specific way. I have further discussed the relationship between moral reasoning and action choices, in particular moral consistency as an indicator of a moral self. Finally the cognitive developmental research on moral feelings in the case of violation of obligations and responsibilities has been outlined. I have argued that the previous focus on research with Western children and adolescents is too narrow to establish an encompassing and culture-fair theory of normative development.

Our own empirical research on socio-moral reasoning about relationships and norms presented in this chapter tries to establish a broader framework by analysing normative development in cultural context, including different components of moral reasoning in an action-theoretical framework. Socio-moral development is described in this framework as involving the descriptive understanding of actions, relationships and norms and the prescriptive evaluation of actions, people and relations in terms of moral norms and principles. The development of the different components of this theory is analysed empirically in a longitudinal study from childhood to adolescence in Iceland and in a cross-cultural comparison in China. The results of this study reveal a complex interaction of context, development and culture. While the developmental sequences of the concepts of social and moral reasoning are the same in both cultures, some stable differences obtain between contexts or issues in the two cultures. In line with other cross-cultural research, some of our findings support stable cultural differences between children from the two cultures, concerning the role of self-interest, interpersonal responsibilities and moral feelings. Some of our findings document that cultural differences are changing over time, such as the difference between moral duties and responsibilities in close friendship. In particular the social and moral importance of close friendship becomes strikingly similar in adolescence. This may indicate the universal importance of close friendship in adolescence. It should be pointed out however that in spite of these similarities the cultural meanings of close friendship may still be slightly different. Thus, while Icelandic adolescents see close friendship as an intimate personal relationship, Chinese adolescents emphasize the interconnection of friendship and society (Keller, 2004a). Friends not only share each other's inner world and help each other with intimate problems but they also have the task of criticizing each other and of helping each other to become socially valuable members of society.

I finally want to mention that we found little variation in the different ecological contexts, such as city and rural children. One small difference concerned the effect that we also found in the not yet fully scored data of the longitudinal follow-up of our Chinese cross-sectional data. A first analysis of these time-lagged assessments reveals an effect that can be taken as an indicator of changes in socio-moral reasoning due to the rapid modernization and the capitalist-individualistic transformation of Chinese society. The most striking difference of the longitudinal follow-up study is a change from altruistic responsibility to more hedonistic self-interest in reasoning about the friendship dilemma: the children in the time-lagged sample used the category of hedonistic self-interest much more frequently than altruistic responsibilities. This is consistent with the finding in the cross-sectional study, that the children from the most modernized school type which children of the elite attained also used hedonistic self-interest more frequently than the children from the two other settings. Thus, a modernization effect was already present at the earlier measurement occasion and became stronger in the time-lagged longitudinal study. Whether this indicates a general change in the normative orientation of youth is a question for future research. However, it is important to see that cultural change can affect the socio-moral reasoning of children even in a rather short timespan. This finding illustrates that normative development is both a universal and a socially dynamic process. When life-patterns change, children's socio-moral learning processes are affected and this is mirrored in what children see as important in morally relevant situations.

8 The multiplicity of social norms: the case for psychological constructivism and social epistemologies

Elliot Turiel

The central issue this volume is meant to address is how the study of the psychology of development can deal with and contribute to understandings of norms. A central problem connected to this issue is that of how norms, which entail 'oughts', can be related to what is the case psychologically. Traditionally, psychologists have implicitly answered the 'is to ought' question by explaining 'ought' as 'is'. That is, oughts take the guise of obligations not because of conceptualizations of norms but because of psychological mechanisms that lead people to behave with compulsion (and often lead people to the supposedly false view that they do so for normative reasons). As is well known, the two primary sources attributed to compulsion in beliefs and behaviours are learning and biology. In one set of positions, it is through conditioning, or social learning, or cultural participation that people develop habits or dispositions that involve constant actions (to paraphrase Martin Luther, 'he cannot do otherwise because that is how he was socially engineered'). Analogously, psychologists have attempted to explain compulsion as due to people's biological make-up stemming from evolutionary forces. These can take the form of hard-wired actions or built-in intuitions due to emotional dispositions ('he cannot do otherwise because that is the way he is biologically engineered'). In some explanations, of course, learning and cultural participation serve to reinforce the biologically given.

Therefore, psychologists often have been able to readily do away with the 'is to ought' problem by implicitly claiming that oughts are nothing but psychological states that give the appearance that people act normatively. Psychologists have been able to eliminate the problem of understanding norms and oughts, however, only by not granting to humans, who are the objects of their explanations, the types of mental activities they use in formulating those very explanations. That is, psychologists use reasoning, inference and evidence to formulate the explanations that human functioning is not based on reasoning. The propositions I put forth in this chapter are based on the assumption that people, starting in childhood, reason about norms and formulate conceptions of different types of norms that may be in conflict with each other. Consequently, it is necessary to understand how different types of norms are applied in situational contexts.

I argue, therefore, that the development of reasoning is central to how humans (not only psychologists) understand norms and that children develop multiple aspects of understanding of norms that divide by domains in social realms. When Martin Luther asserted, 'I cannot do otherwise,' he was talking about what he ought to do and applying it to his actions (Smith, 2003; see also Smith, this volume, Chapter 1). Martin Luther was referring to norms of conscience or the realm of moral obligation. Although the issue of norms is often linked to moral judgments, there are several different types of norms that people maintain. To understand how people make decisions about social norms, which frequently vary by social contexts, it is necessary to understand how they develop distinct domains of social judgments (not only moral judgments) through multiple social interactions. Since children develop judgments by which they discriminate among different categories of norms, it is essential to connect social development with epistemological categories. Moreover, in their everyday lives people oppose, resist and attempt to change societal norms and cultural practices. The process of reflecting upon existing conditions and practices demonstrates that children construct deep moral norms that are not due to social or biological engineering.

Epistemology and domains of social judgment

How we explain the acquisition of different types of social judgments is related less to the question of whether individuals form distinct domains of judgments connected to epistemological categories and more to two other issues: the sources of development and how social decisions are made. Recent propositions of biological engineering (e.g. Haidt, 2001) place little emphasis on development through children's experiences. Usually, two types of criteria are used in claims that moral evaluations and actions are due to built-in intuitions that do not involve reasoning or reflection. The criteria are that evaluations and actions are made in immediate and rapid fashion, and that they appear at early ages, such as three or four years. Each criterion, however, has been used inappropriately.

First, making judgments or taking actions rapidly does not mean that reasoning is uninvolved. The development of reasoning in several realms (e.g. number, mathematics, logic, classification, psychological understandings) can entail errors, incomplete understandings and be-laboured efforts at reaching conclusions. Once formed, children then apply concepts in these realms in rapid ways in many situations (for further discussion, see Pizarro & Bloom, 2003; Turiel, 2006). Reasoning cannot be eliminated through the quantitative dimension of speed of reaction.

More to the point for the present purposes is that the appearance of particular actions or judgments in early childhood is not in any way direct evidence for innatism since children have experienced a good deal of social interaction by the ages of two, three and four years. This obvious point was made many years ago by Piaget (1932), but it has not always been heeded. At the time, Piaget remarked on the fallacy of innatist positions based on studies of young children with reference to propositions put forth by Antipoff (1928). According to Piaget (1932, p. 228), Antipoff conducted a small study showing that young children feel sympathy for the suffering of others. She then concluded that there is 'an innate and instinctive moral manifestation which, in order to develop, really requires neither preliminary experience nor socialization amongst other children' (quoted in Piaget, 1932, p. 228). Antipoff went on to say: 'We have here an inclusive affective perception, an elementary moral "structure" which the child seems to possess very early and which enables him to grasp simultaneously evil and its cause, innocence and guilt. We may say that what we have here is an affective perception of justice' (quoted in Piaget, 1932, p. 228).

For Piaget, this was, in his words, going a little too far. He succinctly summarized the problem in the following way:

We may mention at once that nothing in the very interesting observations quoted by Mme Antipoff goes to show this innateness. She deals with observations on the behavior of children between three and nine, and it is obvious that at the age of three, a child has already come under all sorts of adult influences such as can account for the fact that its polarization is now only in terms of good and evil. (1932, p. 228)

According to Piaget, early emerging emotions of fear, affection and sympathy contribute to the development of moral judgments, but moral judgments are not reducible to those emotional reactions. In the above quoted statement, Piaget specifically stressed that by the age of three years children have come under all sorts of adult influences. He empha-sized adult influences because he thought that in significant ways young children's physical, psychological, social and moral judgments were undifferentiated from each other in ways of thinking that made for what he labelled heteronomous morality. Heteronomous moral thinking is mainly associated with adult influences and includes unilateral (not mutual) respect for adults and rules. The young child's moral thinking does not yet represent moral understandings distinct from other types of understandings since the moral is undifferentiated from other realms (e.g. social, psychological). Nevertheless, Piaget's formulation of morality was domain-specific because he proposed that at later ages children form 'normative autonomy', with moral understandings of justice that differ from other realms of thought (Piaget, 1932, pp. 196, 345). According to Piaget, the cooperation that comes with moral autonomy 'allows for the emancipation of what ought to be from what is' (1932, p. 350). By contrast, the essence of heteronomous moral thinking 'is to identify what is with what ought to be' (1932, p. 347).

Therefore, Piaget did not propose that reasoning about deontic rules is unified or general. It is sometimes thought that the question of whether reasoning about norms is unified or entails differences between domains is closely connected to the proposed age of emergence of the domain. For instance, I have proposed that at young ages children begin to distinguish morality from the social conventional and personal domains (Turiel, 1983), and that these constitute separate developmental paths within the thinking of individuals. This proposition departs from a differentiation model of moral development, like the one proposed by Piaget (1932), with regard to processes and sources of development to autonomous and distinct moral judgments (I return to these issues below). Nevertheless, Piaget implicitly proposed a domain-specific view with regard to both the epistemological bases of morality (i.e. the definitional features) and its distinctive status at the most advanced level of development.

I can further illustrate how a differential model can entail the proposition that morality is a distinct domain with reference to Kohlberg's (1969, 1971) extensions and refinements of Piaget's moral judgment formulation into a six-stage sequence meant to encompass transformations from childhood to adulthood. Kohlberg was more explicit than Piaget about the need for a moral epistemology that entailed definitional properties in analyses of moral development. Kohlberg also recognized that the 'is to ought' problem needed to be addressed by developmentalists, if they take seriously an understanding of norms as part of their psychological investigations. Indeed, he titled one of his major essays 'From is to ought: how to commit the naturalistic fallacy and get away with it in the study of moral development' (Kohlberg, 1971).

Kohlberg (1971, p. 151) argued that two central questions pertaining to epistemology had not been adequately addressed by psychologists. One was: 'What can the psychological study of the development of concepts tell us about their epistemological status?' Kohlberg regarded this question to be connected to the problem of moving from 'is' (the study of what exists psychologically) to 'ought' (moral prescriptions). In the first place, psychological study can tell us whether people do engage in reasoning about moral matters of the sort outlined by philosophers. If it were the case that only (or mainly) philosophers did so while others judged and acted as a consequence of, say, conditioning or biological dispositions, then psychological reality would have a bearing on the validity of epistemological categories. Kohlberg maintained that empirical studies evidenced that moral reasoning was not solely the province of philosophers and that common patterns of reasoning occurred in different cultural settings. Accordingly, one can go from 'is to ought' without committing the naturalistic fallacy by using psychological findings to inform the validity of epistemological considerations. Kohlberg went a little further by also asserting that understanding the ways people reason morally can feed back upon philosophical formulations of the moral realm.

More detailed discussion of issues revolving around the first question about psychology and epistemology are beyond the scope of this chapter. Of greater relevance is the second question claimed by Kohlberg to have been neglected by psychologists: 'What does the psychological study of concept development require in the ways of epistemological assumptions about knowing?' (Kohlberg, 1971, p. 151). The answer is that psychological study of moral development needs to be guided by epistemological considerations – that is, by conceptualizations of the realm under investigation, in part, provided in philosophical analyses (for Kohlberg, these were provided by Kant, Dewey and Rawls). Kohlberg's formulations were based on the criteria of universality, prescriptivity and consistency that defined the distinctive epistemological category of morality.

Kohlberg, therefore, defined morality as a domain with distinctive features and, thereby, as different from other value judgments. However, he also proposed that morality 'is only fully defined by its final or principled stages' (1971, p. 217). This was because he explained the process of development as entailing increasing differentiations of moral judgments from judgments in other realms:

The individual whose judgments are at stage 6 asks 'Is it morally right?' and means by morally right something different from punishment (stage 1), prudence (stage 2), conformity to authority (stages 3 and 4) etc. Thus, the responses of lower-stage subjects are not moral for the same reasons that responses of higher-stage subjects to aesthetic or other morally neutral matters fail to be moral . . .

This is what we had in mind earlier when we spoke of our stages as representing an increased differentiation of moral values and judgments from other types of values and judgments. (1971, p. 216)

So morality possesses the distinctive features of judgment that would render it domain-specific, only among those who have attained the highest stage of development. At that stage moral norms are 'disentangled' from other social issues (which resembles Piaget's formulation of moral judgments). Kohlberg, too, viewed his stage formulation as involving a type of 'differentiation of the morally autonomous or categorical "oughts" from the morally heteronomous "is"' (1971, p. 184). The perspectives of both Piaget and Kohlberg on morality as a distinct domain with particular characteristics are not unimportant to a developmental explanation. It means morality involves reasoning and that development entails a process of construction through social interactions. But what if morality were a distinct domain of judgment from an early age – and separate from other social judgments? Domain-specificity that does not involve increasing differentiations but separate developmental pathways would have implications for explanations of developmental processes, the sources of development (as well as how development could be facilitated) and for how social decisions are made (including the question of how different norms are applied).

My interpretation of research conducted over the past thirty years or so is that the evidence unambiguously shows that the specificity of the domain of morality begins in childhood and that the differentiation model is not an accurate representation of development. A large number of studies, including ones using hypothetical situations and real-life events, have demonstrated that moral judgments are distinctively different from judgments in the personal and social-conventional domains by the ages of five or six years (Turiel, 1983, 1998, 2002). Children as young as three or four years of age do make the distinctions, but by five or six years the distinctions are made consistently on a number of dimensions.

Both the moral and conventional domains involve understandings of different types of norms, and their distinction does not solely involve a simple discrimination between categories. A complex configuration is connected to each domain, including criterion judgments and justifications. The criterion judgments, which are not age-related, refer to whether morality or convention is seen as contingent on rules, dependent on authority dictates, or based on common practice or existing social arrangements. Many studies show that moral norms are judged to be obligatory, and non-contingent on rules, authority, or existing practices and agreements. By contrast, conventional norms are judged to be contingent on rules, authority, common practice, and are based on social agreements. Justifications – or reasons for evaluations and criterion judgments – also differ by domain. Justifications in the moral domain are based on concepts of welfare, justice and rights, whereas in the conventional domain they are based on tradition, social agreement and social coordinations. Age-related changes occur in justifications. Levels of development have been identified for the domain of social convention (Turiel, 1983). Although less is known about development in the moral domain, shifts occur from a focus on harm among younger children to concerns with welfare and justice in later childhood (Davidson, Turiel & Black, 1983; Nucci, 2001; Turiel, 1998).

The propositions regarding domain-specificity recently received further empirical support from research on deontic rules that contrasted the ways cognitive reasoning has been approached with the work on morality and social convention (Fiddick, 2004, 2005). A point of departure of Fiddick's work is the frequent use of the Wason (1968) selection task to assess general cognitive processes in supposedly unified reasoning about deontic rules (obligations, permissions and prohibitions). The Wason task is meant to examine logic regarded to be content-independent. However, Fiddick argued that the Wason task is a 'relatively poor assay of people's reasoning about deontic rules because it reinforces a narrow, logical characterization of reasoning' (2004, 452) and because of the lack of content in tasks where only logical rules of an 'if P then Q' and 'if P then not-Q' nature are invoked. To test these propositions, Fiddick conducted experiments on different types of rules that had yielded similar responses to the Wason selection task: social-contract rules (based on agreements or social conventions) and precautionary rules (of a prudential kind with harmful consequences to the actor). Fiddick found that when presenting participants with the Wason selection task no distinctions were evident for these types of rules. However, when assessments were made of criterion judgments and justifications, reasoning about social contracts differed from reasoning about precautionary rules. Social contracts were generally judged in conventional terms and precautionary rules in prudential terms (having to do with self harm and regulation; see Tisak & Turiel, 1984).

To summarize thus far, I have tried to show that morality is an epistemological category that can be regarded as distinct from other domains within the context of different types of explanations of development. Both Piaget (1932) and Kohlberg (1971) identified and defined morality with distinctive features (hence a form of domain-specificity), but proposed that judgments that include those features do not come about until advanced stages of development (hence differentiation models). In Piaget's formulation, true moral understandings entailing autonomy are not formed until late childhood or early adolescence. In Kohlberg's formulation, true and autonomous moral judgments are not formed until late adolescence or early adulthood. There is very strong evidence, however, that young children distinguish morality from other social domains. The distinction is made by three or four years of age, and it is made across several dimensions by the ages of five or six years.

Domains and social experiences

Although these two approaches have important commonalities (e.g. morality as a distinct epistemological category and development as a constructive process), the differences are not trivial. In the first place, the particular ways development is explained differ from each other. In contrast with a process of differentiating or disentangling morality from other matters (e.g. prudence, convention), in the domain-specific view development is seen to occur within domains. That is, there are different strands of developmental transformations within individuals – in the context of the maintenance of the domain distinctions across ages (there is both stability and change with increasing age).

A second and related difference between the two approaches is in their respective perspectives on the influences of children's social experiences. In the differentiation models distinctions are not drawn between types of social experiences associated with moral judgments and other social judgments. For instance, Kohlberg did not specify, except in general terms, experiences that serve to stimulate development at the later ages of thinking to the highest stages. He discussed experiences like increased role-taking opportunities, discussion or argumentation, and conflicts that allow for increased differentiations. Piaget did specify differences associated with the formation of heteronomous and autonomous morality. Young children's experiences revolve around interactions with adults as authority figures – which are associated with heteronomous thinking. Older children's experiences revolve around interactions with peers – which provide a basis for relationships of equality and autonomous thinking. In both the Piaget and Kohlberg formulations, social experiences that might be associated with the social conventional or other domains are not in the picture.

In the domain-specific view, distinctions are drawn between qualitatively different social interactions associated with the different domains. Piaget seemed to speak to this possibility in work published later than his 1932 volume on moral development. In later writing he stated: 'socialization in no way constitutes the result of a unilateral cause such as the pressure of the adult community upon the child through such means as education in the family and subsequently in the school. Rather . . . it involves the intervention of a multiplicity of interactions of different types and sometimes with opposed effects' (Piaget 1951/1995, p. 276).

I interpret Piaget's statement to mean that children experience a variety of social interactions in many social contexts. Moreover, young children's social experiences are multifaceted in that they go beyond the influences of adults or peers *per se* in the sense that they attend to the substance of events. As examples, children perceive the actions and reactions of those (including the self) involved in acts of physical harm, unequal treatment, helping, sharing, or failing to help or share. A number of studies with pre-school-age children in the home and pre-schools, as well as a few studies with older children in playgrounds and schools (Nucci & Nucci, 1982a, 1982b; Turiel, 2005), have shown that children's interactions with each other and with adults do differ in accord with events in the moral and conventional domains. With regard to moral events, interactions and communications revolve around the effects of acts on people, the perspectives of others, the need to avoid harm, and the pain and emotions experienced. With regard to conventional events, interactions and communications revolve around adherence to rules, commands from those in authority and an emphasis on social order (for further details, see Nucci, 2001 and Turiel, 1998).

The differences in developmental explanations stemming from the differentiation and domain-specific models also have implications for how to influence social and moral development in educational programmes (propositions regarding educational interventions based on domain-specificity have been presented by Nucci, 2001). The domain-specific propositions on thought and experiences have additional implications for the nature of social relationships. The clearest example of how domain distinctions relate to social interactions comes from a body of research on adolescent–parent relationships (see Smetana, 1995, 2002 for reviews). In brief, it has been found that parent–adolescent relationships, including conflicts, differ by the domains involved. Typically, conflicts occur over personal issues and not matters of morality or social conventions.

Another implication of domain-specificity more directly tied to the topics of this volume has to do with how social and moral decisions are made.

Domains and social decisions

The psychological research I have considered thus far poses us with a problem with norms. Norms are judged as entailing obligations that ought to be or have to be followed. The problem is that people hold to more than one type of norm. There are moral norms and there are conventional norms (nor are norms restricted to these two types). As we have seen, beginning at young ages the organization of moral norms is distinct from the organization of conventional norms. This is a problem for issues of normativity because often enough these different types of norms can be in conflict so that upholding one type means the other is violated. The problem is further compounded by the possibility that different norms within the moral domain can be in conflict with each other (e.g. welfare vs rights or welfare vs trust).

One of the appeals of the types of differentiation models I discussed above is that these problems with normativity are eliminated through the propositions that moral norms displace other categories of social norms and that true moral understandings involve overarching moral principles that serve to organize priorities among moral considerations and result in consistency in their application in different contexts. Within the context of Kohlberg's differentiation model, for instance, moral principles will have priority over other domains because the process of development involves a formation of judgments out of prior confusions (i.e. lack of differentiation) of morality and other judgments. At less advanced levels moral judgments are not equilibrated or consistently applied because matters like personal choice, prudence and convention are not disentangled from moral principles. In part, development involves disentangling these different considerations such that the greater adequacy of moral judgments over those other considerations is understood. Armed with such understandings, moral norms will be given priority over what are now conceptualized as non-moral realms. In other words, at the highest level of development moral concepts trump everything else social and are understood in ways that are manifested in their consistent application (criteria sometimes used in a circular way for assessing levels of development).

People's concepts of rights have been approached in this way. Rights are seen as part of the formation of moral principles at the highest level or stage of development. And the expectation is that rights as understood at that stage of thinking would be upheld consistently across situations. Conversely, insofar as rights are not upheld in some situations, it is taken to reflect an inadequately developed understanding of rights (and moral judgments, more generally). In this way, consistency across situations is a benchmark for attainment of an advanced level of moral reasoning. There is a counterpart to this developmental approach in the ways rights have been discussed by some political scientists and philosophers. Several large-scale public-opinion surveys, taken at various times during the twentieth century (Hyman & Sheatsley, 1953; McClosky & Brill, 1983; Stouffer, 1955), of attitudes towards rights have consistently yielded the finding that American adults endorse rights in some situations but fail to do so in other situations. To some analysts, this is a clear indication that most Americans do not adequately understand the concept of rights (Protho & Grigg, 1960; Sarat, 1975). The claim is that although Americans give lip service to the value of rights, inadequate understandings lead them to the failure to uphold rights in many situations (in turn, the failure to uphold rights in some situations is taken to indicate that rights are not adequately understood).

Others have provided an alternative interpretation of rights and their application. From a philosophical perspective, Dworkin (1977) and Gewirth (1982) have viewed rights as one type of norm that needs to be weighed against other competing moral or social considerations. An adequate understanding of rights does not mean that they must always be applied regardless of other goals. Dworkin (1977, p. 93) stated this position as follows: 'An abstract right is a general political aim the statement of which does not indicate how that general aim is to be weighed or compromised in particular circumstances against other political aims.'

Dworkin's position on rights is consistent with the developmental framework and findings on domains, which lead to the idea that decisions in particular contexts involve weighing, balancing and attempting to coordinate different components (including norms) of situations. Even when rights are well understood, they are not necessarily given priority over all other personal, social or moral considerations. The co-existence of different domain understandings means that people attempt to take various issues into account when arriving at decisions. Therefore, in endorsing a particular norm, like that of rights, consistency across situations would not be a valid criterion for developmentally advanced levels. The findings on rights show that variations by contexts (reflecting neither situationalism nor inconsistencies) are not particular to any age period.

As already indicated, seeming inconsistencies are abundantly evident among adults. Consider the findings from the most recent national survey of several thousand adults (McClosky & Brill, 1983). Respondents were presented with a large number of items pertaining to rights and civil liberties (e.g. freedom of speech, press, assembly, association, religion, dissent), which were couched sometimes in abstract or general terms and sometimes in the context of particular circumstances. To briefly summarize the findings, rights were endorsed by most people when stated in general terms, but often subordinated to other considerations when put into particular situations. The nature of these findings can be conveyed through a few examples from the surveys. Examples of items couched in abstract or general terms are: (1) 'I believe in free speech for all no matter what their views might be,' and (2) 'We would never be free if we gave up the right to criticize our government.' These statements were endorsed by 89 per cent and 82 per cent, respectively, of the respondents. However, most did not uphold rights when asked: (1) 'Should a community allow the American Nazi party to use its town hall to hold a public meeting?' or (2) Should a group be allowed to 'use a public building to hold a meeting denouncing the government?' In these contexts the liberties were endorsed by 18 per cent and 23 per cent, respectively, of the respondents.

One consistency in the findings is that rights, when stated in general terms, were endorsed by the large majority of respondents. Another consistency in these findings is that there was variability in the endorsement of rights when placed in contexts. The findings indicate that very few adults treat rights as an inviolable norm that always ought to be upheld. It depends on circumstances. Since large-scale public-opinion surveys assess attitudes (i.e. accept or not, uphold or not) only on items presented to respondents, they yield no direct information on whether or how they were coordinating rights and other moral or social considerations. Other research has attempted to more closely examine the types of judgments involved in responses to rights stated in general terms and embedded in situations with particular circumstances (Helwig, 1995, 1997; Turiel & Wainryb, 1998).

In studies conducted in the United States and Canada, children, adolescents and adults made judgments about rights in general and within particular contexts. At all ages, rights pertaining to such matters as freedom of speech and religion were endorsed in the abstract. Moreover, rights were regarded as obligatory norms in that they were judged to generalize across groups or cultures and that they should not be legally restricted. Moreover, rights were understood as serving democratic principles, and needs for self-expression and autonomy. Nevertheless, in some contexts these same rights were subordinated, across ages, to preventing matters like psychological harm (e.g. a public speech with racial slurs), physical harm (e.g. a speech advocating violence) and inequality (e.g. a speech advocating exclusion of people of poverty from political participation). Some age differences were found. The younger children, overall, were more likely than older people to subordinate rights to other considerations. The age differences, however, were not in accord with what would be expected from the differentiation models. At all ages there was an attempt to take into account the different considerations posed by a given situation and to draw priorities between conflicting norms. In addition, the older ones (later adolescence and adulthood) did not always give priority to rights. A shift in the severity of a consideration pertaining to, say, physical harm, resulted in a greater likelihood of subordination of rights on the part of the older ones. It should also be noted that similar results have been obtained outside North America, including the Middle East (Turiel & Wainryb, 1998), Costa Rica, France, Italy and Switzerland (Clémence et al., 1995; Doise, Clémence & Spini, 1996).

Therefore, research that has examined understandings of rights and their application in particular situations speaks against the idea that individuals fail to give rights priority because of an inability to adequately grasp the concept. The research shows that even where there are clear indications that people grasp the concept well, they subordinate it to other considerations in some situations. It is probably safe to say that it is when people understand a concept well enough not to apply it rigidly that they are able to weigh and coordinate different considerations. In forming understandings of the distinct domains, individuals make decisions by coordinating different moral and social considerations.

More of the same: the norm of honesty

It could be said that the concept of rights is not a good example. Perhaps concepts of rights are not representative of what typically occurs in moral judgments because they involve the types of abstract issues that make them operate in people's minds unlike other norms. It has also been maintained that the concept of rights is particular to think-ing in modern Western societies (for counter-arguments see Dworkin, 1977 and Gewirth, 1982; I have already referred to counter-evidence). It turns out, however, that the pattern of findings in research on rights is obtained for other moral issues – so that it takes on the flavour of a rule rather than the exception.

Even the moral precept that harm should be prevented is not consist-ently upheld across situations. There are commonly discussed examples like actions in self-defence or during wartime. Variability regarding harm (erroneously) led Ruth Benedict (1934, pp. 45–6) to the well-known statement in support of cultural relativism: 'in a matter of homicide, it may be held that one is blameless if diplomatic relations have been severed between neighboring countries, or that one kills by custom his first two children, or that a husband has a right of life and death over his wife, or that it is the duty of the child to kill his parents before they are old'. (For alternative views, see Asch, 1952; Hatch, 1983; Turiel, 2002; Wertheimer, 1935.)

A clear example of a pattern similar to the issue of rights is the norm of honesty. Honesty is often seen as a binding value or virtue, and usually is not seen as particular to any given culture. Honesty is treated as an ought! It is always listed among the moral virtues and responsibilities by those who go about the business of listing virtues, traits of character or responsibilities. Thou shalt not lie is considered a binding rule. And among those who approach the issue from the perspective of moral concepts or principles, trust is regarded as framing an obligatory norm. Laypersons, too, view honesty as a binding norm. If they were to be posed with a general question, like should you tell the truth, undoubtedly most would answer in the affirmative (Perkins, 2003). Nevertheless, people the world over frequently lie.

When I say that people lie frequently I do not have in mind lies for self-serving reasons or for selfish gain. Also, I am not talking about a discrepancy between what people say and what they do. People lie frequently for what they perceive to be justified reasons. Philosophical discourse has dealt with these issues in discussions about Kant's dictum that the prohibition against lying is absolute (see Bok, 1978/1999). In questioning Kant's position, philosophers have posed the following question: Suppose a murderer asks you to tell him which way an intended victim has gone. Do you tell the truth? Some maintain that the moral norm, 'you ought to tell the truth', is transformed in this situation into the moral norm, 'you ought not tell the truth'. I hasten to add that the problem of truth-telling is not limited to the speculation of philosophers. A clear and dramatic example comes from decisions many had to make (and did make) during World War II when Nazis came looking for their intended victims to send to concentration camps. In those instances, the moral obligation could be seen as to engage in deception and that one ought not to tell the truth.

There are many less serious instances in which lying is seen as acceptable in order to spare people's feelings. These are the so-called white lies that people tell and that parents even encourage their children to tell. Several types of more complicated instances are documented in studies showing that the application of the norm of honesty varies by the situational context. One study addressed the issue of honesty in connection with the physical welfare of persons in the context of medical decisions (Freeman et al., 1999). In this research, the issue was investigated by assessing how physicians would judge deception as a means of obtaining a treatment of one type or another for patients. A sample of physicians were presented with hypothetical situations in which a doctor considers deceiving an insurance company as the only way to obtain a particular treatment or diagnosis for a patient. Six hypothetical situations were used in the study, designed to contain conditions of varying severity or seriousness. As examples, the most serious conditions required coronary-bypass surgery and arterial revascularization – both life-threatening situations. The least serious situation involved cosmetic surgery. The majority of physicians thought that deception of the insurance company was justified for the two serious conditions (58 per cent and 56 per cent of them), and very few (3 per cent) thought it would be legitimate in the case of the least severe condition. Predictably, the number of physicians judging deception legitimate was in between for the other conditions (intravenous pain medication, mammography and psychiatric referral for depression).

There is also evidence that physicians act on these types of judgments in their medical practices (Wynia et al., 2000). It would be incorrect to assume that physicians are for some reason a dishonest lot. We can assume that most of them are considered by others to be honest people. More than likely, honesty is of value to them. Most people will violate the norm of honesty and lie when it is in conflict with the norm of welfare for those in their charge. Honesty is also a norm weighed against other considerations even when the type of physical welfare at stake in medical or other situations is not involved. Studies show that deception is considered by many to be legitimate to resist injustices and to combat inequalities in power and control in marital relationships, and in adolescents' relationship with parents.

One study examined the judgments of college students and married adults about the use of deception in the context of inequalities in marital relationships (Turiel, Perkins & Mensing, in preparation). A few details as to how these judgments were elicited are necessary to describe the findings. Individuals participating in the research were asked to judge examples of one spouse deceiving the other about four different matters (presented in different stories). In each case the marital relationship was described as involving inequality in that one spouse works while the other does not, and the working member exerts a substantial degree of control over the other. In one set of conditions it is the husband who works and in a second set of conditions it is the wife who works. As an example, in one story the non-working spouse maintains a bank account kept secret from the working spouse, who exerts a great deal of control over the finances of the family. Results for this situation are particularly interesting because deception on the part of a wife was judged acceptable by the majority of participants and more often than deception on the part of a husband (recall that in the latter case the wife works and controls the finances). Therefore, deception is judged acceptable as a means to combat what are perceived as unfair restrictions and deprivations in relationships of inequality. The inequality, however, is not solely determined by the specific conditions in the particular relationship. Deception by a wife is judged more acceptable than deception by a husband because the general structure of power and inequality in society is taken into account.

Two other situations revealed similar but less pronounced differences in evaluations of deception by wife or husband. Those two situations depicted a spouse who deceives the other with regard to shopping for clothes and seeing a friend the other does not like. The fourth situation used in the study pitted honesty against welfare. A person deceptively attends meetings of Alcoholics Anonymous in order to deal with a drinking problem even though the spouse insists that she or he not do so. Virtually all participants judged that deception to deal with a drinking problem is acceptable regardless of whether it was the wife or husband who engaged in it.

Again, we see a pattern of contextual variability in judgments about obligations to the norm of honesty. The findings suggest that in addition to sometimes subordinating honesty to promoting people's welfare, inequalities in relationships and matters of social control have a bearing on judgments about the application of norms. A study of judgments about adolescents' relationships with parents and friends shows that the type of relationship and the domain of action intersect in evaluations of honesty and deception (Perkins, 2003). The study examined judgments about acts of deception on the part of adolescents in the face of directives from their parents or friends about matters having to do with morality, personal jurisdiction and prudence.

Hypothetical situations were presented to adolescents depicting parents or friends directing the protagonist (an adolescent) to refrain from chosen activities. In some situations the adolescent was directed to engage in what might be considered acts that violate moral norms (to fight another child, to discriminate against a person of another race). In the end (after other efforts), the protagonist continues the activity, but lies about it. Almost all adolescents in the study evaluated deception of parents in these situations as the correct course of action on the grounds that it would promote welfare or prevent injustices. Most also positively evaluated deception of parents when the adolescent was directed to refrain from choices in the personal domain (i.e. who to date, what club to join). Deception was justified in these situations on the grounds that the activities involved personal choices. By contrast, most gave negative evaluations of deception of parents regarding their directives about prudential matters (doing homework, not riding a motorcycle). Prudential concerns were viewed as within the legitimate authority of parental responsibility. In turn, deception of friends regarding the moral and personal issues was judged less acceptable than deception of parents. Directives from friends were not considered more legitimate than directives from parents. Rather, it was thought that the situations should be dealt with openly with friends because of the equality and mutuality in those relationships (in contrast with inequalities of power and control in relationships with parents).

The three studies I have discussed reveal the same pattern of varying judgments as to whether honesty is a norm that ought to be upheld. Whether it should be upheld depends on other moral, personal and social considerations in a situation. These findings are consistent with findings in the studies of concepts of rights – which also show that rights are, in general or in the abstract, valued and endorsed. I believe we can safely assume that the adults in the studies on deception in medical contexts and in marital relationships accepted the value of honesty in general. The study with adolescents (Perkins, 2003) directly demonstrated that they value and endorse honesty through responses to a direct and general question that lying is wrong. The adolescents also evaluated deception for self-gain (e.g. to cover up a misdeed) as wrong.

The study with adolescents also provides evidence that speaks against the differentiation models of development. The adolescents participating in the research, who ranged in age from twelve to seventeen years, do not confuse authority, prudence or personal interests with morality. In the first place, they did not accept the legitimacy of the dictates of an authority regarding issues of harm or unfairness. In their minds, such dictates ought to be opposed, even with reliance on deception to do so. Prudence was treated differently from moral issues, since they regarded deception unjustified in these cases. Although deception of parental directives to circumvent restrictions on decisions in the personal realm was judged as acceptable as for the moral realm, the reasons for each were different. The adolescents distinguished between deception aimed at furthering moral goals of welfare and fairness from deception aimed at preserving personal choices in the context of a relationship of inequality. Adolescents think differently about each of these domains and apply their judgments with flexibility of mind in relation to honesty in the context of different types of social relationships.

Conclusion: norms about norms

The norm about norms that emerges from the considerations discussed in this chapter is that norms are not and should not be applied consistently across situations. This is because in social thought and social lives there is no general or unified norm that would handle all situations. The different domains of social thought that apply to social interactions make for a multiplicity of norms important for different aspects of social life.

We cannot adequately frame norms through specific dictums like, 'it is wrong to lie' or 'you should always tell the truth'. In the moral domain norms are structured by concepts of welfare, justice and rights. As such, it is in the aim of achieving goals of welfare, justice and rights that an issue like honesty is understood and applied. One problem is that a norm like honesty and its underlying basis in trust and fairness can be in conflict with other moral considerations. Another problem is that moral norms can be in conflict with norms stemming from judgments about conventions in the social system and realms of perceived legitimate personal jurisdiction. One task, then, is to explain social decisions from the perspective of coordinations of different domains. As the research on rights and honesty shows, we cannot rely on the idea that one realm (say morality) trumps all others – as might follow from a differentiation model that does not give sufficient weight to distinct domains in development.

The study of psychological development in children has contributed to our understanding of norms by pointing the way to analyses that account for multiple types or domains of reasoning and associated norms. Analyses of domains demonstrate the importance of definitional matters; that is, of grounding research in epistemological categories. Researchers who look to a general or unified cognitive process in deontic rules have given insufficient attention to defining epistemological categories. In some of the research on moral development there have been efforts to define the realm of morality, but insufficient attention to other realms that develop alongside morality.

A system of classification of different social domains provides an alternative perspective on development (i.e. occurring within domains), the influences of a multiplicity of social experiences, and coordinations in social decision-making. The research on concepts of rights and honesty in connection to the domains further reinforces the idea that individuals are not ready to simply accept societal or cultural norms as given or to always adjust to social conditions. The flexibility of thought, which is not locked into one type (unified) of cognitive system, also means that individuals reflect upon social conditions and cultural practices. The norms of society come under scrutiny and defying societal norms deemed wrong could be seen as obligatory. We saw this in the findings on honesty and deception. Deception was judged by adolescents as a legitimate way to counteract the unfairness of social conditions that provide greater power to one group over another. More generally, people in subordinate positions in the social hierarchy oppose, resist and attempt to change such conditions in their everyday lives (Abu-Lughod, 1993; Turiel, 2002, 2003; Turiel & Perkins, 2004; Wikan, 1996).

Opposition and resistance add another complication to analyses of norms. Psychologists have tended to emphasize the importance of adjustment or adaptation to social conditions. The emphasis on adjustment and adaptation comes with the assumption that social development primarily involves compliance and accommodation to the norms and values of society. Evidence that people, including children and adolescents, oppose and resist societal norms and cultural practices from a moral standpoint poses a serious challenge to such views. It is a challenge that was posed in 1967 by Martin Luther King, Jr when he addressed an assemblage of psychologists at the annual meeting of the American Psychological Association (King, 1968, 185): 'there are some things in our society, some things in our world, to which we should never be adjusted. There are some things concerning which we must always be maladjusted if we are to be people of good will.'

Of course, Martin Luther King, Jr recognized that maladjustment can result from serious clinical problems of understandable concern to psychologists. However, he also recognized that people as autonomous beings make choices about things to accept and things to combat.

Part III

Norms in cognitive development

9   Can psychology be a quantitative science, or is Kant right after all? Normative issues in psychometrics

Peter C. M. Molenaar

In a recently published collection of essays on the collapse of the fact/ value dichotomy, Hilary Putnam (2004) presents an 'eloquent demolition of the dichotomy between judgments of fact and judgments of value' (Martha Nussbaum's commentary cited in Putnam, 2004). In those essays the dichotomy between fact and value judgment is accused of having 'corrupted our thinking about both ethical reasoning and description of the world, not least of all by preventing us from seeing how evaluation and description are interwoven and interdependent' (Putnam, 2004, p. 3). Compelling arguments are given against the tenability of both the classical empiricist (Hume) and the logical positivist (Carnap) definition of 'facts' in terms of 'observation terms'. Putnam concludes that 'from Hume on, empiricists – and not only empiricists but many others as well, in and outside of philosophy – failed to appreciate the ways in which factual description and valuation can and must be *entangled*' (2004, pp. 26–7; italics in original).

This demolition of the fact/value *dichotomy* into nothing more than a *distinction* concerning mutually entangled fact–value complexes (e.g. thick ethical concepts; Putnam, 2004, pp. 34–43) is of great importance for social scientists who have been raised in the long era in which logical positivism reigned. It extends the domain of social-scientific research to facts *and* values, whereas previously value judgments were banned from scientific consideration because of their subjectivity. Putnam is not the only player in the recent re-evaluation of the scientific status of values (e.g. Oddie, 2005, who also discusses the causal powers of values). In fact, in the essay entitled 'Values and norms' Putnam (2004, pp. 111–34) extensively refers to the theoretical work on communicative action of Jürgen Habermas (1987), aimed at the reintegration of science and ethics. The critical social theory of Habermas itself is strongly influenced by Max Weber's *Wissenschaftslehre* (see the excellent monograph of George McCarthy, 2001). With Weber we are back in the times of the *Psychologismusstreit* (Kusch, 1995), the *Methodenstreit* in economics (McCarthy, 2001) and all the fundamental questions that accompanied the establishment of psychology as an independent science (see Heidelberger, 2004): questions that have not been answered satisfactorily, that have been neglected for a long time as being metaphysical (i.e. not amenable to scientific methodology), but that tend to resurface again in recent times now that psychology is under siege (see Erneling & Johnson, 2005).

Within the confines of this chapter it is not possible to consider these important developments in the philosophy of science. I will focus only on one particular aspect in the argumentation of Putnam (2004), namely his criticism of the way in which logical positivists divided reality into two parts: 'facts' and 'non-facts'. According to Putnam (2004, p. 21): 'In the writings of the positivists, in the case of . . . the dualism of ethical and factual judgments, it is the conception of the "factual" that does all the philosophical work.' Everything that does not obey the criteria of being 'factual' is collected into a single, presumably homogeneous, class of 'non-facts'. The elements of this class of 'non-facts' are, according to the logical positivists, not reducible to 'observation terms' and hence fall outside the range of science. Putnam not only takes issue with the crispness of the two classes involved (he shows that their elements are entangled), but also criticizes the presumed homogeneity of the class that is not of central interest (he shows that the class of 'non-facts' itself is heterogeneous).

In what follows I will transpose the gist of Putnam's criticism of the logical-positivist categorization of reality to a critical evaluation of the foundations of modern test theory. In test theory (psychometrics) we also encounter a division of a given universe of discourse into two parts, akin to the 'fact' versus 'non-fact' division in logical positivism. In test theory the class of focal interest involves the reliable, 'structural' part of test scores (as expressed in validity and reliability indices taken to be invariant across subjects; see Lord & Novick, 1968). The remaining parts of observed test scores, the parts that deviate from the invariant 'structural' part of focal interest, are collected into a single, presumably homogeneous, class of 'individual differences'. I will show that this psychometric paradigm, which has become the gold standard of modern test theory (and according to which almost all of our psychological tests in current use have been constructed), is seriously flawed.

Normative aspects of mental test theory

When the observed responses of an individual subject to the questions of a mental test are decomposed into two distinct parts, true score and measurement error, respectively, it may occur that this particular subject's true score is considered to lie outside the 'normal range'. The latter verdict can have serious consequences for this subject (affecting, e.g., her school career, clinical treatment, etc.). The decomposition into true score and measurement error corresponds to the division of a universe of discourse into two distinct classes, where here the class of focal interest comprises the true scores. The decomposition concerned, including the computational formulas to implement it, constitute the heart of modern test theory.

Lord & Novick (1968) define the class of focal interest, i.e. the class of true scores, as follows. Consider a single, fixed, individual person P. The true score of P is defined as the expected value (mean) of the observed scores of this person with respect to her propensity distribution of observed scores. The latter propensity distribution is characterized as a 'distribution function defined over repeated statistically independent measurements on the same person' (Lord & Novick, 1968, p. 30). It is assumed that the repeated measurements do not affect the person in that in each replication she responds without any after-effects of previous assessments (e.g. due to memory, habituation, etc.).

This definition of true score focuses on the single, individual person P, who is measured repeatedly under ideal circumstances (no habituation or memory effects, etc.). Elsewhere I have taken issue with details of this definition (Molenaar, 2003); for instance, it is not necessary to require sequential independence of the repeated measurements concerned (memory effects can be allowed to occur). One can validly generalize the definition of true score to a time series of sequentially dependent repeated measurements obtained with a single person P. This generalized definition of true score is compatible with measurement theories in the physical sciences. In particular it conforms to psychophysical experimental designs (e.g. Heidelberger, 2004).

The definition of true score in terms of the expected value of repeated measurements of a single subject P pertains to intra-individual variation (IAV). In particular, the propensity distribution characterizing P's responses to the test describes variation within P's repeated responses (IAV). With respect to this definition, Lord & Novick (1968, p. 32) make the following remark: 'The true . . . scores defined above are not those primarily considered in test theory . . . They are, however, those that would be of interest to a theory that deals with individuals rather than with groups (counseling . . . rather than selection).'

Obviously, Lord & Novick consider true scores defined on the basis of IAV of importance for the purpose of individual assessment and prediction. However, they then proceed by raising practical objections against the feasibility of a mental test theory based on the IAV definition of true score, pointing to the presumably disturbing effects of repeated testing (memory effects). I already indicated that these objections are not decisive (see Molenaar, 2003, ch. 3). What is even more noteworthy is that the rejection of the IAV definition of true score is not based on principled arguments, but on *ad hoc* contingencies that could have been accommodated by means of adequate statistical techniques. Despite this lack of sufficient reasons to abandon the IAV definition of true score, it is replaced by a completely different definition based on inter-individual variation (IEV): 'Primarily, test theory treats individual differences or, equivalently, measurements over people' (Lord & Novick, 1968, p. 32).

The alternative IEV definition of the class of true scores is based on individual differences between persons. According to the original IAV definition of true score, a single person is repeatedly measured an arbitrarily large number of times (sufficient to determine this person's propensity distribution). According to the alternative IEV definition, an arbitrarily large number of persons is measured once. It will be shown below that these two distinct definitions of true score are fundamentally different, if not irreconcilable. At present, it is noted that in order to arrive at the standard IEV test theory that is currently almost universally accepted, individual differences have to be collected into a single, presumably homogeneous, class. It will turn out, as in Putnam's criticism of the presumed homogeneity of the class of non-facts in logical positivism, that this homogeneity assumption is unwarranted in many cases of prime psychological interest.

Homogeneity assumptions

Standard test theory (based on the IEV definition of true score) requires the postulation of strong homogeneity assumptions. Basically, it has to be assumed that all differences between every possible pair of persons in some population are qualitatively equivalent (constitute a homogeneous class) and can be validly located in a common space. I will consider in somewhat more detail what this means, using the standard 1-factor model as illustration. For a useful description of the close relationship between the 1-factor model and test theory, the reader is referred to Lord & Novick (1968, ch. 24).

Let y_i denote the p-variate vector of observed scores of person i, i=1, 2, . . . Then the standard 1-factor model is given by

(1) $y_i = Lf_i + e_i$

where f_i denotes the univariate common factor score of person i, e_i denotes the p-variate vector of measurement errors, and L is the p-dimensional vector of factor loadings. The homogeneity assumptions associated with this IEV model are the following. The vector of observed scores of each person i in the population is assumed to obey the same 1-factor model. In particular, the vector of factor loadings is assumed to be invariant (fixed) across persons. Last but not least, it is assumed that the measurement errors have a common (usually Gaussian) distribution.

The homogeneity assumptions associated with the standard 1-factor model are crucial for its solution; without these assumptions the model cannot be properly fitted to the data and no parameter estimates (e.g. reliabilities) can be obtained. One therefore would expect that violation of these assumptions in one way or another would lead to substantial lack of fit, or problems in obtaining a reasonably fitting 1-factor model solution. Yet, perhaps surprisingly, this is not the case. To wit, Lord & Novick (1968, Theorem 2.7.3) already proved that the measurement errors e_i are allowed to have person-dependent variances. Hence the variance of the measurement error of different persons i and j are allowed to differ in magnitude (while the distributional form, e.g. Gaussian, still is assumed to be invariant across persons). The allowance of person-specific variances of the measurement errors already has awkward implications, as will be discussed at the close of this section. But first I consider more serious violations of the necessary homogeneity assumptions associated with the standard 1-factor model.

Suppose that the factor loadings also are person-specific. That is, the true model in the population of persons i = 1, 2, . . ., is

(2) $y_i = L_i f_i + e_i$

where now the p-variate vector of factor loadings is no longer fixed (as in the standard 1-factor model) but person-specific, i.e. L_i, i = 1, 2, . . . Hence the population of persons is substantially heterogeneous in that each person has her own instance of the 1-factor model (with factor loadings that characterize only this particular person). If data are generated by means of model (2) with person-specific factor loadings, and consecutively the standard 1-factor model (1) with fixed factor loadings is fitted to the data thus simulated, what will be the result?

In a series of such simulation studies it was found that the fit of model (1) to data generated according to model (2) always yields a satisfactory fit of the standard factor model (1). For further details about these simulation studies the reader is referred to Molenaar (2004), where also a mathematical-statistical proof is given of the formal equivalence of the second-order moments associated with models (1) and (2) in case the person-specific factor loadings have Gaussian distribution across persons. The implications of these findings are quite dramatic, especially in the context of individual counselling and prediction. I will give some examples.

Suppose again that the true model in the population is given by model (2) with person-specific factor loadings. For instance, let the factor loadings L_i in (2) be Gaussian distributed with mean L and (p,p)-dimensional covariance matrix $\text{cov}[L_i]$. In addition suppose that, instead of the true model (2), the standard 1-factor model (1) with fixed factor loadings is fitted to the observed data. The latter (incorrect) model (1) will fit the data satisfactorily, irrespective of the magnitude of the true variation $\text{cov}[L_i]$ of factor loadings across persons (see Molenaar, 2004). It therefore will happen that the actual person-specific factor loadings for person P, L_P, can differ in arbitrary ways from the estimated fixed factor loadings in model (1). Suppose that the estimated fixed factor loadings obtained in the fit of model (1) are all positive and significant, i.e. indicative of a highly reliable test. Then, given that the true $\text{cov}[L_i]$ is sufficiently high, it may occur that none of the true person-specific factor loadings making up L_P for person P are significant, or even positive. It then is obvious that the qualities assigned to the test based on the fit of model (1), such as having high reliability, do not at all pertain to person P. If the true person-specific factor loadings of P are negative, while the fit of the standard 1-factor model (1) yields a satisfactory solution with significantly positive factor loading estimates, it will be obvious that the factor score for person P, as determined from the latter model, will be severely biased. In fact, it will have the wrong polarity (being negative while the true factor score is positive, or vice versa). Again it will be obvious that individual counselling or prediction based on this test can be severely misdirected.

The essential role of idiographic psychology

In the previous section it was shown that test theory based on IEV (individual differences) requires the introduction of severe homogeneity constraints. Empirical results obtained in this way can only be interpreted unambiguously if these homogeneity assumptions are met. Yet, the standard 1-factor model associated with IEV-based test theory is shown to be entirely insensitive to the presence of substantial heterogeneity (person-specific factor loadings). This implies that in empirical applications, where we do not know the true model generating the data, we are entirely uncertain whether, and if so, how much, heterogeneity is actually present in the population. A satisfactorily fitting standard 1-factor model (1) with fixed factor loadings is uninformative in this important respect. Hence the question arises how the presence of such heterogeneity can be determined empirically.

To answer this question, I go back to the two definitions of true score discussed above. The initial definition given by Lord & Novick (1968) is IAV based: true score is defined as the mean of a time series of observed scores obtained with a fixed person P. The second definition of true score is IEV based, in terms of the distribution of individual differences of observed scores in a homogeneous population of persons. As I indicated earlier, these two definitions are fundamentally different, leading to qualitatively different types of test theory. The proof that these two definitions of true score are different follows directly from the so-called classical ergodic theorems (see Molenaar, 2004). The content of these theorems can be summarized as follows: the structure of intra-individual variation (IAV) is equivalent to the structure of inter-individual variation (IEV) only under very stringent homogeneity conditions, namely, only if the structure of IAV is homogeneous in time (no trends, cycles, or other forms of time-dependent changes of the characteristics of the time serial IAV). If the structure of IAV is heterogeneous in time, then it can no longer be analysed by changing to the IEV perspective, because the two types of variation (intra-individual versus inter-individual) are no longer comparable. It then is necessary to study the structure of IAV for its own sake, i.e. by means of dedicated time-series analysis.

The dedicated investigation of the structure of IAV constitutes the basic tenet of idiographic psychology (Molenaar, 2004, 2003, ch. 3). The first step in idiographic psychology is to determine a valid, appropriate model of the structure of IAV characterizing each fixed person. After having obtained these person-specific models, usually by means of time-series analysis, the usual inductive tools of nomothetic science are applied to derive commonalities among the time-series models thus obtained (see Nesselroade & Molenaar, 2003).

Discussion and conclusion

Currently, the norms for assessing persons are derived from data pertaining to inter-individual variation (IEV). On the basis of the content of this chapter, it follows that such norms are invalid for the proper assessment (prediction) of individual developmental (lifespan) trajectories. To arrive at proper norms for such kinds of assessment one needs to focus on intra-individual variation (IAV) within an idiographic context. This will require a paradigm change in the sense of Thomas Kuhn regarding the ways in which we construct our psychological measures and tests. Yet it is, I claim, our ethical duty as psychologists to rectify the current state of affairs in which decisions are being made concerning the fate of individual persons based on IEV-norms which now have been proven (by means of the classical ergodic theorems) to be incorrect for these purposes. The time-series analytical tools to accomplish this paradigm change in psychometrics, or better: this extension of IEV-based psycho-metrics with appropriate IAV-based approaches is in principle available. So we should not wait any longer to start implementing these.

Psychometrics in general, and test theory in particular, can no longer neglect the proven fact that the structures of IAV and IEV are different for most psychological characteristics of interest. All psychological pro-cesses that change their characteristics in time (dynamic heterogeneity, due to homeostasis, learning, development, etc.) have to be investigated by idiographic paradigms. This is the basic message obtained from the classical ergodic theorems. It will require a major reorientation and extension of the experimental paradigms, statistical-analysis techniques and educational programmes in psychology. The reader is referred to the excellent monograph of Borsboom (2005) for an in-depth discussion of some of the issues involved.

One reason why heterogeneity, of the kind as expressed by the factor model (2) with person-specific factor loadings, can be expected to be present in human populations has been sketched in Molenaar (2004). Modern mathematical-biological models of the growth of neural networks show that epigenesis is characterized by endogenous variation. The precise connectivity of neurons in a growing network is not specified genetically, but is the result of a self-organizing epigenetic process. Such epigenetic processes create irreducible variation that is distinct from the usual genetic and environmental influences. More specifically, this epigenetically induced variation occurs also when genetic and envir-onmental influences are kept constant (for instance, in computer simu-lations). Hence even the brains of identical twins or clones will not be identical because the influence of this epigenetic source of irreducible variation has been shown to be substantial in empirical quantitative genetic studies.

In closing I should emphasize that my use of the denotation 'idio-graphic psychology' differs from earlier definitions mentioned in the published literature. Idiographic psychology, as understood in this chap-ter, concerns the dedicated study of (nomothetic commonalities among replicated) structures of IAV by means of modern time-series analysis techniques (including applications to nonlinear and chaotic dynamics). Yet, use of this denotation inevitably is associated with aspects of the intellectual setting in which it was first put forward. That was the time in which psychology established itself as an independent science, already referred to in the introductory section, the time also in which fundamental questions were considered, such as the issue whether the mind constitutes a genuine (nomothetic) scientific object (see Heidelberger, 2004; Kusch, 1995). At present, we are witnessing a renewed consideration of these fundamental issues (Erneling & Johnson, 2005). It is expected that idiographic psychology, because of its distinct pedigree and its focus on intra-individual variation, will contribute to a better understanding of the issues concerned. Only the use of idiographic paradigms can avoid the severe homogeneity assumptions underlying our current psychometrical techniques, thus bringing into clear focus the unique characteristics of human persons. In standard test theory and psychometrics, norms are defined at the level of populations. In contrast, in idiographic psychology norms are defined at the level of individual persons. For application to individual persons (assessment, counselling, prediction), only the latter paradigm can yield useful results.[1]

---

[1] I thank Les Smith for his encouragement and support in preparing this chapter.

10 Norms and intuitions in the assessment of chance[1]

Vittorio Girotto and Michel Gonzalez

Are children able to draw normatively correct probabilistic inferences? The readers may find this question rather odd given the well-documented difficulties of intelligent adults to solve various sorts of probability problems. The aim of this chapter is to show that children do possess an elementary competence to reason about uncertain events, and that the existence of such a competence sheds light on the properties of adults' reasoning and its relation to the normative models of probability.

There is an ongoing controversy in the adult literature about the factors that hinder correct probabilistic reasoning in naive individuals (i.e. those who have not mastered the probability calculus or other formal calculi, like standard logic). According to an influential, evolutionary view, naive individuals fail simply because the human mind is inherently unable to reason about the probability of single events, and only individuals trained in probability calculus can succeed. Besides empirical evidence, a normative argument appears to support such a view: since a norm for measuring chance (i.e. the probability calculus) emerged only in the seventeenth century, it follows that probabilistic reasoning is not a natural, mental capacity and that before the seventeenth century individuals could not even consider the possibility of such a yardstick. An alternative is the extensional competence view. Under this view, untutored individuals are able to draw correct probabilistic inferences, even if they have not learnt the probability calculus. Instead of applying the rules of such a calculus, these individuals evaluate chance in an *extensional* way, by considering and numbering the various possibilities in which an event may or may not occur (Johnson-Laird et al., 1999).

[1] Preparation of this paper was funded by a COFIN (2003–5) grant from the Italian Ministry of Universities. We thank Les Smith for his helpful comments on a previous version of this paper.

In this chapter we contrast the extensional competence view with the evolutionary view. In particular, we question the basic assumption of the evolutionary view that learning normative rules is the only way to reason about the probability of single events. To this end, we examine evidence of an intuition of probability in two groups of individuals who are unlikely to possess a culturally based ability to reason normatively, one comprising children, and the other comprising individuals who lived before the advent of the probability calculus.

In the first part of the chapter, we briefly present the debate about the source and the normative status of erroneous inferences in adults' probabilistic reasoning. In the second part, we present the extensional reasoning hypothesis and some supporting results obtained with adult participants. In the third part, we discuss results showing that children possess a basic intuition of probability, according to which an outcome is more likely than another one, if the former can be produced in more ways than the latter. In the fourth part, we discuss written evidence that, as early as the fourteenth century, individuals solved problems of decision under uncertainty by means of an extensional assessment of expectations. We conclude that formal education on the relevant norms may improve it, but that everyday probabilistic reasoning is grounded on basic extensional intuitions.

1   Norms and errors in probabilistic reasoning

From at least the age of eight, children presented with forty black marbles and two white marbles and asked whether there are more black marbles or more marbles, correctly answer that there are more marbles (Piaget & Szeminska, 1952). In other words, school children correctly solve problems asking them to compare the size of a set and of one of its subsets. Given children's understanding of the part–whole logical relation, one might puzzle about the discovery that adults fail the famous Linda problem (adapted from Tversky & Kahneman, 1983):

Linda is 31 years old, single, outspoken and very bright. She majored in philosophy. As a student, she was deeply concerned with issues of discrimination and social justice, and also participated in anti-nuclear demonstrations. Indicate which of the following alternatives is more probable:
Linda is a bank teller (T).
Linda is a bank teller and is active in the feminist movement (T & F).

A large majority of adult participants judge T & F more likely than T. This judgment is an error, called the *conjunction fallacy*. According to a basic property of probability, T & F cannot be more likely than T: If

Linda is a bank teller, she can be either feminist or not. Hence, the probability that she is a bank teller should be equal to the sum of the probabilities that she is a feminist bank teller *and* that she is a non-feminist bank teller (for a more detailed analysis of the problem, see Appendix). Therefore, from a probabilistic perspective, concluding that T & F is more likely than T is equivalent to answering that there are more black marbles than marbles. Adults, of course, do master the part–whole relation. Why then do they commit the conjunction fallacy? According to Tversky & Kahneman (1983), naive inferences often depend on the application of some intuitive procedures (aka non-extensional heuristics). One of these procedures leads individuals to evaluate the probability of an event on the basis of its representative-ness. Since T & F fits the description of Linda better than T, individuals judge T & F more likely than T.

The finding that adults' judgments violate elementary rules of prob-ability has been used to question normative models of rational choice, and more generally any view that presupposes the existence of coherent inferential systems in the human mind (for reviews on adults' judgments and choices, see Gilovich, Griffin & Kahneman, 2002; Kahneman & Tversky, 2000). Not surprisingly, this sort of finding has stimulated an animated debate about the fundamental properties of human reasoning and the normative status of its products.

A common criticism of the studies that have documented defective probabilistic reasoning is that they have not conclusively demonstrated the existence of genuine reasoning errors. It is now widely agreed that the way in which participants interpret the verbal premises and the verbal instructions of reasoning problems may affect the inferences they draw (for reviews, see Hilton, 1995; Girotto, 2004). In particular, if the statement of a problem contains pragmatic anomalies, participants are likely to misinterpret it and to produce apparently erroneous judgments. According to some authors (e.g. Politzer & Noveck, 1991), the request to compare a class and a subclass is pragmatically anomalous for adult participants. Indeed, they are obviously able to make such a comparison at least from the age of eight, and in ordinary conversations they are not normally asked questions whose answers are obvious to both speaker and hearer. Consequently, in order to make plausible the requested comparison in the Linda problem, participants may reinterpret the statement expressing the event T as 'Linda is a bank teller and is *not* active in the feminist movement' (i.e. T & not-F). Under this interpret-ation, the request becomes a standard comparison between two cate-gories (T & F vs T & not-F), and judging that T & F is the more likely event cannot be considered an erroneous answer. Pragmatic factors undoubtedly affect reasoning. It is difficult, however, to believe that all normatively incorrect answers are appropriate solutions to pragmatically anomalous problems. For instance, it has been shown that individuals fail problems similar to the Linda one even when they cannot interpret T as T & not-F (e.g. Tentori, Bonini & Osherson, 2004).

A different line of criticism is based on a normative argument. The nature of probability is a controversial issue in philosophy (for a review, see Howson & Urbach, 1993). According to a 'subjectivist' view, probabilities should be considered degrees of beliefs about single events, whereas according to a 'frequentist' view probabilities are limits of frequencies of repeated events (see Appendix). Since there are different meanings given to probability, one has to establish whether naive individuals and researchers share the norm that the latter use to assess the inferences of the former. If naive individuals are not committed to that particular norm, one cannot conclude that they fail on a given reasoning problem. Consider the Linda problem. According to Gigerenzer (1993), the conjunction fallacy is an error from a subjectivist view, but it is *not* an error from a strict frequentist view, given that probabilities do not concern a single event such as whether Linda is a feminist, but only multiple, repeatable events. The point is that participants of reasoning studies are likely to hold a frequentist view:

The frequency view has been dominant since the nineteenth century, and teaching in statistics departments today as well as in undergraduate psychology courses is still predominantly frequentist in philosophy . . . One should be careful not to evaluate reasoning against some norm, unless subjects have been committed to that particular norm. Thus, choosing T & F in the Linda problem is *not* [author's emphasis] a reasoning error. (Gigerenzer, 1993, p. 293)

Of course, if norms are controversial, and if individuals have learnt just one norm, it is difficult to evaluate the correctness of their inferences. However, the claim that the errors discovered in adults 'only look like errors from a narrow normative view about what is right and wrong in reasoning' (Gigerenzer, 1993, p. 308) leads to a paradoxical conclusion. If individuals' commitment to a given norm is a necessary condition to evaluate reasoning against that norm, then one should not investigate totally naive individuals, like children, because they have not been committed to *any* particular norms of reasoning. For the same reason, their inferences can never be considered erroneous.

The assumption that normative issues matter is the basis of another interpretation of reasoning errors, according to which the human mind is intrinsically unable to deal with probabilities. Following the normative claim that the probability of a single event is meaningless, and the evolutionary premise that no organism can evolve mental mechanisms designed to reason about unobservable information (like single-event probability), some authors argue that individuals are doomed to reason poorly about probabilistic information (e.g. Cosmides & Tooby, 1996; Gigerenzer & Hoffrage, 1995). In other words, individuals fail the standard probability problems because single-case probabilities were never encountered in the natural environments in which the human species evolved. For instance, one cannot imagine our hominoid ancestors observing the probability that the neighbouring tribe has hostile intentions. By contrast, it is easy to imagine that they observed the repetition of similar events and recorded their frequencies, that is they could gather such data in a 'natural', sequential way. For instance, they could observe that they were successful five out of the last twenty times they hunted in a given place.

The finding that participants solve problems that convey 'natural' frequency information, and fail the same problems when they convey probability information, has corroborated this evolutionary-frequentist view (Gigerenzer & Hoffrage, 1995). For instance, consider the following problem:

A screening test of an infection is being studied. Here is the information about the infection and the test results: 4 of the 100 people tested were infected. 3 of the 4 infected people had a positive reaction to the test. 12 of the 96 uninfected people also had a positive reaction to the test. Imagine that this test is given to a new group of people. Among those who have a positive reaction, how many will actually have the infection?   (Girotto & Gonzalez, 2001, pp. 248–9)

In this problem, participants have to predict the frequency of infected people among those who have a positive reaction. In order to do so, they have simply to consider the set of positive and infected people (3) and to compare it to the total set of positive people (3+12). Most participants do solve this problem. By contrast, they fail the following version of the same problem:

There is a 4% chance that a person who is tested has the infection. If the person is infected, there is a 75% chance that he/she will have a positive reaction to the test. If the person is not infected, there is still a 12.5% chance that he/she will have a positive reaction to the test. Imagine that Pierre is tested now. If Pierre has a positive reaction, what is the probability that he actually is infected? ___ %
(Girotto & Gonzalez, 2001, p. 248)

In this case, participants have to deal with single-case probability information and have to evaluate the probability of a single event, that is, the conditional probability that Pierre is infected, given that he is positive (see Appendix). As predicted by the evolutionary-frequentist view, very few participants solve it. In sum, experimental evidence seems to support the view that naive individuals cannot draw normatively correct inferences if they are required to reason about a type of information to which natural selection has not adapted the human mind.

2   Naive extensional reasoning

Pessimistic views of naive probabilistic reasoning are based on the implicit assumption that the only way to solve single-case probability problems, like the test-disease problem, consists in applying the rules of probability calculus. Naive individuals, however, draw probabilistic inferences in a much simpler way. They often make *extensional* judgments, inferring the probability of an event from the various possible ways in which it can occur (Johnson-Laird et al., 1999). Consider the problem:

Two dice are thrown at random. You do not see how they land, but a friend tells you that the number of points is 7. What is the probability that one of the two dice landed with 1 uppermost?

One can easily answer this question without applying the rules of probability calculus, by considering and counting the different ways in which the indicated events can occur. There are three pairs of points summing up to 7: {1, 6}, {2, 5} and {3, 4}. Given that in only one of them a die lands with 1 uppermost, it is easy to obtain the correct answer: 1 chance in 3, that is, a probability of 1/3. Indeed, it has been shown that notorious probability problems become easy to solve if they prompt individuals to reason extensionally. Consider the following version of the test-disease problem:

A person who was tested had 4 chances out of 100 of having the infection. 3 of the 4 chances of having the infection were associated with a positive reaction to the test. 12 of the remaining 96 chances of not having the infection were also associated with a positive reaction to the test. Imagine that Pierre is tested now. Out of a total of 100 chances, Pierre has ___ chances of having a positive reaction, ___ of which will be associated with having the infection.

(Girotto & Gonzalez, 2001, p. 253)

In this case, as in the standard probability version considered above, participants have to deal with probabilities and to evaluate the probability of a single event. Unlike the standard one, however, this version presents probability data as numbers of chances rather than as percentages. To solve it, participants have to reason as in the frequency problem: they have to count the total number of chances of being positive (3+12), and, in this set, they have to consider the number of chances of being infected (3). As in the frequency problem, most participants do produce the correct solution (Girotto & Gonzalez, 2001, 2002; see also Sloman et al., 2003). In sum, contrary to the evolutionary-frequentist view, individuals solve problems asking for a single-event evaluation if they can reason extensionally about finite sets of countable units, as possibilities, chances, cases and observations.

These results clearly corroborate the extensional competence hypothesis. They have been obtained, however, with the usual participants of experimental studies on reasoning, that is, college undergraduates untutored in the probability calculus. Now, these individuals cannot be considered completely naive about the normative way of thinking about uncertainty, given that they live in a culture that prescribes thinking in this way, at least about some events like those produced by randomized devices (see e.g. Nisbett et al., 1983). In order to obtain a stronger test of the claim that untutored individuals do possess an intuitive sense of chance, we have to examine individuals who are unlikely to possess a culturally based ability to reason normatively. Two obvious classes of candidates for such a test are children and individuals who lived before the advent of the probability calculus. In the following two sections, we will present evidence of correct reasoning about chances even in these individuals.

3   Children's extensional reasoning

Are children able to draw correct probability inferences about single events? According to the evolutionary-frequentist view, the answer is, of course, negative, given that all individuals, including adults, are supposed to be unable to deal with single-case probabilities. According to the traditional Piagetian view, the answer is partially negative (see Piaget & Inhelder, 1975). The basic assumption of such a view is that there is a parallel development of logical and probabilistic reasoning. Consequently, the lack of basic logical abilities is the main source of children's failure to solve probability problems. On the one hand, young children do not base their judgments on correct probability ratios, which relate the number of favourable outcomes to the total number of outcomes, because they do not master part–whole logical relation. For instance, before the age of about seven children fail the class-inclusion problem, judging that there are more black marbles than marbles overall in a set of forty black marbles and two white marbles (Piaget & Szeminska, 1952). Likewise, children of the same age fail problems whose solution requires them to take into account probability ratios. For instance, Piaget and Inhelder (1975) observed that their six-year-old participants judge that if one takes at random a chip from a bag containing one red chip and three white chips, one is more likely to get a red than a white chip. According to Piaget and Inhelder, these erroneous judgments illustrate young children's inability to reason about probability: they focus on one possibility (e.g. drawing of a red chip), and fail to consider its relation to the set of all possibilities (e.g. the entire set of possible draws). On the other hand, older children fail probability problems in which they have to compare proportions or to consider combinations of possibilities, because they do not have the logical ability to conduct a combinatorial analysis until adolescence. For instance, Piaget and Inhelder observed that, according to their ten-year-old participants, one is more likely to get a marked chip from a set composed of two unmarked and one marked chips, than from a set composed of three unmarked and two marked chips. Likewise, Piaget and Inhelder reported observations according to which nine-year-olds were unable to predict the sort of marble pairs that one could draw from a bag containing twenty red marbles and twenty blue marbles. Only after a certain number of drawings, did these children understand that one is more likely to draw a mixed pair (i.e. one red and one blue marble) than a one-colour pair (i.e. two red marbles, or two blue marbles). Both pessimistic views are contradicted by experimental evidence that children can correctly assess the probability of single events by means of extensional reasoning.

As reported, adults reason extensionally about uncertain events by considering and counting chances, possibilities or frequencies. Children appear to treat quantities before knowing the symbolic numerical system. In particular, comparing quantities is a basic cognitive skill of even very young children (for a review, see Dehaene, 1997). Therefore, children should be able to compare chances, even if they are unable to express them numerically, and to make correct evaluations of probability. This prediction has already been corroborated by the results of a series of studies, which unfortunately have been neglected in the literature on adult reasoning. In particular, Brainerd (1981) has shown that pre-school children are able to solve extensionally problems in which they have to predict a single event. His five-year-old participants were asked to put seven chips representing monkeys and three chips representing birds in an opaque container (i.e. 'Take seven monkeys and put them in here. Then take three birds and put them in here'). The experimenter shook the container, announcing that this would 'mix the monkeys and the birds up', and asked children, 'If I close my eyes and take one chip from the container, do you think I will get a monkey or a bird?' The majority of children correctly answered 'monkey', that is, the animal represented by most chips. They performed particularly well when they were asked to name the most numerous animal class in the container just before making the prediction (e.g. 'Do you think that there are more monkeys or more birds now?') The large majority (80 per cent) of children correctly answered this question (i.e. 'more monkeys'). All successful children were then able to predict correctly that the experimenter was more likely to get a monkey than a bird from the container. These results are at odds with Piaget and Inhelder's (1975) observations on children's performance in similar tasks (e.g. predicting which kind of chip one is more likely to get from a bag). The former have been obtained in experimental situations more controlled than the latter. They are also consistent with those obtained in studies in which young children were asked to make a choice, rather than a verbal judgment (e.g. Yost, Siegel & Andrews, 1962). In sum, evidence exists that even pre-school children make predictions based on correct evaluations of chances, especially when they are probed to retrieve the relative size of the relevant event classes.

In Brainerd's (1981) studies, children had to make a prediction by comparing the respective possibilities of two alternative outcomes in a single set. It has also been shown that children are able to draw correct probabilistic inferences even when they have to compare the possibilities of two alternative outcomes in two different sets. For example, seven-year-olds judge that a bug that loves to eat flowers is happier if it lands at random in a box containing five flowers and five spiders, than in one containing two flowers and four spiders (Acredolo et al., 1989). In other words, middle primary school children are able to evaluate the likelihood of an event by means of a comparison of proportions. Evidence exists that primary school children are even able to solve probability problems in which they have to construct possible *combinations*. Girotto & Gonzalez (2003) presented participants of various ages, including primary school children, with probability problems, like the following one:

As you see, I have a white die and a red die. Each die has six sides, each with a number from 1 to 6. Now I play a game with these two puppets, Paolo and Maria. I throw the dice, and when they land on the table I cover them, so that Paolo and Maria cannot see the sum the dice made. (The experimenter throws the dice and covers them.) Paolo says that I got 3 with the two dice. Maria says that I got 5 with the two dice. According to you, who is more likely to win their bet?

(Girotto & Gonzalez, 2005, p. 164)

In order to solve problems of this sort, individuals have to consider the various combinations that make up a sum, to count them and to conclude that the sums produced in more combinations are more likely to occur. In other words, unlike the monkey–bird or the flower–spider problems, in which each elementary possibility corresponds to a perceptual unit, the dice problem requires individuals to construct mentally the relevant possibilities. In the version above, the correct answer is to name the puppet that predicts the sum that can be obtained in more ways (i.e. 5, which can be obtained with a 3 and a 2, and with a 4 and a 1). From the age of nine, children perform better than chance in this sort of problem. Moreover, from the same age they are also able to produce all possible combinations for each of the two outcomes (i.e. {3, 2} and {4, 1} for 5; {2, 1} for 3). Few children, however, are able to consider arrangements (or permutations). In other words, few of them distinguish the two possible arrangements of each combination (e.g. 5 is obtained with a 3 and a 2, or with a 2 and a 3). Adults too, sometimes, fail to consider relevant possibilities, by treating different arrangements as one and the same possibility (see Girotto & Gonzalez, 2005). Untrained children's success in combinatorial problems contradicts the claim that even adolescents need an explicit training in combinatorial procedures in order to solve problems of this sort (Fischbein, 1975).

The ensemble of these finding is at odds with the Piagetian view according to which children are able to compare proportions, and to reason about combinations of possibilities only when they have attained the alleged level of formal operations, that is, during adolescence (Piaget & Inhelder, 1975). Of course, these findings cannot be considered evidence in favour of an early emergence of the entire system of formal operations as defined in Piaget's theory (see Inhelder & Piaget, 1964). They simply indicate that even before adolescence children are able to solve extensionally probability problems that, according to Piaget's theory, depend on the mastering of some complex logical abilities.

Finally, it has recently been shown that children also solve problems, similar to those used to assess adults' competence, in which they have to combine numerical values. Consider the following problem:

Pingping goes to a small village to ask for directions. In this village, 10 out of every 100 people will lie. Of the 10 people who lie, 8 have a red nose. Of the remaining 90 people who don't lie, 9 also have a red nose. Imagine that Pingping meets a group of people in the village with red noses. How many of these people will lie? ___ out of ____.

This problem requires participants to indicate the frequency of people who lie among those who have a red nose. In order to do so, they have simply to consider the set of people who lie and who have a red nose (8) and to compare it to the total set of people who have a red nose (8+9). Most eleven-year-olds solve this problem (Zhu & Gigerenzer, 2006). Not surprisingly, no eleven-year-old is able to solve the following version of the same problem:

Pingping goes to a small village to ask for directions. In this village, the probability that the person he meets will lie is 10%. If a person lies, the probability that he/she has a red nose is 80%. If a person doesn't lie, the probability that he/she also has a red nose is 10%. Imagine that Pingping meets someone in the village with a red nose. What is the probability that the person will lie?

According to the advocates of the evolutionary-frequentist hypothesis, these results demonstrate that children reason correctly only about one type of information, that is, natural frequencies. One problem with this interpretation is that it neglects the finding that children (as well as adults) do have correct intuitions about the probability of single events, like the outcome of drawing a chip or throwing two dice. A more parsimonious interpretation is that children are able to solve extensionally problems requiring them to reason about finite sets of cases, possibilities or observations.

Taken together, the evidence presented in this section shows that children are able to assess probabilities by considering and enumerating the various possibilities in which an event may occur. They do so when each possibility corresponds to a physical unit (Brainerd, 1981; Acredolo et al., 1989), when it is a mentally constructed combination of possible outcomes (Girotto & Gonzalez, 2003), and when it is an observation (Zhu & Gigerenzer, 2006).

4   Normative reasoning before the creation of norms

How do individuals who live in a culture in which no normative system of reasoning has been formalized reason? Are these individuals able to draw inferences that an external observer could consider normatively correct? Some followers of Aristotle answered no, since they assumed that using the Aristotelian syllogistic system was the only way to draw correct inferences. John Locke answered yes:

He that will look into many parts of Asia and America, will find men reason there perhaps as acutely as himself, who yet never heard of a syllogism, nor can reduce any one argument to those forms . . . Syllogism [is] not the great instrument of reason . . . if syllogisms must be taken for the only proper instrument and means of knowledge; it will follow, that before Aristotle there was no man that did or could know anything by reason; and that since the invention of syllogisms there is not one of ten thousand that doth. But God has not been so sparing to Men to make them barely two-legged creatures, and left to Aristotle to make them rational.   (Locke, 1975, p. 671)

According to the advocates of the evolutionary-frequentist view, the recent invention of the probability calculus supports the thesis that probabilistic reasoning is not intuitive and that before the seventeenth century individuals dealt with frequencies but not probabilities: 'probabilities and percentages took millennia of literacy and numeracy to evolve; organisms did not acquire information in terms of probabilities and percentages until very recently' (Gigerenzer & Hoffrage, 1995, 686). This argument echoes the one criticized by Locke: if applying the probability calculus is the only way to reason about probabilities, it follows that human beings living in pre-modern times could not reason about probabilities. There are two problematic assumptions at the basis of this argument. First, the theory of probability is the only branch of mathematics that has been developed lately. Second, in pre-modern times there was no intuitive assessment of chance. We consider these assumptions in turn.

There are various speculations about the factors that may have hindered the emergence of the probability calculus before the seventeenth century. The most plausible explanation is simply that basic mathematical culture was deficient before the seventeenth century. Scholars lacked some fundamental mathematical tools like decimal notation, negative numbers, combinatorics and algebraic symbolism, whose common availability by 1650 made possible the creation of mathematical probability. Moreover, the amount of shared mathematical knowledge was very low, given that scholars worked in isolation, rather than in networks. 'But this explanation has nothing to do with probability, since it happened in all fields equally' (Franklin, 2001, p. 332). Consequently, the late development of a theory of probability cannot be used to maintain the intrinsic difficulty of naive probabilistic reasoning.

Hacking's (1975) seminal book has popularized the idea that before the seventeenth century individuals lacked even the basic notions of logical probability (e.g. the notion of evidential support). Franklin (2001), however, has demonstrated that logical probability arguments were used in pre-modern times. For example, medieval jurists and theologians distinguished conclusive and inconclusive evidence, and related the certainty of conclusions to the grades of evidence. Even aleatory probability, concerning chance devices such as the throwing of dice or coins, was conceptualized before modern times. Dante (*Purgatory*, Canto VI, 1–4) mentioned a popular medieval game, the *Zara*, which consisted in guessing the sum of points in a throw of three dice. In the fourteenth century, Dante's commentators gave an account of the game in which they applied an elementary combinatorics to obtain the number of ways in which a given sum can occur. They used this number as an indicator of the expected frequency of the sum. According to Della Lana (1866–7; for an English translation of the entire passage, see Girotto & Gonzalez, in press): 'the die is a cube which can land on each of its faces, so that the number made up in more ways must occur more often.' Da Buti (1852–62) used the same extensional principle: 'reasonably, the sum that can be made up in more ways must occur more often than those that can be made up in one or two ways'. These commentators reasoned as if the partitions of a sum describe completely the ways in which it can occur: 'three . . . can occur in only one way, that is, when all three dice land one; four . . . when one die lands two and two dice land one' (Della Lana, 1866–7; see also Ottimo, 1827–9); '14 can be made up in three ways: 6, 6, 2; 4, 4, 6; 5, 5, 4' (Da Buti, 1852–62). In other words, these authors did not take into account the various arrangements of the dice corresponding to a given combination. As indicated in the previous section, such failures occur in the extensional reasoning of modern-day children and adults. Nevertheless, these medieval authors understood that the expectation of an event should depend on the number of ways in which it may occur.

More complete analyses, referring to the distribution of the 216 possible throws of three dice, are presented in the thirteenth-century poem *De vetula* (see Kendall, 1956), in Cardano's (circa 1568, see Ore, 1965) and Galileo's (circa 1613, see David, 1962) writings. Galileo noticed that sums like 9 and 10 could be obtained in the same number of ways, given that both correspond to six partitions. Still, long observation had made dice players consider 10 to be more advantageous than 9. Galileo explained this fact pointing out that partitions can be obtained by throws of variable numbers. For instance, while the partition 3–3–3 of 9 can be obtain in only one throw since each die has to land 3, the partition 2–3–5 of 10 can be obtained in six throws since each die can land on each of these three numbers. Given that the six partitions of 10 correspond to 27 throws and those of 9 only to 25, 10 is more advantageous than 9. According to Franklin (2001), Galileo made the first clear reference to gamblers observing long-run frequencies in games of chance. This reference, however, should be considered as a rhetorical point. Galileo's demonstration that one has to consider throws rather than partitions is not based on observing that long-run frequencies of partitions vary, whereas those of throws are stable. Rather, Galileo refers to the material structure of the game: 'a die has six faces, and when thrown it can equally well (*indifferentemente* in the original text) fall on any one of these' (Eng. trans. in David, 1962, p. 192). In short, Galileo established that the 'advantage' (the probability, in modern terms) of a sum depends on the number of ways in which it can be obtained, and that its long-run frequency should follow from its advantage. From a phenomenological point of view, the way in which Galileo presents his solution differs from Pascal's excitement on discovering a science of chance (Franklin, 2001), and from Galileo's own astonishment on discovering counter-intuitive phenomena like the pendulum isochronism (Bozzi, 1990). Indeed, presenting his solution as a 'very obvious' one, Galileo writes as if everybody could understand his argument. His attitude implies that an extensional evaluation of chances was considered as a natural form of reasoning.

In sum, written traces exist that before the seventeenth century individuals could solve problems of decision under uncertainty by means of an extensional treatment of possibilities. As we have seen in the previous section, modern-day children solve similar problems using the same extensional procedures. Taken together, these results show that naive individuals do not need to know the normative models of probabilistic reasoning to reason about chance.

5   Conclusions

In this chapter, we have defended the thesis that naive individuals have an intuition of chance supported by extensional procedures (Johnson-Laird et al., 1999). Following this view, we have defended the strong claim that even individuals who are totally naive about the normative models of probabilistic reasoning, like children and individuals who lived before the creation of the probability calculus, can draw correct inferences about uncertain events (for an illustration of the normative character of these inferences, see Appendix). We have discussed experimental evidence that children solve probability problems in which they have to compare the chances of two alternative outcomes (e.g. Brainerd, 1981; Acredolo et al., 1989), including problems asking for a combinatorial analysis of possibilities (Girotto & Gonzalez, 2003, 2005). We have then presented historical evidence of extensional reasoning about chances before the advent of the probability calculus in the seventeenth century.

Under our interpretation, these findings contradict alternative views of naive probabilistic reasoning. In particular, according to the influential evolutionary-frequentist view, individuals can reason correctly only about natural frequencies of data gathered in a sequential way (Gigerenzer & Hoffrage, 1995; Cosmides & Tooby, 1996). Contrary to such a view, evidence exists that both children and adults solve problems in which they are asked for the evaluation of a single event. Moreover, child participants of the above reviewed studies were unlikely to have observed long-run frequencies in actual games of chance resembling the bug problem (Acredolo et al., 1989), or even the dice problem

(Girotto & Gonzalez, 2003). Yet, they succeeded in such unfamiliar problems. The reviewed results also call into question the hypothesis that intuitive reasoning about chance depends on cultural prescriptions. On the one hand, the finding that untrained children solve problems in which they have to assess combinations of possibilities contradicts the claim that children and even adolescents need an explicit training in combinatorial procedures in order to succeed (*pace* Fischbein, 1975). On the other hand, the correct probabilistic inferences of people living in the Middle Ages contradict the hypothesis that before the seventeenth century individuals did not deal with probabilities (*pace* Gigerenzer & Hoffrage, 1995).

It is plausible that cultural evolution has improved everyday reasoning about uncertainty (see Nisbett et al., 1983). However, the finding that untutored individuals can solve probability problems extensionally shows that formal education may improve it, but that naive probabilistic reasoning is grounded on basic extensional intuitions.

APPENDIX: PROBABILITIES AS NORMS

Some of the chapters in this volume focus on children's acquisition of rules that individuals ought to follow in order to avoid moral or social sanctions. The focus of our chapter is on children's intuitions about a different sort of norm, that is, probability theory. In this Appendix, we will show that its rules too have an 'ought' character, by showing why one has to follow them: individuals who fail to respect rules such as these act against their own interests.

In general terms, a probability is a numerical measure of the expectancy about an uncertain event. There is an ongoing debate about the kinds of events that probabilities can deal with. Following the frequentist approach, probabilities deal only with repeatable events. Accordingly, the probability of an event is the limit of its frequency when it is repeated indefinitely. In this sense, probabilities are the foundation of the sampling model, which allows one to measure the risks connected to the predictions and decisions under uncertainty, by means of statistical inferences (e.g. Neyman & Pearson, 1967). Various disciplines, such as biology, economics and psychology, routinely apply this model to exploit their data. Following this perspective, probabilities are the norm to respect in order to make informed decisions. Following the subjectivist approach, probabilities deal with single events too. Accordingly, a probability conveys the degree of belief about the occurrence of a specific event, on the basis of all available knowledge. The notion of coherent (or rational) decision is the building block of this approach (Savage,

1954). Decisions form a coherent set when they do not lead decision-makers to act against their interest. In a set of coherent decisions, each decision is a function of both the probability of the possible outcomes, and the utility of their consequences. Accordingly, probabilities are the norm of coherent decisions.

Regardless of the way in which it is interpreted, probability is characterized by the same set of rules, the most important of which is the *additivity rule*. If A and B are two incompatible events (i.e. A & B cannot occur), it follows that the probability that A or B happens is the probability that A happens added to the probability that B happens. In more formal terms, $p(A \lor B) = p(A) + p(B)$. For instance, the probability of drawing a King or a Queen from a regular deck of cards equals the probability of drawing a King (i.e. 4/52) plus the probability of drawing a Queen (4/52), that is, 8/52. Another basic rule of probability is the *conditional probability rule*. Given that one knows B, one can infer the probability of A, that is $p(A|B)$, as follows: $p(A|B) = p(A \& B)/p(B)$. For instance, if one knows that the card drawn from a deck is a Court card, one can infer that the probability that it is a King equals 1/3.

In what follows, we will illustrate the normative character of probabilities, by analysing two of the problems presented above.

Linda problem

Let L define everything one knows about Linda, T the hypothesis that she is a bank teller and F the hypothesis that she is feminist. Given the additive property of probabilities, $p(T|L) = p(T \& F|L) + p(T \& \text{not-}F|L)$. Given that $p(T \& \text{not-}F|L)$ cannot be negative, $p(T \& F|L)$ cannot be greater than $p(T|L)$. Individuals who judge that T & F is more likely than T can make decisions that go against their interests. Suppose you make a bet about Linda's status. If you think that T & F is more likely than T, you should bet on T & F rather than on T. It follows that you miss a chance to win the bet: the one in which Linda is T & not-F. In sum, in the Linda problem, individuals who do not conform to basic probabilistic norms are doomed to make disadvantageous decisions.

Test-disease problem

A way to solve this problem consists in applying the conditional probability rule. Let us call H the hypothesis that Pierre is infected, not-H the hypothesis that he is not infected, E the evidence of a positive reaction. The probability that Pierre is infected, given that he is positive, can be computed as follows: $p(H|E) = p(H \& E)/p(E)$. Now, the probability that a person is infected *and* positive (H & E) equals the prior probability that a person is infected (4%) times the probability of a positive reaction when a person is infected (75%), that is 3%. Similarly, the probability that a person is not infected *and* positive (not-H & E) equals the prior probability that a person is not infected (96%) times the probability of a positive reaction when a person is not infected (12.5%), that is 12%. Given the additive property of probabilities, the probability that a person has a positive reaction whether or not a person is infected (E) is the sum of the probability that a person is infected and positive (3%) and the probability that a person is not-infected and positive (12%). It follows that $p(H|E) = 3\% /(3\% + 12\%) = 20\%$.

In fact, most people fail this problem. Typically, participants answer: '75%', which is the inverse conditional probability of a positive reaction when a person is infected. This evaluation is incorrect, and so may have detrimental effects. Suppose that the disease is mortal, if the infected person is not treated. Suppose that the only available treatment has lethal side effects, so that a treated person has a 50% chance of dying whether or not the person is infected. Now, individuals who have a positive reaction and judge that they have a 75% chance of being infected will probably decide to receive the treatment. They will make this decision, considering that a 50% chance of dying because of the treatment side effect is smaller than a 75% chance of dying because of a not-treated infection. In fact, they will make a wrong decision. Since the probability that a person with a positive reaction has the disease is actually 20%, the person who decides to receive the treatment will considerably increase the probability of dying.

11   Making conditional inferences: the interplay between knowledge and logic

Henry Markovits

Conditional (if-then) reasoning occupies a central place in the study of logical reasoning. Reasoning with conditionals is a part of everyday thinking (e.g. Scholnick & Wing, 1991) and is important to activities such as reading (Lea et al., 1990). In addition, the ability to make 'if-then' inferences that are hypothetical and logical underlies much of formal mathematics and underpins many of the physical sciences. Understanding the nature and the corresponding developmental trajectory of conditional reasoning abilities is thus crucial to the basic understanding of the nature of logical reasoning. This is also important for very practical reasons, since promoting the ability to reason logically must be an important educational goal.

Conditional reasoning is one of the key components of a system of logical norms referred to as propositional logic. Although modern logic acknowledges the existence of different forms of logic, there is an intuitive presumption that standard propositional logic constitutes a template for logical reasoning. This can be seen in textbooks that teach logic and reasoning, where propositional logic is an explicit or implicit model for good reasoning. There is also a clear link between the idea that standard propositional logic is the norm for good reasoning and psychological theories of the nature and development of reasoning abilities. This can be seen most clearly in two important theories that share a common biological theme. Piaget's theory of logical (formal) reasoning (Inhelder & Piaget, 1958) and Braine's (1990) theory of natural logic both consider (although in different ways) that some forms of propositional logic become embedded in people's minds through the workings of basic biological processes that tend to create 'optimal' forms of reasoning. In these theories, there is a clear identity between development and normative reasoning, to the extent that biological processes are supposed to drive development to some optimal state that is identified with propositional logic. However, more recent theories of the nature of reasoning explicitly dispute this identity (e.g. Evans & Over, 2004; Johnson-Laird & Byrne, 1991; Oaksford, Chater & Larkin, 2000). These theories focus

237

on observed variability in reasoning performance in both children and adults and deny both that there is a clear direction to development and the normative nature of propositional logic. In other words, these theories deny that reasoning that is consistent with propositional logic is 'good' reasoning, since there are other ways of reasoning that could be seen as leading to better conclusions, in some sense.

While we will go into the detail of these theories and their underlying conception of the nature of good reasoning later on, it is clear that what is considered to be the norm for 'good' reasoning and the nature of the development of reasoning abilities appear to be intertwined in some basic way. Underlying this is the fundamental idea that development tends towards some state that is 'better', or at least, not worse, than earlier states. An explicit use of this basic argument can be found in Stanovich's recent programme concerning the nature of heuristic and normative reasoning in adults (e.g. Stanovich & West, 2000). Kahneman & Tversky (1996) have found that adults very often give normatively 'wrong' answers to many kinds of problems, and have claimed that people use some simple (and not-so-good) heuristics that give quick and easy answers to complex problems, but that effectively make them 'bad' reasoners. Stanovich has found that higher IQ reasoners tend to give more normative answers, i.e. answers that correspond to standard propositional logic or standard mathematical 'norms'. Since high IQ is a surrogate for development in these studies (see also Kokis et al., 2002), these results are interpreted as showing that normative reasoning is the end-state of development (even though this might be reached only by a small subset of a population). This is in turn interpreted to indicate that reasoning according to the norms of standard propositional logic and mathematics is in fact better reasoning. Of course, these same results could be interpreted as indicating that development results in a deterioration of reasoning abilities, and that heuristic use is 'better' reasoning, but there does not appear to have been any attempt to do so (although see Gigerenzer & Goldstein, 1996 for an argument that heuristics may be 'good' reasoning).

Before continuing, it is useful to define just what is meant by conditional reasoning. Conditional reasoning in its most basic sense involves making inferences with a given major premise of the form 'If P then Q' and one of four possible minor premises. Modus ponens (MP) is the logical principle that involves reasoning with the premises 'If P then Q, P is true' and leads to the logically correct conclusion 'Q is true.' Modus tollens (MT) involves reasoning with the premises 'If P then Q, Q is false' and leads to the logically correct conclusion 'P is false.' These two are valid logical forms, since they both lead to a single, logically correct conclusion. Affirmation of the consequent (AC) involves reasoning with the premises 'If P then Q, Q is true.' Denial of the antecedent (DA) involves reasoning with the premises 'If P then Q, P is false.' In both cases the implied conclusions, 'P is true' for AC and 'Q is false' for DA are not logically correct. Neither of these forms leads to a single, logically correct conclusion and the correct response would be to deny the implied (biconditional) conclusion in both cases.

Development, biology and normative thinking

A critical consideration in understanding the possible relationship between development and logical norms is the underlying mechanism that can allow an equation between the direction of development and 'good' thinking. One of the most important of these is biological adaptation. There are however two quite distinct ways that biology has been used. The first relies on an evolutionary process that is assumed to act directly upon the specific algorithms used by the mind to make inferences. According to this general argument, if there is some underlying genetic basis to these algorithms, then they will be subject to selection pressure. Over time, use of less good inference rules or procedures will result in lowered reproductive fitness, and the species will retain alternative rules or procedures that increase reproductive fitness. Thus, consistently used inference rules reflect the workings of this process and can be considered to be normative to the extent that they will have resulted in increased reproductive fitness in the past. This argument has been used however in two different ways. The first, which is probably best represented by Braine's (1990) theory of natural logic, claims that at least some (if not all) components of propositional logic are hard-wired. For example, Braine (1990) has claimed that the MP inference is biologically primitive in just this way. Thus, an early human might have information stored that says: 'If a lion, then dangerous.' Upon meeting a lion, an individual who possessed the inference rule: 'If P then Q, P is true, thus Q is true' will immediately, and rightly, conclude that the lion is dangerous and run away. An individual who possessed a different inference rule, say: 'If P then Q, P is true, thus maybe Q is true' might be eaten while evaluating whether or not the lion is really dangerous.

This general viewpoint might then claim that the rules of propositional logic generally lead to the best inferences, and that they are normative as a result of this. One would expect that many of these rules would be available quite early in development (as Braine claims is the case for the MP inference), but it is also consistent with a biological perspective to suppose that some maturational process is required for more complex rules to come on-line. This would then lead to the idea that development would tend towards normative reasoning.

There is however another way of using this same general argument that potentially goes in a very different direction. The underlying idea here is that selection does not produce abstractly optimal designs, in many cases it produces 'solutions' to problems of adaptation that are not optimally engineered (e.g. Dawkins, 1999). Thus, it is possible to argue that biological selection underlies some forms of inferential processes, but that these may well have led to the evolution of the kinds of heuristics that have been identified as non-normative. Gigerenzer (e.g. Gigerenzer & Goldstein, 1996) has made just this argument, i.e. that evolution may have developed 'quick and dirty' algorithms which function to make the best inferences that can be made rapidly. Such inferential procedures would profit from statistical patterns that characterize familiar situations and would thus give conclusions that are often accurate, but are not necessarily correct. In this version of the strong argument from biology, if normative reasoning is the result of evolution, then reasoning by common heuristics must be considered to be normative. Development would then tend towards increasingly efficient use of these heuristics (there is some evidence of such developmental effects, e.g. Cahan & Artman, 1997). Logical reasoning as instantiated by propositional logic would then be the result of some other kind of process, and its normative status correspondingly in doubt. Related to this viewpoint is the more specific idea that if-then reasoning is performed by some form of statistical calculation of the probability of a potential conclusion (Cummins, 1995; Oaksford, Chater & Larkin, 2000; Evans & Over, 2004). Thus, even seemingly basic inferential processes can be considered to be the result of some statistical heuristic that leads to plausible, although not necessarily true, conclusions.

In other words, a biological argument can be used to argue both for and against the idea that some strong form of logical reasoning is normative, if the principle criterion for normativity is biological. There is however another form of an argument from biology that is less constrained. Piaget's theory of cognitive development (Piaget, 1970) considers that the basic processes underlying development are biologically determined. These include the classic forms of assimilation and accommodation, and to this list must really be added the basic capacity for what Piaget (2001) referred to as 'reflective abstraction'. According to this theory, the mind is an organ that is programmed to adapt to basic patterns in the external world. Piaget also claimed that cognitive development follows a basically invariant, and universal, sequence. One of the more advanced points of this sequence is a set of cognitive procedures that allow a formal operational reasoner to make consistently logical inferences that correspond to the rules of propositional logic. Now, there is nothing in the description of the basic biological processes that allow any conclusion as to the universality of the resulting cognitive procedures. Certainly, there is a large amount of highly variable information about specific contexts that cannot be universal. However, Piaget made two claims about the way that cognitive development proceeds that underlie the larger claim about universality. The first is the idea that there is a clear distinction to be made between what might be referred to as factual knowledge and underlying concepts. This derives from a Kantian analysis of cognition which identifies some key concepts, such as causality, classification, etc., as absolutely basic to understanding. These concepts are then used to 'assimilate' any specific bits of information that might be acquired. It is thus these basic concepts that are assumed to follow an invariant sequence of development. However, while restricting the notion of invariance to basic concepts narrows the focus of the invariance argument, this alone provides no reason for this argument. The critical idea here concerns the origins of these basic concepts. Piaget claimed that these concepts are extracted by the cognitive system from the basic structure of action, via an ongoing process of reflective abstraction. Given that this structure is the same irrespective of the specific content upon which actions are performed, then it can be reasonably concluded that these base concepts will develop in very similar ways despite differences in experience and context. For example, the concept of classification is derived from the original sensori-motor schemas that allow young children to group objects together on the basis of some form of perceptual similarity. These schemas work in the same way, i.e. they have the same basic structure, irrespective of the specific nature of the objects that are available in a young child's environment. Thus, the internal structure of the classification schemas that are developed at the end of the sensori-motor period will be identical across children and contexts. Critically, development of more symbolic forms of concepts is assumed to depend tightly upon this universal base. This is due to the functioning of the process of reflective abstraction (Piaget, 2001), which results in older children being able to (1) construct abstract internal representations of action structures that reflect some key underlying properties of these actions, and (2) to manipulate these internal representations in order to construct increasingly complex and coordinated concepts at any given level of abstraction. For example, the concept of classification by some criteria at a concrete level is instantiated by representations of the kinds of perceptual similarities that might be used by young children, e.g. the concepts of grouping by colour, form, etc. These are relatively abstract concepts that are somewhat independent of the specific nature of the objects that have been classified in these ways. Once these kinds of concepts have been developed, then a further process of reflective abstraction is employed to construct representations that allow manipulation of concepts that correspond to formal criteria, such as those underlying biological taxonomies.

Thus, this theory claims that formal logic represents some basic structural properties of the real world that are gradually reconstructed at a very abstract level by the workings of the basic processes of the mind. Both the invariance of the developmental sequence and the normative status of these abstract inferential procedures derive from this basic assumption. More specifically, the ability to make logically appropriate if-then inferences is assumed to characterize the end-point of development. These inferences are normative since they reflect critical (although abstract) characteristics of the way that actions are structured in the real world.

What these approaches have in common is the idea that biology directly or indirectly provides access to some set of inferential procedures, or rules that can be used to make inferences in the real world. The normative status of these procedures similarly derives from the nature of the underlying biological processes. Specifically, if-then inferences can be seen as being the result of the use of some sort of procedure. In the case of theories such as Braine's and Piaget's, these procedures are assumed to be, or to develop, a high degree of consistency with at least some of the rules of formal logic. In other cases, the hypothesized procedures can be assumed to develop consistency, although their relation to formal logic remains undetermined.

It is also worth noting in this context how another major theory of reasoning deals with the relationship between normative reasoning and development. Johnson-Laird's mental model theory (e.g. Johnson-Laird & Byrne, 1991, 2002) is a very influential theory of adult reasoning, with the theory of if-then reasoning a critical component. We will not go into detail about the more general workings of the theory. What is important in our present context is the idea that when making an if-then inference, reasoners possess an underlying semantics of 'if' that, if used appropriately, will invariably lead to making inferences that are the same as those of propositional logic. The specific inferences that are made are the result of working memory limitations that make manipulation of this semantics difficult. Thus, development is basically explained by differences in working memory capacity, and there is some assumption that age-related increases in working memory will lead to a tendency to make more logical inferences (Barrouillet & Lecas, 1999). The key question here is the origin of this base semantics. Although this is not totally explicit from the theory, there is an assumption that this is derived from language. Thus, it can be considered that people will develop a capacity to reason in a way that is more consistent with propositional logic, and that this logic is normative since it is captured by the semantics of language. There is a further question here of the potential universality of this analysis, and what this might mean for the question of normativity. For example, it might be the case that the underlying semantics of 'if' might differ between languages. In this case, there would be no specific status to the propositional form of if-then inferences. If, on the other hand, it were argued that the meaning of 'if' were universal, then this might suggest some underlying biological origins to this. Thus, to some extent, mental model theory would stake a claim to the normative status of propositional logic that would depend on the biological origins of the meaning of logical connectives that is similar to previously discussed theories.

The discussion of these theories points out the often critical relationship between the development of reasoning from childhood to adolescence and what is seen as normative reasoning. The specific question of the nature of if-then reasoning and the way that it develops has been extensively researched and there is now a great deal of empirical data that can shed some important light upon the nature of this form of reasoning and its developmental course. I shall look at some of these studies and use their conclusions to suggest a somewhat alternative view of the nature of if-then reasoning, and its potential relationship to logical norms.

Conditional reasoning and knowledge

There is now a very large body of empirical research that has looked at if-then reasoning both developmentally and in adults. Early studies looked at whether or not children and adults were able to reason according to the norms of propositional logic. Conclusions were in fact quite disparate, with some researchers interpreting their results as showing that very young children were in fact capable of reasoning logically well at a very early age (Hawkins et al., 1984; Leevers & Harris, 1999). Other researchers found that even well-educated adults were not able to reason logically with any degree of consistency (Markovits, 1985; Wason, 1968, etc.). Such results appear, on the surface, to be disconcerting, since they lead to quite contradictory conclusions. However, these conclusions are contradictory only if it is assumed that the processes actually used by people to make inferences will consistently lead to either 'logical' or non-logical conclusions. Thus, evidence that young children can make 'logical' inferences is interpreted as indicating that children possess the requisite logical competence. Similarly, evidence that adults do not make 'logical' inferences is interpreted as indicating that adults do not possess the requisite competence. Clearly, these conclusions are incompatible. Unless the basic empirical data are put into doubt, one can infer that the processes used to make inferences can sometimes lead to 'logical' conclusions and sometimes not. Thus these seemingly contradictory results can be explained by variability in performance. And in fact many studies have indeed shown that inferential performance in both children and adults is subject to a great deal of variability.

The key question then is what factors determine the kinds of inferences that are made to what appear to be identical logical arguments. It soon became clear that the specific content of the premises exerts a strong effect on inferential performance. For example, work on the Wason selection task (e.g. Wason & Shapiro, 1971) showed enormous differences in rates of 'logical' responding for different classes of premise. In the specific case of conditional inferences, there has been similar variation. In this case, however, empirical studies have provided some very clear indications of exactly which dimensions affect the kinds of inferences that are made. The first such dimension refers to potential alternatives to the antecedent. Specifically, when reasoning with a familiar conditional premise, e.g. If a rock is thrown at a window, then the window will break, examples of alternative antecedents are those other than rocks that could result in a window breaking. There are now a great many studies that have shown that when reasoning with premises for which there are relatively many potential alternative antecedents, reasoners will tend to reject the AC and DA inferences (Bucci, 1978; Cummins et al., 1991; Markovits & Vachon, 1990). The second dimension refers to what Cummins et al. (1991) referred to as disabling conditions. In this case, this refers to information that allows the antecedent to be true, but implies that the consequent might not be true. In the case of the previous example, a window made of plexiglass would be a disabling condition, since a rock thrown at a plexiglass window might not break the window. Studies have shown that when there are relatively many available disabling conditions, reasoners will tend to reject the MP and MT inferences (Cummins, 1995; Cummins et al., 1991; Janveau-Brennan & Markovits, 1999).

These two dimensions appear able to explain a great deal of the observed variability in conditional reasoning with concrete premises. A further question is then the mechanism by which these dimensions affect reasoning. While there are many possible ways to model such effects, the most direct explanation is that reasoners are simply retrieving information about alternative antecedents and disabling conditions from memory during the inferential process. There is in fact a variety of empirical evidence that this is indeed the case.

The first indicator that active retrieval underlies the observed effects is the observation that the effect of numbers of alternative antecedents is modulated by the strength of association between a given antecedent and the consequent of the major premise. For example, adult reasoners will reject the AC and DA inferences more often with the premise 'If a dog is dirty, then it will scratch constantly' than with the premise 'If a dog has fleas, then it will scratch constantly' (Quinn & Markovits, 1998). In the former, 'having fleas' is an alternative antecedent that is very highly associated with 'scratching', while alternatives for the latter premise are less highly associated. Similar effects have been found with children (Barrouillet, Markovits & Quinn, 2002). In addition, the associative strength effect has also been found with respect to the effects of disabling conditions on MP and MT inferences (De Neys, Schaeken & d'Ydewalle, 2002). Thus, both the number and associative strength of potential alternative antecedents and disabling conditions affect reasoning. The fact that these are the basic factors that determine retrieval of information from long-term memory suggests that retrieval underlies the observed effects.

A second set of observations concerns the relationship between measures of retrieval efficiency and reasoning. Janveau-Brennan & Markovits (1999) found that individual differences in retrieving alternative causes for given effects were correlated to reasoning on the AC and DA forms in children. Specifically, children who were able to retrieve a greater number of causes in a fixed time period showed higher rates of rejection of these inferences. Similarly, Markovits & Quinn (2002) found that retrieval efficiency, measured using latencies for retrieval, also correlated with reasoning on the AC and DA forms, in a similar way. Reasoners who were able to retrieve information more rapidly from memory rejected the AC and DA inferences more often. Once again, similar results have been obtained when access to disabling conditions and performance on the MP (and MT) forms are examined (De Neys, Schaeken & d'Ydewalle, 2002). Thus, reasoners who are able to retrieve information more efficiently from memory are also more likely to spontaneously reject the AC and DA inferences. Although such correlations are not by themselves convincing, since they might be mediated by factors such as working memory, etc., coupled with the previously described results concerning associative strength, they strongly suggest that some form of active retrieval occurs during reasoning.

Now, the most direct interpretation of these results is that when people make inferences about concrete content, they will retrieve and use stored knowledge in order to evaluate these inferences in some way. Basically, the results that have been described suggest that if alternative antecedents are retrieved, then there is a strong likelihood of denying the AC and DA inferences. If disabling conditions are retrieved, then there is a strong likelihood of denying the MP and MT inferences. At this point, we can look at potential models of reasoning in order to understand just how these relationships between retrieval and reasoning might be understood. One model for what goes on in reasoning that can be applied very directly is the idea that reasoning is essentially probabilistic (Cummins, 1995; Evans & Over, 2004; Oaksford, Chater & Larkin, 2000). Essentially these models claim that information about premises is used to evaluate the likelihood of a putative conclusion. This is then used as a basis for making inferences. For example, when evaluating an inference such as 'If an animal is a dog, then it has legs. An animal has legs. Is it a dog?', people might retrieve cases of animals with legs, and then estimate what proportion of these are dogs. This would give a probabilistic evaluation of the conclusion, i.e. it might be concluded that if an animal has legs, then it is not very probable that it is a dog. Such a model is clearly consistent with many of the observed effects of content.

Of course, if reasoning is essentially probabilistic then people do not reason in a way that corresponds to the norms of propositional logic. This has in fact been explicitly claimed by Oaksford, Chater & Larkin (2000). In this perspective, reasoners who give 'logical' responses to inferential problems are doing so only when the statistical properties of real-world knowledge happen to be consistent with the logical responses to a given problem. If this were the case, then development would simply lead to greater efficiency in retrieving and using information in order to make increasingly accurate likelihood evaluations. Inferences generated in this way would become better real-world predictors, but there is little reason to suppose that they would become more normative. In other words, the developmental pattern of probabilistic reasoning would lead to people making inferences that more accurately reflect statistical patterns governing real-world events. Reasoning would not have any specific relationship to standard propositional logic, which could then be seen as a sort of academic exercise.

However, while a straightforward probabilistic model is appealing on many levels, it does have some major problems in explaining actual inferential performance in a variety of ways. The clearest cases are those of contrary-to-fact and abstract reasoning, which will be discussed later. A more immediate problem concerns the way that probabilistic reasoning could be used to generate responses to inferential problems that use standard logical instructions, which ask for certain, as opposed to probable, conclusions. This is a critical point, since even young children are able to understand simple logical instructions, and distinguish between certain and uncertain conclusions in ways that are often 'logical' (e.g. Markovits, 2000). There is, at the moment, no satisfactory model that could explain how reasoners will translate probabilistic evaluations into deductive conclusions. In fact, there is evidence that a probabilistic model may be unable to account for inferential performance under logical instructions, even with concrete content (Markovits & Handley, in press).

Despite the problems with using a purely probabilistic model to explain inferential reasoning performance, it remains the case that reasoning under deductive instructions is subject to the same kinds of content effects that underlie the probabilistic model. In other words, deductive reasoning with concrete content shows variability consistent with the retrieval and use of knowledge about premises, something which is clearly a problem with respect to any form of normative model. On the other hand, developmental studies often show a consistent pattern of increased frequency of 'logical' responding with age (Markovits & Vachon, 1990; O'Brien & Overton, 1980, 1982; Overton et al., 1987), despite some exceptions (e.g. Janveau-Brennan & Markovits, 1999; Klaczynski & Narashimham, 1998). What is needed is an idea of the kinds of processes that could explain both the tendency to use knowledge about premises in an increasingly efficient way with the tendency to produce an increasing level of 'logical' responses. The most revealing form of reasoning in this context, is reasoning with premises that are empirically false, or contrary-to-fact.

Reasoning with contrary-to-fact premises

Reasoning with false premises is an archetypal example of Piaget's stage of formal thinking. What makes logical reasoning with false premises particularly interesting is that it explicitly requires the reasoner not to use their knowledge that the premises are not in fact true. Thus, in this case, being able to reason logically cannot depend on some process of evaluating the real-world status of a potential conclusion. For example, 'If ice is put into water, then the water will become hot.' is an example of this kind of premise. The logical conclusion that 'ice is put into water' necessarily implies that 'the water will become hot' is completely contrary to our knowledge of the world. When a reasoner makes the logical inference, they are doing so despite their available knowledge.

What is particularly intriguing in the case of contrary-to-fact premises is that real-world knowledge can play contradictory roles with respect to logical reasoning. On the one hand, knowledge that the premises are not true clearly is an obstacle to reasoning logically. However, in many cases at least, knowledge about alternative antecedents remains useful when the AC and DA inferences are considered. Thus, when reasoning with the above-mentioned premise, in order to conclude that 'water becomes hot' does not necessarily imply that 'ice has been put into the water', it is useful to be able to generate other ways of making water hot. Thus, retrieval of alternative antecedents will assist the process of making 'logical' inferences.

This makes contrary-to-fact reasoning a very useful test case for developmental theories. Now, there are several studies that have examined young children's ability to make simple inferences on the basis of false premises. There is a clear tendency for children to introduce their real-world knowledge into these inferences (Dias & Harris, 1988, 1990; Hawkins et al., 1984; Markovits & Vachon, 1989). Thus, it is common to conclude that 'ice has been put into water' implies that 'the water will become cold'. However, a variety of simple manipulations can eliminate this form of empirical reasoning, varying from using abstract terms (Hawkins et al., 1984) to inserting premises into a fantasy context (Dias & Harris, 1988; Markovits & Vachon, 1989) to simply asking children to concentrate on the premises (Leevers & Harris, 1999). One straightforward interpretation that has been made of these kinds of results is that there are essentially two separate systems of reasoning, one which relies intrinsically on everyday knowledge and is pragmatic in nature, and another which is abstract and analytic (e.g. Braine, 1990; Hawkins et al., 1984; Leevers & Harris, 1999). Children (and many adults) will spontaneously reason pragmatically, and will use their real-world knowledge as much as possible. The various contextual effects that allow children to make simple logical inferences to contrary-to-fact premises work by cuing the analytic processes which then allow the making of logical inferences that are not affected by knowledge. This basic analysis mirrors more recent dual-process theories (Evans & Over, 1996; Sloman, 1996; Stanovich & West, 2000), and distinguishes between knowledge-based processes (such as are assumed in probabilistic theories) and analytic processes, which allow logical reasoning. This basic distinction allows a very elegant way of explaining both content-related variability and logical reasoning, the former being a consequence of use of pragmatic forms of inference, while the latter is the result of use of analytic processes.

However, there are some problems with this basic idea. The first is theoretical and simply concerns the origins of the analytic processes and their relation to logical reasoning. None of the existing theories specify what these processes are, and why they should allow making the kinds of normative inferences that we are referring to as logical. Thus separating out a pragmatic element from the inferential process allows some potential explanation for the observed variability, but the basic developmental problem remains intact. Specifically, there is no explanation for what people might be doing when not reasoning pragmatically, and why, when they do this, they might tend to produce more normative inferences. The second problem is even more serious and concerns the extended effects of the same contextual manipulations that are interpreted as priming logical processes. If context serves to prime a global form of analytic, and logical, reasoning, then one would expect its effects to be relatively wide-ranging. However, this is unfortunately not the case. When performance on all four logical forms is examined, the following pattern is observed. Embedding contrary-to-fact premises into a fantasy context increases the proportion of logical responses to the MP and MT forms, as has been mentioned (e.g. Dias & Harris, 1988). However, performance on the AC and DA forms becomes less logical with both contrary-to-fact (Markovits, 1995) and believable premises (Markovits et al., 1996). The results of this manipulation mirror the basic developmental pattern that is found in contrary-to-fact reasoning with simple deductive instructions. In this case, there is a clear trend towards responding logically to the MP and MT inferences, but the rate of logical responding to the AC and DA inferences is less high with contrary-to-fact premises than with believable premises (Markovits & Vachon, 1989). Even more striking are results that show that the rate of logical responding to the AC and DA forms with abstract premises is actually lower when these premises are embedded into a fantasy context, than when they are embedded into a realistic context (Venet & Markovits, 2001). These results certainly are not consistent with the idea that context can prime a separate, analytic and logical system; unless it is assumed that this system does not in fact make normative inferences.

There is however another way of looking at the relation between the kind of retrieval process that appears to be related to reasoning and normative logic. This derives from the fact, which has been previously mentioned, that retrieving alternative antecedents and retrieving disabling conditions have opposite effects when considered in the context of standard propositional logic. Specifically, when alternative antecedents are retrieved, then reasoners tend to deny the AC and DA inferences, which results in logically consistent inferences. When disabling conditions are retrieved, reasoners tend to deny the MP and MT inferences, which results in logically inconsistent inferences. The available results concerning the effects of using a fantasy context indicate that this increases the rates of logical responding to the MP and MT forms, but decreases the rates of logical responding to the AC and DA forms. But this apparent contradiction can be simply resolved if we restate these results in terms of information retrieval. Then, we can interpret the effects of fantasy as decreasing retrieval of disabling conditions, and also of alternative antecedents.

The most straightforward explanation of these results would claim that use of a fantasy context results in some form of generalized inhibition of real-world knowledge. In fact, there has been much recent interest in the function of inhibition as an important modulator of general retrieval processes. While the exact nature of inhibitory processes are a subject of debate (Neil, 1997; Tipper, 2001), it does seem clear that inhibition is an important component of cognitive development in general (Bjorklund & Harnishfeger, 1995). Inhibition can be seen as the necessary correlate of the general increase in retrieval efficiency found in development. Specifically, as children begin to have access to a larger quantity of information, it becomes necessary to avoid activation of information that is not directly relevant to a specific problem. This certainly suggests that inhibition in some form could be a useful mechanism to modulate the effects of retrieval when reasoning with false premises. Markovits & Barrouillet (2001) have specifically hypothesized that inhibitory processes are required to explain reasoning performance with contrary-to-fact premises.

When seen in the light of retrieval and inhibitory processes, the nature of contrary-to-fact reasoning and the way that this is affected by context becomes much clearer. When making a MP inference, using a minor premise such as 'ice is put into water', it can be assumed that normal retrieval processes will ordinarily result in the activation of something like 'the water will get cold'. In order to prevent this, the reasoner must inhibit this process, at some stage. Thus, when told to suppose that it is true that 'ice into water will make the water hot', inhibition will be required to reduce interference between real-world knowledge and the logical conclusion. However, when making an AC inference such as 'If ice is put into water, then the water will become hot. Water is hot', it is necessary both to inhibit knowledge that ice makes water cold, and to retrieve potential alternative ways of making water hot, in order to correctly deny the inference that 'ice is put into the water'. Thus, the difficulty in making logical inferences with contrary-to-fact premises comes from the somewhat antagonistic requirements of simultaneously inhibiting access to some real-world knowledge about the premises and allowing retrieval of other forms of knowledge.

Recent studies have provided evidence that individual differences in inhibitory processes in both children (Simoneau & Markovits, 2003) and adults (Markovits & Doyon, 2004) are related to the tendency to make logical inferences on the MP and MT forms with contrary-to-fact premises. These studies also allow some idea of the developmental patterns that characterize the interplay between retrieval and inhibitory processes in this kind of reasoning. Simoneau & Markovits (2003) observed, in line with some previously mentioned results, that children who were more efficient inhibitors make more correct MP and MT inferences, but also rejected the AC and DA inferences less often. However, educated adults who are more efficient inhibitors show a more selective pattern, since they make the MP and MT inferences more often, with no effect on the AC and DA inferences (Markovits & Doyon, 2004).

The sum of the empirical data on inferences with concrete content thus allows a clearer specification of the processes that are in play when logical reasoning is called for. Specifically, even quite young children can interpret logical instructions as requiring both inhibition of information that puts into doubt the truth of the major premise and retrieval of information about alternative antecedents that can result in denial of the AC and DA inferences (see Markovits & Barrouillet, 2002 for a mental model account of these processes). Development results in both increasing efficiency of retrieval (Kail, 1992) and increasing selectivity of inhibition (Bjorklund & Harnishfeger, 1990). The combined results of these two developmental trends is an increasing tendency to make normative inferences when asked to make logical inferences with concrete premises, whether these are believable or not. When explicit logical instructions are not used, there is a trend towards increasingly denying the MP inference (Janveau-Brennan & Markovits, 1999), which is mirrored in adults (Cummins et al., 1991). Thus, there is a clear distinction between the processes used in simply evaluating the real-world probability of inferences and those used in making logical inferences, despite the fact that in both cases there is variability due to the specific properties of premises used for reasoning.

The development of logical reasoning can be explained, at least partially, by the increasingly efficient use of retrieval and inhibitory processes in order to facilitate and target information retrieval during the reasoning process. The general tendency towards production of normative responses can be seen as the result of the interplay of these two processes. However, these do not, of themselves, explain developmental trends towards increasing normativity when making conditional inferences. Retrieval and inhibition simply allow better use of information that is stored in long-term memory, and their functioning reflects the specific way that this information is stored. Thus, any developmental trend towards making normative inferences must ultimately be based on the way that information is stored in memory. In other words, the increasing ability of children and adolescents to make normatively correct conditional inferences reflects the basic way that the mind stores information about the world. This conclusion is reinforced by results that indicate that the ability to reason logically with purely abstract premises is facilitated by the insertion of these premises into a realistic context and that underlying abstract reasoning is a process that capitalizes on the structure of stored information (Venet & Markovits, 2001). In this perspective, what is considered normative may be defined, at least partly, by the structure of information about the world in long-term memory. Development would then tend towards more normative inferences since it increases the efficiency and focus of information retrieval, and allows inferential processes to more clearly reflect how information is stored.

References

1. NORMS IN HUMAN DEVELOPMENT: INTRODUCTION

Anastasi, A. (1982). *Psychological testing.* 5th edition. New York: Macmillan Publishing Co. Inc.

Anderson, J. A. (1957). Significance of growth and development to the practicing physician. In Harris (1957).

Armstrong, L. (2003). *Every second counts: from recovery to victory.* London: Yellow Jersey Press.

Axtell, G. (2000). *Knowledge, belief, and character: readings in virtue epistemology.* New York: Rowman & Littlefield Publishers Inc.

Bainton, R. H. (1950). *Here I stand: a life of Martin Luther.* New York: Signet.

Baldwin, J. (2005). www.inspirationalstories.com/0/91.html

Bickhard, M. (2003). Process and emergence: normative function and representation. In J. Seibt (ed.), *Process theories: crossdisciplinary studies in dynamic categories.* Dordrecht: Kluwer Academic.

Bjorklund, D. & Pellegrini, A. (2002). *The origins of human nature.* Washington, DC: American Psychological Association.

Blank, G. (2002). www.drblank.com/slaws.htm

Bornstein, M. & Lamb, M. (1992). *Developmental psychology: an advanced textbook.* Hillsdale, NJ: Erlbaum.

Brandom, R. (1994). *Making it explicit: reasoning, representing, and discursive commitment.* Cambridge, MA: Harvard University Press.

(2000). *Articulating reasons: an introduction to inferentialism.* Cambridge, MA: Harvard University Press.

Brown, T. & Weiss, L. (1987). Structures, procedures, heuristics and affectivity. *Archives de Psychologie,* 55, 59–94. Reprinted in L. Smith (1992), *Jean Piaget: critical assessments,* vol. IV. London: Routledge.

Changeux, J-P. (2000). Co-author. In J-P. Changeux & P. Ricoeur, *What makes us think?* Princeton: Princeton University Press.

Cole, M., Cole, S. & Lightfoot, C. (2005). *The development of children.* 5th edition. New York: Worth Publishing.

Cosmides, L. & Tooby, J. (2004). *What is evolutionary psychology? Explaining the new science of the mind.* New Haven, CT: Yale University Press.

Cresswell, M. & Hughes, G. (1996). *A new introduction to modal logic.* London: Routledge.

Damasio, A. (2003). *Looking for Spinoza.* London: William Heinemann.

Damon, W. (1998). *Handbook of child psychology*. 5th edition. New York: Wiley.

Dawkins, R. (1999). *The extended phenotype: the long reach of the gene*. Revised edition. Oxford: Oxford University Press.

Durkheim, E. (1901). *The rules of sociological method*. In S. Lukes (1982). London: Macmillan Press Ltd.

Flavell, J., Miller, P. & Miller, S. (1993). *Cognitive development*. 3rd edition. Englewood Cliffs, NJ: Prentice Hall.

Frege, G. (1964). *The basic laws of arithmetic*. Berkeley, CA: University of California Press.

Gardner, H. (1982). *Developmental psychology: an introduction*. Boston: Little, Brown & Co.

Gigerenzer, G. & Selten, R. (2001). *Bounded rationality: the adaptive toolbox*. Cambridge, MA: MIT Press.

Goldman, A. (2001). *Pathways of knowledge: public and private*. Oxford: Oxford University Press.

Goswami, U. (2002). *Blackwell handbook of childhood cognitive development*. Oxford: Blackwell.

Habermas, J. (1992). *Between facts and norms: contributions to a discourse theory of law and democracy*. Cambridge, MA: MIT Press.

Harris, D. B. (1957). *The concept of development*. Minneapolis: University of Minnesota Press.

Hawking, S. (2001). *The universe in a nutshell*. London: Bantam Press.

Horty, J. F. (2001). *Agency and deontic logic*. Oxford: Oxford University Press.

Hume, D. (1965). *Treatise of human nature*. Oxford: Oxford University Press.

Humphrey, G. (1963). *Thinking*. New York: John Wiley.

Inhelder, B. & Piaget, J. (1958). *The growth of logical thinking*. London: Routledge & Kegan Paul.

Isaacs, N. (1951). Critical notice. *British Journal of Psychology*, 42, 185–8.

Kant, I. (1780). *On universal practical philosophy*. In P. Heath & J. Schneewind (1997), *Lectures on ethics*. Cambridge: Cambridge University Press.

   (1785). *Groundwork of the metaphysics of morals*. In H. J. Paton (1948), *The moral law*. London: Hutchinson.

   (1800). *Introduction to logic*. In T. K. Abbott (1972), *Kant's Introduction to logic*. Westport, CT: Greenwood Press.

King, M. L. (1968). The role of the behavioural scientist in the Civil Rights movement. *American Psychologist*, 23, 180–6.

Kitcher, P. (1992). The naturalists return. *The Philosophical Review*, 101, 53, 114.

Korsgaard, C. (1996). *The sources of normativity*. Cambridge: Cambridge University Press

Kuhn, T. S. (2000). *The road beyond structure*. Chicago: University of Chicago Press.

Laudan, L. (1996). *Beyond positivism and relativism*. Boulder, CO: Westview Press.

LeTour (2005). www.letour.fr/indexus.html

Longuenesse, B. (1998). *Kant and the capacity to judge*. Princeton, NJ: Princeton University Press.

MacIntyre, A. (1998). *A short history of ethics*. 2nd edition. London: Routledge.

Mandler, J. (1998). Babies think before they speak. *Human Development*, 41, 116–26.

Marcus, R. B. (1993). *Modalities: philosophical essays.* New York: Oxford University Press.

Mason, H. E. (1996). *Moral dilemmas and moral theory.* Oxford: Oxford University Press.

Milgram, S. (1974). *Obedience to authority: an experimental view.* London: Tavistock Publications Ltd.

(1992). *Individual in a social world.* New York: McGraw-Hill.

Mooney, C. (2003). www.csicop.org/doubtandabout/polling/

Nadel, I. (2002). *Double act: a life of Tom Stoppard.* London: Methuen.

Neisser, U. (1998). *The rising curve.* Washington, DC: American Psychological Association.

Nozick, R. (2001). *Invariances.* Cambridge, MA: Harvard University Press.

Peng, K. & Nisbett, R. E. (1999). Culture, dialecticism, and reasoning about contradiction. *American Psychologist*, 54, 741–54.

Piaget, J. (1918). *Recherche.* Lausanne: La Concorde.

(1953). *Origins of intelligence in the child.* London: Routledge & Kegan Paul.

(1976). *The grasp of consciousness.* Cambridge, MA: Harvard University Press.

(1995). *Sociological studies.* London: Routledge.

Plotkin, H. (1997). *Evolution in mind.* London: Allen Lane Press.

Popper, K. R. (1968). *The logic of scientific discovery.* London: Hutchinson.

(1979). *Objective knowledge.* 2nd edition. Oxford: Oxford University Press.

Pufendorf, S. (1703). *Of the law of nature and nations.* Oxford: Lichfield.

Putnam, H. (2002). *The collapse of the fact/value dichotomy, and other essays.* Cambridge, MA: Harvard University Press.

Quine, W. (1972). *Methods of logic.* 3rd edition. London: Routledge & Kegan Paul.

Ricoeur, P. (2000). Co-author. In J-P. Changeux & P. Ricoeur, *What makes us think?* Princeton: Princeton University Press.

Ross, A. (1968). *Directives and norms.* London: Routledge & Kegan Paul.

Sainsbury, R. M. (1991). *Logical forms.* Oxford: Blackwell.

Searle, J. (1969). *Speech acts: an essay in the philosophy of language.* Cambridge: Cambridge University Press.

(1995). *The construction of social reality.* New York: The Free Press.

Shayer, M. (2007). 30 years on – a large anti-'Flynn effect'? The Piagetian test volume & heaviness norms 1975–2003. *British Journal of Educational Psychology.*

Siegler, R. S. (1991). *Children's thinking.* 2nd edition. Englewood Cliffs, NJ: Prentice Hall.

Simon, H. A. (1981). *Sciences of the artificial.* 2nd edition. Cambridge, MA: MIT Press.

Skinner, B. F. (1974). *About behaviourism.* London: Jonathan Cape.

Slater, A. & Muir, D. (1999). *Blackwell reader in developmental psychology.* Oxford: Blackwell.

Sloman, S. A. (1996). The empirical case for two systems of reasoning. *Psychological Bulletin*, 119, 3–22.

Smith, L. (1993). *Necessary knowledge*. Hove, UK: Erlbaum Associates.

(2002). *Reasoning by mathematical induction in children's arithmetic*. Oxford: Pergamon Press.

(2003). From epistemology to psychology in the development of knowledge. In T. Brown & L. Smith (eds.), *Reductionism and the development of knowledge*. Mahwah, NJ: Erlbaum.

Spencer, R. (1957). Evolution and development: a view of anthropology. In Harris (1957).

Spinoza, B. (1963). *Short treatise*. New York: Russell & Russell.

Summers, L. H. (2005). Remarks at NBER conference on diversifying the science & engineering workforce. President, Harvard University homepage.

Wason, P. (1977). Self-contradictions. In P. Johnson-Laird & P. Wason (eds.), *Thinking: readings in cognitive science*. Cambridge: Cambridge University Press.

Watson, J. B. (1930). *Behaviorism*. New York: Norton & Company Inc.

von Wright, G. H. (1963). *Norm and action*. London: Routledge & Kegan Paul.

(1968). *The varieties of goodness*. London: Routledge & Kegan Paul.

(1983). *Practical reason*. Oxford: Blackwell.

2. THE IMPLICIT NORMATIVITY OF DEVELOPMENTAL PSYCHOLOGY

Aristotle (1928). περι ψυχήγ. In *Oeuvres complètes*. Paris: Guillaume Budé.

Baldwin, J. M. (1902). *Development and evolution*. New York: Macmillan.

(1906, 1908, 1911). *Thoughts and things or genetic logic*. 3 vols. New York: Macmillan.

Bergson, H. (1911). *Creative evolution* (trans. A. Mitchell). New York: Holt.

Bosanquet, B. (1888). *On the morphology of knowledge*. 2 vols. London/New York: Oxford University Press.

Cassirer, E. (1903–20). *Das Erkenntnisproblem*. 3 vols. Berlin: B. Cassirer.

(1953, 1955, 1957). *Philosophy of symbolic forms*. 3 vols. New Haven: Yale University Press.

Damasio, A. (2003). *Looking for Spinoza*. London: William Heinemann.

Darwin, C. (1859). *On the origin of species by means of natural selection, or the preservation of favoured races in the struggle for life*. London: Murray.

Durkheim, E. (1897). *Le suicide*. Paris: Félix Alcan.

Furth, H. (1986). The social function of Piaget's theory: a response to Apostel. *New Ideas*, 4 (1), 23–9.

Hobhouse, L. T. (1888). *Theory of knowledge*. London: Macmillan.

(1912). *Mind in evolution*. London: Macmillan.

Huxley, T. H. (1881). *Science and culture*. London: Macmillan.

James, W. (1890). *Principles of psychology*. New York: Henry Holt, vol. II.

Kant, I. (1972). *Introduction to logic*. Westport, CT: Greenwood Press.

Liard, L. (1873). *De Democrito philosopho*. Paris.

Lovejoy, A. O. (1936). *The great chain of being*. Cambridge, MA: Harvard University Press.

Maturana, H. R. & Varela, F. J. (1980). *Autopoiesis and cognition*. Dordrecht: Reidel.

Piaget, J. (1936). *La naissance de l'intelligence chez l'enfant*. Paris: Delachaux et Niestlé.

(1953). *The origins of intelligence in the child*. London: Routledge & Kegan Paul.

Popper, K. (1928). Die Methodenfrage der Denkpsychologie. Vienna: unpublished doctoral dissertation, Vienna University.

Russell, E. (1946). *The defectiveness of organic activities*. Cambridge: Cambridge University Press.

Sigwart, C. (1894–5). *Logic*. 2 vols. New York: Macmillan.

Thompson, D. A. W. (1942). *On growth and form*. Cambridge: Cambridge University Press.

Werner, H. & Kaplan, B. (1963). *Symbol formation*. New York: Wiley.

von Wright, G. H. (1983). *Practical reason*. Oxford: Blackwell.

Wundt, W. (1880). *Logik*. Stuttgart: Enke.

3. DEVELOPMENTAL NORMATIVITY AND NORMATIVE DEVELOPMENT

Aristotle (1908). *De anima* (*On the soul*). In W. D. Ross (ed.), *The works of Aristotle*. Oxford: Clarendon Press, §424a, pp. 17–22.

Bickhard, M. H. (1980). A model of developmental and psychological processes. *Genetic Psychology Monographs*, 102, 61–116.

(1988). Piaget on variation and selection models: structuralism, logical necessity, and interactivism. *Human Development*, 31, 274–312.

(1989). The nature of psychopathology. In Lynn Simek-Downing (ed.), *International psychotherapy: theories, research, and cross-cultural implications*. Westport, CT: Praeger Press, pp. 115–40.

(1992a). How does the environment affect the person? In L. T. Winegar & J. Valsiner (eds.), *Children's development within social contexts: metatheory and theory*. Hillsdale, NJ: Lawrence Erlbaum Associates, pp. 63–92.

(1992b). Scaffolding and self scaffolding: central aspects of development. In L. T. Winegar & J. Valsiner (eds.), *Children's development within social contexts: research and methodology*. Hillsdale, NJ: Lawrence Erlbaum Associates, pp. 33–52.

(1992c). Piaget on variation and selection models: structuralism, logical necessity, and interactivism. In L. Smith (ed.), *Jean Piaget: critical assessments*, vol. IV. London: Routledge, ch. 83, pp. 388–434. (Reprint of 1988)

(1992d). Commentary on the age 4 transition. *Human Development*, 35 (3), 182–92.

(1993). Representational content in humans and machines. *Journal of Experimental and Theoretical Artificial Intelligence*, 5, 285–333.

(2000a). Motivation and emotion: an interactive process model. In R. D. Ellis & N. Newton (eds.), *The caldron of consciousness*. Amsterdam: J. Benjamins, pp. 161–78.

(2000b). Emergence. In P. B. Andersen, C. Emmeche, N. O. Finnemann & P. V. Christiansen (eds.), *Downward causation*. Aarhus, Denmark: University of Aarhus Press, pp. 322–48.

(2001). Why children don't have to solve the frame problems: cognitive representations are not encodings. *Developmental Review*, 21, 224–62.

(2003a). An integration of motivation and cognition. In L. Smith, C. Rogers & P. Tomlinson (eds.), *Development and motivation: joint perspectives*. Leicester: British Psychological Society, Monograph Series II, pp. 41–56.

(2003b). Process and emergence: normative function and representation. In J. Seibt (ed.), *Process theories: crossdisciplinary studies in dynamic categories.* Dordrecht: Kluwer Academic, pp. 121–55.

(2003c). The biological emergence of representation. In T. Brown & L. Smith (eds.), *Reductionism and the development of knowledge.* Mahwah, NJ: Erlbaum, pp. 105–31.

(in preparation). *The whole person.*

Bickhard, M. H. & Campbell, R. L. (1989). Interactivism and genetic epistemology. *Archives de Psychologie*, 57 (221), 99–121.

(1996). Topologies of learning and development. *New Ideas in Psychology*, 14 (2), 111–56.

Bickhard, M. H. & Richie, D. M. (1983). *On the nature of representation: a case study of James Gibson's theory of perception.* New York: Praeger Publishers.

Brady, G. (2000). *From Peirce to Skolem.* Amsterdam: Elsevier.

Campbell, D. T. (1974). Evolutionary epistemology. In P. A. Schilpp (ed.), *The Philosophy of Karl Popper.* LaSalle, IL: Open Court, pp. 413–63.

(1990). Levels of organization, downward causation, and the selection-theory approach to evolutionary epistemology. In G. Greenberg & E. Tobach (eds.), *Theories of the evolution of knowing.* Hillsdale, NJ: Erlbaum, pp. 1–17.

Campbell, R. (1992). *Truth and historicity.* Oxford: Oxford University Press.

Campbell, R. L. & Bickhard, M. H. (1986). *Knowing levels and developmental stages.* Contributions to Human Development. Basel, Switzerland: Karger.

(1992). Types of constraints on development: an interactivist approach. *Developmental Review*, 12 (3), 311–38.

Caston, V. (1997). Epiphenomenalisms, ancient and modern. *Philosophical Review*, 106 (3), 309–63.

Christensen, W. D. & Bickhard, M. H. (2002). The process dynamics of normative function. *Monist*, 85 (1), 3–28.

Coffa, J. A. (1991). *The semantic tradition from Kant to Carnap.* Cambridge: Cambridge University Press.

Fodor, J. A. (1987). A situated grandmother? *Mind and Language*, 2, 64–81.

(1990a). Information and representation. In P. P. Hanson (ed.), *Information, language, and cognition.* Vancouver: University of British Columbia Press, pp. 175–90.

(1990b). Fodor's guide to mental representation. In J. A. Fodor (ed.), *A theory of mental content and other essays.* Cambridge, MA: MIT Press.

(2003). *Hume variations.* Oxford: Oxford University Press.

Gill, M-L. (1989). *Aristotle on substance.* Princeton, NJ: Princeton University Press.

Hume, D. (1978). *A treatise of human nature.* Index by L. A. Selby-Bigge; Notes by P. H. Nidditch. Oxford: Oxford University Press.

Hylton, P. (1990). *Russell, idealism, and the emergence of analytic philosophy.* Oxford: Oxford University Press.

Juarrero, A. (1999). *Dynamics in action: intentional behavior as a complex system.* Cambridge, MA: MIT Press.

Olson, K. R. (1987). *An essay on facts.* Stanford, CA: Center for the Study of Language and Information.

Piaget, J. (1954). *The construction of reality in the child.* New York: Basic Books.
(2001). *Studies in reflecting abstraction,* ed. and trans. Robert L. Campbell.
Hove, UK: Psychology Press.

Plato (1892). *Theaetetus.* In *The dialogues of Plato,* vol. IV, ed. and trans.
B. Jowett. Oxford: Clarendon Press, p. 191.

Rouse, J. (2002). *How scientific practices matter: reclaiming philosophical naturalism.*
Chicago: University of Chicago Press.

4. GENETIC EPISTEMOLOGY: NATURALISTIC EPISTEMOLOGY VS NORMATIVE EPISTEMOLOGY

Alston, W. (1989). *Epistemic justification.* Ithaca: Cornell University Press.

Apostel, L. et al. (1957). Les liaisons analytiques et synthétiques dans les
comportements du sujet. In *Etudes d'épistémologie génétique,* vol. IV. Paris:
Presses Universitaires de France.

Aristotle (1984). Nichomachean ethics. In J. Barnes (ed.), *The complete works of
Aristotle,* vol. II. Princeton: Princeton University Press, pp. 1, 729–867.

Armstrong, D. (1973). *Belief, truth and knowledge.* New York: Cambridge
University Press.

Axelrod, R. (1984). *The evolution of cooperation.* New York: Basic Books.

Axtell, G. (2000). *Knowledge, belief, and character.* Lanham, MD: Rowman.

Bicchieri, C. (1993). *Rationality and coordination.* Cambridge: Cambridge
University Press.

Bonjour, L. (1985). *The structure of empirical knowledge.* Cambridge, MA:
Harvard University Press.

Chisholm, R. (1977). *Theory of knowledge.* 2nd edition. Englewood Cliffs, NJ:
Prentice Hall.

Churchland, P. (1979). *Scientific realism and the plasticity of mind.* New York:
Cambridge University Press.

Clifford, W. (1999). *The ethics of belief and other essays.* Amherst, NY: Prometheus.

Conee, E. & Feldman, R. (2004). *Evidentialism.* New York: Oxford University
Press.

Copp, D. (2001). *Morality, normativity, and society.* Oxford: Oxford University
Press.

Dancy, J. & Sosa, E. (eds.) (1992). *A companion to epistemology.* Oxford: Blackwell's.

Danielson, P. (1992). *Artificial morality.* London: Routledge.

Descartes, R. (1984). *Meditations on first philosophy.* In J. Cottingham et al. (eds.,
trans.), *The philosophical writings of Descartes,* vol. II. New York: Cambridge
University Press, pp. 1–62. (Original work published 1641.)

Fairweather, A. & Zagzebski, L. (eds.) (2001). *Virtue epistemology: essays on
epistemic virtue and responsibility.* New York: Cambridge University Press.

Gauthier, D. (1986). *Morals by agreement.* Oxford: Clarendon Press.

Ginet, C. (1975). *Knowledge, perception and memory.* Dordrecht: D. Reidel.

Goldman, A. I. (1986). *Epistemology and cognition.* Cambridge, MA: Harvard
University Press.

(1992). *Liaisons: philosophy meets the cognitive and social sciences.* Cambridge,
MA: MIT Press.

Goldman, A. (2001). Social epistemology. *Stanford Encyclopedia of Philosophy.*
http://plato.stanford.edu/entries/epistemology-social

Hamlyn, D. (1971). Epistemology and conceptual development. In T. Mischel
(ed.), *Cognitive development and epistemology.* New York: Academic Press,
pp. 3–24.

Inhelder, B. (1981). Some aspects of Piaget's genetic approach to cognition. In
H. Furth (ed.), *Piaget and knowledge: theoretical foundations.* 2nd edition.
Chicago: University of Chicago Press, pp. 22–39.

Kitchener, R. F. (1986). *Piaget's theory of knowledge: genetic epistemology and
scientific reason.* New Haven, CT: Yale University Press.

    (1999). *The conduct of inquiry: an introduction to logic and scientific method.*
Lanham, MD: University Press of America.

    (ed.) (2000). Special issue: Piaget's *Sociological studies. New Ideas In Psychology,*
18, 119–275.

    (2003). Piaget's social epistemology. In J. Carpendale & U. Müller (eds.),
Social interaction and the development of knowledge. Mahwah, NJ: Lawrence
Erlbaum, pp. 45–67.

    (forthcoming). Developmental epistemology: cognitive development and nat-
uralistic epistemology. (Book manuscript.)

Kitcher, P. (1992). The naturalists return. *Philosophical Review,* 101, 53–114.

Kripke, S. A. (1982). *Wittgenstein on rules and private language.* Cambridge, MA:
Harvard University Press.

Laudan, L. (1987). Progress or rationality? The prospects for normative naturalism. *American Philosophical Quarterly,* 24, 19–31.

Locke, J. (1975). *An essay concerning human understanding* (ed. P. H. Niddith,
4th edition). Oxford: Clarendon Press.

Maffie, J. (1990). Recent work on naturalized epistemology. *American Philosophical Quarterly,* 27, 281–93.

Opp, D. (1983). *Die Enstehung der sozialer Normen.* Tübingen: J. C. B. Mohr.

Piaget, J. (1942). Les trois structures fondamentales de la vie psychique: rythme,
régulation et groupement. *Schweizerische Zeitschrift für Psychologie und ihre
Anwendungen,* 1, 9–21.

    (1950). *Introduction à l'épistémologie génétique.* Paris: Presses Universitaires de
France, vol. I.

    (1955). Les lignes générales de l'épistémologie génétique. In *Actes du deuxième
Congrès international de l'Union internationale de philosophie des sciences,
Zurich, 1954,* vol. I. Neuchâtel: de Griffon, pp. 26–45.

    (1957). Programme et méthodes de l'épistémologie génétique. In *Etudes
d'épistémologie génétique,* vol. I. *Epistémologie génétique et recherche psychologi-
que.* Paris: Presses Universitaires de France, pp. 13–84.

    (1962). Défense de l'épistémologie génétique. In *Etudes d'épistémologie génét-
ique,* vol. XVI. *Implication, formalization et logique naturelle.* Paris: Presses
Universitaires de France, pp. 165–91.

    (1967a). Nature et méthodes de l'épistémologie. In J. Piaget (ed.), *Logique et
connaissance scientifique.* Paris: Gallimard, pp. 3–61.

    (1967b). Les méthodes de l'épistémologie. In J. Piaget (ed.), *Logique et con-
naissance scientifique.* Paris: Gallimard, pp. 62–126.

(1971a). *Psychology and epistemology*. New York: Viking.
(1971b). *Genetic epistemology*. New York: W. W. Norton.
(1972a). *Insights and illusions of philosophy* (trans. W. Mays, 2nd edition). New York: World Publishing Co. (Original work published 1968.)
(1972b). *The principles of genetic epistemology* (trans. W. Mays). London: Routledge & Kegan Paul. (Original work published 1970.)
(1985). *The equilibration of cognitive structures: the central problem of intellectual development* (trans. T. Brown & K. J. Thampy). Chicago: University of Chicago Press. (Original work published 1975.)
(1986). Essay on necessity (trans. L. Smith & F. Steel). *Human development*, 29, 301–14.
(1995). *Sociological studies* (ed. L. Smith, trans. L. Smith et al.). London/New York: Routledge.
Plantinga, A. (1993a). *Warrant and proper function*. New York: Oxford University Press.
(1993b). *Warrant: the current debate*. New York: Oxford University Press.
Quine, W. V. O. (1951). Two dogmas of empiricism. *Philosophical Review*, 60, 20–43.
(1969). Epistemology naturalized. In his *Ontological relativity and other essays*. New York: Columbia University Press, pp. 69–90.
Rawls, J. (1971). *A theory of justice*. Cambridge, MA: Harvard University Press.
Schmitt, F. (1994). Socializing epistemology: an introduction through two sample issues. In F. Schmitt (ed.), *Socializing epistemology: the social dimensions of knowledge*. Lanham, MD: Rowman & Littlefield, pp. 1–27.
Smith, L. (1993). *Necessary knowledge*. Hove: Lawrence Erlbaum.
(1995). Introduction. In L. Smith (ed., trans. L. Smith et al.), *Jean Piaget: sociological studies*. London: Routledge, pp. 1–22.
Sosa, E. (1991). *Knowledge in perspective*. Cambridge: Cambridge University Press.
Sugden, R. (1986). *The economics of rights, cooperation and welfare*. Oxford: Blackwell's.
Taylor, M. (1984). *The possibility of cooperation*. New York: Cambridge University Press.
Ullmann-Margalit, E. (1977). *The emergence of norms*. Oxford: Clarendon Press.
Zagzebski, L. (1996). *Virtues of the mind*. Cambridge: Cambridge University Press.

5. NORMS AND NORMATIVE FACTS IN HUMAN DEVELOPMENT

Adey, P. & Shayer, M. (2002). Cognitive acceleration comes of age. In M. Shayer & P. Adey (eds.), *Learning intelligence*. Buckingham: Open University Press.
Aristotle (1987). On the soul. In J. Ackrill (ed.), *New Aristotle reader*. Oxford: Oxford University Press.
Audi, R. (1999). *The Cambridge dictionary of philosophy*. 2nd edition. Cambridge: Cambridge University Press.
Bell, V. & Johnson-Laird, P. N. (1998). A model theory of modal reasoning. *Cognitive Science*, 22, 25–51.

Bereiter, C. (2002). *Education and mind in the knowledge age*. Mahwah, NJ: Erlbaum.

Bickhard, M. (2003). The biological emergence of representation. In T. Brown & L. Smith (eds.), *Reductionism and the development of knowledge*. Mahwah, NJ: Erlbaum.

Bjorklund, D. & Pellegrini, A. (2002). *The origins of human nature*. Washington, DC: American Psychological Association.

Braine, M. & O'Brien, D. (1998). *Mental logic*. Mahwah, NJ: Erlbaum.

Brandom, R. (1994). *Making it explicit: reasoning, representing, and discursive commitment*. Cambridge, MA: Harvard University Press.

(2000). *Articulating reasons: an introduction to inferentialism*. Cambridge, MA: Harvard University Press.

Bruner, J. (1966). *Toward a theory of instruction*. Cambridge, MA: Harvard University Press.

Bryant, P. (2001). Learning in Geneva: the contribution of Bärbel Inhelder and her colleagues. In A. Typhon & J. Vonèche (eds.), *Working with Piaget: essays in honour of Bärbel Inhelder*. Hove: Psychology Press.

Byrnes, J. & Duff, M. (1989). Young children's comprehension of modal expressions. *Cognitive Development*, 4, 369–87.

Carl, W. (1994). *Frege's theory of sense and reference: its origins and scope*. Cambridge: Cambridge University Press.

Carroll, L. (1895). What the tortoise said to Achilles. *Mind*, 4, 278–80.

Chalmers, D. (1996). *The conscious mind: in search of a fundamental theory*. New York: Oxford University Press.

Changeux, J-P. (2000). Co-author. In J-P. Changeux & P. Ricoeur, *What makes us think?* Princeton: Princeton University Press.

Cheng, P. & Holyoak, K. (1985). Pragmatic reasoning schemas. *Cognitive Psychology*, 17, 391–416.

Cosmides, L. (1989). The logic of social exchange: has natural selection shaped how humans reason? Studies with the Wason selection task. *Cognition*, 31, 187–276.

Cosmides, L. & Tooby, J. (2004). *What is evolutionary psychology? Explaining the new science of the mind*. New Haven: Yale University Press.

Cresswell, M. & Hughes, G. (1996). *A new introduction to modal logic*. London: Routledge.

Damon, W. (1977). *The social world of the child*. San Francisco: Jossey-Bass.

Dawkins, R. (1999). *The extended phenotype: the long reach of the gene*. Revised edition. Oxford: Oxford University Press.

Descartes, R. (1931). Meditations on first philosophy. In E. Haldane & G. Ross (eds.), *Philosophical works of Descartes*, vol. I. New York: Dover Publications.

Dummett, M. (1981). *Frege: philosophy of language*. 2nd edition. London: Duckworth.

Evans, J. (2002). Logic and human reasoning: an assessment of the deduction paradigm. *Psychological Bulletin*, 128, 978–96.

Ferrari, M., Pinard, A. & Runions, K. (2001). Piaget's framework for a scientific study of consciousness. *Human Development*, 44, 195–213.

Fiddick, L. (2003). Is there a faculty of deontic reasoning? A critical re-evaluation of abstract deontic versions of the Wason selection task. In D. Over (ed.). *Evolution and the psychology of thinking*. Hove: Psychology Press.

(2004). Domains of deontic reasoning: resolving the discrepancy between the cognitive and moral reasoning literatures. *The Quarterly Journal of Experimental Psychology*, 57A, 447–74.

Flavell, J., Miller, P. & Miller, S. (1993). *Cognitive development*. 3rd edition. Englewood Cliffs, NJ: Prentice Hall.

Frege, G. (1950). *The foundations of arithmetic*. Oxford: Blackwell.

(1964). *The basic laws of arithmetic*. Berkeley, CA: University of California Press.

(1977). *Logical investigations*. Oxford: Blackwell.

(1979). *Posthumous papers*. Oxford: Blackwell.

Goldman, A. (2001). *Pathways of knowledge: public and private*. Oxford: Oxford University Press.

Gruber, H. & Vonèche, J. (1995). *The essential Piaget*. Northvale, NJ: Jason Aronson Inc.

Harris, P. L. & Núñez, M. (1996). Understanding of permission rules by preschool children. *Child Development*, 67, 1572–91.

Hawking, S. (2001). *The universe in a nutshell*. London: Bantam Press.

Holbo, J. (2002). Moral dilemma and the logic of obligation. *American Philosophical Quarterly*, 39, 259–74.

Horty, J. F. (2001). *Agency and deontic logic*. Oxford: Oxford University Press.

Humphrey, G. (1951). *Thinking*. New York: John Wiley.

Huxley, T. H. (1868). *A liberal education*. In C. Bibby (1971), *Huxley on education*. Cambridge: Cambridge University Press.

Isaacs, N. (1951). Critical notice. *British Journal of Psychology*, 42, 185–8.

Johnson-Laird, P. (1983). *Mental models*. Cambridge: Cambridge University Press.

(1999). Deductive reasoning. *Annual Review of Psychology*, 50, 109–35.

Kant, I. (1993). *Critique of practical reason*. 3rd edition. Upper Saddle River, NJ: Prentice Hall.

(1997). *Lectures on ethics*. In *Collected works*. Cambridge: Cambridge University Press.

Kenny, A. (1995). *Frege*. London: Penguin Books.

Kitcher, P. (1992). The naturalists return. *The Philosophical Review*, 101, 53–114.

Klahr, D. (1999). The conceptual habitat: in what kind of system can concepts develop? In E. Scholnick, K. Nelson, S. Gelman & P. Miller (eds.), *Conceptual development: Piaget's legacy*. Mahwah, NJ: Erlbaum.

Korsgaard, C. (1996). *The sources of normativity*. Cambridge: Cambridge University Press.

Kripke, S. (1982). *Wittgenstein on rules and private language*. Cambridge, MA: Harvard University Press.

Kuhn, T. (1977). *The essential tension*. Chicago: University of Chicago Press.

Kusch, M. (1995). *Psychologism: a case study in the sociology of philosophical knowledge*. London: Routledge.

Lakatos, I. (1974). Falsification and the methodology of scientific research programmes. In I. Lakatos & A. Musgrave (eds.), *Criticism and the growth of knowledge*. Cambridge: Cambridge University Press.

Macnamara, J. (1994). *The logical foundations of cognition*. New York: Oxford University Press.

Mason, H. E. (1996). *Moral dilemmas and moral theory*. New York: Oxford University Press.

Morf, A. (1957). Les relations entre la logique et la langage lors du passage du raisonnement concrèt au raisonnement formel. In L. Apostel, B. Mandelbrot & A. Morf, *Logique, langage, et théorie de l'information*. Paris: Presses Universitaires de France.

Morgan, P. (2005). *The insider*. London: Ebury Press.

Moser, P. (1999). Epistemology. In R. Audi (ed.), *The Cambridge dictionary of philosophy*. 2nd edition. Cambridge: Cambridge University Press.

Nagel, T. (1995). *Other minds: critical essays 1969–94*. New York: Oxford University Press.

Peng, K. & Nisbett, R. (1999). Culture, dialectics, and reasoning about contradiction. *American Psychologist*, 54, 741–54.

Piaget, J. (1918). *Recherche*. Lausanne: La Concorde.

(1932). *The moral judgment of the child*. London: Routledge & Kegan Paul.

(1950). *Introduction à l'épistémologie génétique*. Paris: Presses Universitaires de France, vol. I.

(1952). *The child's conception of number*. London: Routledge & Kegan Paul.

(1953). *Logic and psychology*. Manchester: Manchester University Press.

(1962). *Play, dreams and imitation in childhood*. London: Routledge & Kegan Paul.

(1965). Discussion: genèse et structure en psychologie. In M. de Gandillac & L. Goldman (eds.), *Entretiens sur les notions de genèse et de structure*. Paris: Mouton & Co.

(1966). Part II. In E. Beth & J. Piaget, *Mathematical epistemology and psychology*. Dordrecht: Reidel.

(1970a). *Genetic epistemology*. New York: Columbia University Press.

(1970b). A conversation with Jean Piaget. *Psychology Today*, 3, 25–32.

(1971). *Biology and knowledge*. Edinburgh: Edinburgh University Press.

(1973). *Main trends in psychology*. London: George Allen & Unwin.

(1974). *The child and reality*. London: Frederick Muller Ltd.

(1985). *Equilibration of cognitive structures*. Chicago: University of Chicago Press.

(1986). Essay on necessity. *Human Development*, 29, 301–14.

(1995). *Sociological studies*. London: Routledge.

(2001). *Studies in reflecting abstraction*. Hove, UK: Psychology Press.

(2006). Reason. *New Ideas in Psychology*.

Piaget, J. & Garcia, J. (1991). *Toward a logic of meanings*. Hillsdale, NJ: Erlbaum.

Popper, K. (1979). *Objective knowledge*. 2nd edition. Oxford: Oxford University Press.

Priest, G. (1998). What is so bad about contradictions? *The Journal of Philosophy*, 95, 410–26.

Putnam, H. (2002). *The collapse of the fact/value dichotomy, and other essays.* Cambridge, MA: Harvard University Press.

Quine, W. (1972). *Methods of logic.* 3rd edition. London: Routledge & Kegan Paul.

Ricoeur, P. (2000). Co-author. In J-P. Changeux & P. Ricoeur, *What makes us think?* Princeton: Princeton University Press.

Ross, A. (1968). *Directives and norms.* London: Routledge & Kegan Paul.

Sainsbury, R. M. (1991). *Logical forms.* Oxford: Blackwell.

Scholnick, E. & Wing, C. (1995). Logic in conversation: comparative studies of deduction in children and adults. *Cognitive Development,* 10, 319–45.

Searle, J. (1995). *The construction of social reality.* New York: The Free Press.

(1999). *Mind, language and society.* London: Weidenfeld & Nicolson.

(2001). *Rationality in action.* Cambridge, MA: MIT Press.

Shayer, M. (1997). Piaget and Vygotsky: a necessary marriage for effective intervention. In L. Smith, J. Dockrell & P. Tomlinson (eds.), *Piaget, Vygotsky and beyond.* London: Routledge.

Shayer, M. & Adey, P. (1981). *Towards a science of science teaching.* London: Heinemann.

(2002). *Learning intelligence.* Buckingham, UK: Open University Press.

Shayer, M. & Adhami, M. (2003). Realising the cognitive potential of children 5–7 with a mathematics focus. *International Journal of Educational Research,* 39, 743–75.

Sluga, H. (1980). *Gottlob Frege.* London: Routledge & Kegan Paul.

Smith, L. (1993). *Necessary knowledge.* Hove, UK: Erlbaum Associates.

(1998). On the development of mental representation. *Developmental Review,* 18, 202–27.

(1999a). What Piaget learned from Frege. *Developmental Review,* 19, 133–53.

(1999b). Epistemological principles for developmental psychology in Frege and Piaget. *New Ideas in Psychology,* 17, 83–117, 137–47.

(1999c). Representation and knowledge are not the same thing. *Behavioural and Brain Sciences,* 22, 784–5.

(2002a). *Reasoning by mathematical induction in children's arithmetic.* Oxford: Pergamon Press.

(2002b). Piaget's model. In U. Goswami (ed.), *Blackwell handbook of childhood cognitive development.* Oxford: Blackwell.

(2003). From epistemology to psychology in the development of knowledge. In T. Brown & L. Smith (eds.), *Reductionism and the development of knowledge.* Mahwah, NJ: Erlbaum.

(2004). Developmental epistemology and education. In J. Carpendale & U. Müller (eds.), *Social interaction and the development of knowledge.* Mahwah, NJ: Erlbaum.

Turiel, E. (1983). *The development of social knowledge.* Cambridge: Cambridge University Press.

Wason, P. (1966). Reasoning. In B. Foss (ed.), *New horizons in psychology.* Harmondsworth, UK: Penguin.

(1977). The theory of formal operations: a critique. In B. Gerber (ed.), *Piaget and knowing.* London Routledge & Kegan Paul.

Wittgenstein, L. (1958). *Philosophical investigations.* 2nd edition. Oxford: Blackwell.
(1978). *Remarks on the foundations of mathematics.* 3rd edition. Oxford: Blackwell.
von Wright, G. H. (1963). *Norm and action.* London: Routledge & Kegan Paul.
(1983a). *Practical reason.* Oxford: Blackwell.
(1983b). *Truth, knowledge, and modality.* Oxford: Blackwell.
(1985). *The tree of knowledge.* Leiden: E. J. Brill.

6. CONTEXTUALIZING MORAL JUDGMENT

Boesch, E. E. (1991). *Symbolic action theory and cultural psychology.* Berlin: Springer.
Breit, H. & Eckensberger, L. H. (2004). Die Faktizität des Normenbewusstseins: eine entwicklungs psychologische Perspektive. In C. Lütge & G. Vollmer (eds.), *Fakten statt Normen? Zur Rolle einzelwissenschaftlicher Argumente in einer naturalistischen Ethik.* Baden-Baden: Nomos-Verlag, pp. 207–24.
Cole, M. (1998). *Cultural psychology: a once and future discipline.* Cambridge, MA: The Belknap Press of Harvard University Press.
Dasen, P. R. & Heron, A. (1981). Cross-cultural tests of Piaget's theory. In H. C. Triandis & A. Heron (eds.), *Handbook of cross-cultural psychology,* vol. IV: *Developmental psychology.* Boston: Allyn & Bacon, pp. 295–342.
Day, J. & Tappan, M. (1996). The narrative approach to moral development: from the epistemic subject to dialogical selves. *Human Development, 32,* 67–82.
Eckensberger, L. H. (1986). Handlung, Konflikt und Reflexion: zur Dialektik von Struktur und Inhalt im moralischen Urteil. In W. Edelstein & G. Nunner-Winkler (eds.), *Zur Bestimmung der Moral: philosophische und sozialwissenschaftliche Beiträge zur Moralforschung.* Frankfurt am Main: Suhrkamp, pp. 409–42.
(1990). From cross-cultural psychology to cultural psychology. *The Quarterly Newsletter of the Laboratory of Comparative Human Cognition, 12 (1),* 37–52.
(1993). Normative und deskriptive, strukturelle und empirische Anteile in moralischen Urteilen: ein Ökonomie-Ökologie Konflikt aus psychologischer Sicht. In L. H. Eckensberger & U. Gähde (eds.), *Ethische Norm und empirische Hypothese.* Frankfurt: Suhrkamp Verlag, pp. 328–79.
(1995). Activity or action: two different roads towards an integration of culture into psychology? *Culture & Psychology, 1,* 67–80.
(1996). Agency, action and culture: three basic concepts for cross-cultural psychology. In J. Pandey, D. Sinha & D. P. S. Bhawuk (eds.), *Asian contributions to cross-cultural psychology.* New Delhi: Sage Publications, pp. 72–102.
(2003). Wanted: a contextualized psychology: a plea for cultural psychology based on actual psychology. In T. S. Saraswathi (ed.), *Cross-cultural*

perspectives in human development: theory, research, and application. New Delhi: Sage Publications, pp. 70–101.

Eckensberger, L. H. & Emminghaus, W. B. (1982). Moralisches Urteil und Aggression: zur Systematisierung und Präzisierung des Aggressionskonzeptes sowie einiger empirischer Befunde. In R. Hilke & W. Kempf (eds.), *Aggression: naturwissenschaftliche und kulturwissenschaftliche Perspektiven der Aggressionsforschung.* Bern: Huber, pp. 208–80.

Eckensberger, L. H. & Meacham, J. (1984). The essentials of action theory: a framework for discussion. *Human Development,* 27, 166–72.

Eckensberger, L. H. & Plath, I. (in press). Soziale Kognitionen. In W. Schneider & B. Sodian (eds.), *Enzyklopädie für Psychologie, Kognitive Entwicklung, C Theorie und Forschung,* Serie V *Entwicklung,* vol. II. Göttingen: Hogrefe, pp. 407–91.

Eckensberger, L. H. & Reinshagen, H. (1980). Kohlbergs Stufentheorie der Entwicklung des moralischen Urteils: ein Versuch ihrer Reinterpretation im Bezugsrahmen handlungstheoretischer Konzepte. In L. H. Eckensberger & R. K. Silbereisen (eds.), *Entwicklung sozialer Kognitionen: Modelle, Theorien, Methoden, Anwendung.* Stuttgart: Klett-Cotta, pp. 65–131.

Eckensberger, L. H. & Zimba, R. F. (1997). The development of moral judgment. In P. Dasen & T. S. Saraswathi (eds.), *Handbook of cross-cultural psychology.* 2nd edition, vol. II. *Developmental psychology.* Boston: Allyn & Bacon, pp. 299–338.

Eckensberger, L. H., Breit, H. & Döring, T. (1996). Moral judgments in the context of ecological and economical value orientations: the case of a coal-fuelled power station. Paper read at the 22nd Annual Conference of the Association for Moral Education (AME) Ottawa, November, 1996.

(1997). Moral judgments and knowledge in the context of ecological and economical value orientations: the case of a coal-fuelled power plant. Paper read at the 23rd Annual Conference of the Association for Moral Education (AME) Atlanta, November, 1997.

(1999a). Ethik und Barrieren in umweltbezogenen Entscheidungen: eine entwicklungspsychologische Perspektive. In V. Linneweber & E. Kals (eds.), *Umweltgerechtes Handeln.* Heidelberg: Springer, pp. 165–90.

(1999b). The role of affects in contextualized moral judgments. Paper read at the 25th Annual Conference of the Association for Moral Education (AME) Minneapolis, November, 1999.

Eckensberger, L. H., Döring, T. & Breit, H. (2001). Moral dimensions in risk evaluation. *Research in Social Problems and Public Policy,* 9, 137–63.

Engelhardt, H. D. (1975). *Umweltstrategie: Materialien und Analysen zu einer Umweltethik in der Industriegesellschaft.* Gütersloh: Mohn.

Erikson, E. H. (1959). *Identity and the life-cycle.* New York: International University Press.

Fowler, J. W. (1981). *Stages of faith.* New York: Harper & Row.

Gigerenzer, G. (1998). Surrogates for theories. *Theory & Psychology,* 8 (2), 195–204.

Haan, N. (1977). *Coping and defending: processes of self-environment organization.* New York: Academic Press.

Habermas, J. (1981). *Theorie des kommunikativen Handelns*, vol. I: *Handlungsrationalität und geschlechtliche Rationalisierung*. Frankfurt am Main: Suhrkamp.

Kant, I. (1966). *Groundwork of the metaphysics of morals*. In H. Paton (ed.), *The moral law*. London: Hutchinson.

Kasper, E., Sieloff, U., Nieder, A. & Eckensberger, L. H. (1987). Entwicklung eines Tests zur Erfassung des Wissens über die Kraftwerksproblematik. *Arbeiten der Fachrichtung Psychologie*, Universität des Saarlandes, 114.

Kegan, R. (1982). *The emerging self*. Harvard: Harvard University Press.

Kesselring, T. (1981). *Entwicklung und Widerspruch: ein Vergleich zwischen Piagets genetischer Erkenntnistheorie und Hegels Dialektik*. Frankfurt am Main: Suhrkamp.

Kohlberg, L. (1973). The claim to moral adequacy of a highest stage of moral judgment. *Journal of Philosophy*, 70, 630–46.

Lazarus, R. S. & Launier, R. (1978). Stress-related transactions between person and environment. In L. A. Pervin & M. Lewis (eds.), *Perspective in interactional psychology*. New York: Plenum, pp. 287–327.

Leontiev, A. N. (1977). *Tätigkeit, Bewusstsein, Persönlichkeit* (Activity, consciousness, personality). Stuttgart: Klett-Cotta.

Lourenço, O. (1996). Reflections on narrative approaches to moral development. *Human Development*, 39, 83–99.

Meggle, G. (1993). Semantische, empirische und normative Aspekte eines Begriffs des kommunikativen Handelns. In L. H. Eckensberger & U. Gähde (eds.), *Ethische Norm und empirische Hypothese*. Frankfurt am Main: Suhrkamp, pp. 197–221.

Oser, F. & Gmünder, P. (1984). *Der Mensch: Stufen seiner religiösen Entwicklung*. Zürich: Benziger.

Piaget, J. (1918). *Recherche*. Lausanne: La Concorde.

(1932). *The moral judgment of the child*. London: Routledge & Kegan Paul.

(1970). Piaget's theory. In P. H. Mussen (ed.), *Carmichael's handbook of child psychology*, vol. I. New York: Wiley, pp. 703–32.

(1977). The grasp of consciousness. London: Routledge & Kegan Paul ((1974). *La prise de conscience*. Paris: Presses Universitaires de France).

(1981). *Intelligence and affectivity: their relationship during child development*, trans. and ed. T. A. Brown & C. E. Kaegi. Palo Alto, California: Annual Reviews Inc.

(1995). *Sociological studies*. London: Routledge ((1965). *Etudes sociologiques*. Geneva: Droz).

(2001). *Studies in reflecting abstraction*. Hove, UK: Psychology Press.

Rosnow, R. L. & Georgoudi, M. (1986). The spirit of contextualism. In R. L. Rosnow & M. Georgoudi (eds.), *Contextualism and understanding in behavioral science*. New York: Praeger, pp. 3–22.

Schwartz, L. (1951). *Die Neurosen und die dynamische Psychologie von Pierre Janet*. Basel, Switzerland: Schwabe.

Shweder, R. A. (1990). Cultural psychology – what is it? In J. W. Stigler, R. A. Shweder & G. Herdt (eds.), *Cultural psychology: essays on comparative human development*. Cambridge: Cambridge University Press, pp. 1–43.

Sieloff, U., Schirk, S., Kasper, E., Nieder, A. & Eckensberger, L. H. (1988). Eine textanalytische Auswertungstechnik zur Erfassung von Abwehr und Bewältigung beim moralischen Argumentieren. *Arbeiten der Fachrichtung Psychologie*, 118, Saarbrücken: Universität des Saarlandes.

Valsiner, J. (1987). *Culture and the development of children's action*. Chichester: Wiley.

Wittgenstein, L. (1972). *Tractatus logico-philosophicus*. 2nd edition. London: Routledge & Kegan Paul.

von Wright, G. H. (1971). *Explanation and understanding*. Ithaca, NY: Cornell University Press.

7. THE DEVELOPMENT OF OBLIGATIONS AND RESPONSIBILITIES IN CULTURAL CONTEXT

Arsenio, W. F. & Lover, A. (1995). Children's conceptions of sociomoral affect: happy victimizers, mixed emotions, and other expectancies. In M. Killen & D. Hart (eds.), *Morality in everyday life*. New York: Cambridge University Press, pp. 87–128.

Barrett, C. D., Keller, M., Takezawa, M. & Wichary, S. (submitted). Children's understanding of social emotions: a study in ecological rationality.

Berndt, T. J. (1993). The morality of friendship versus the morality of individual autonomy. Paper presented at the symposium 'Spheres of Morality' at the 60th anniversary meeting of the Society for Research in Child Development, New Orleans, March, 1993.

Bersoff, D. M. & Miller, J. G. (1993). Culture, context and the development of moral accountability judgments. *Developmental Psychology*, 29, 664–76.

Blasi, A. (1980). Bridging moral cognition and moral action: a critical review of the literature. *Psychological Bulletin*, 88, 1–45.

(2004). Moral functioning: moral understanding and personality. In Lapsley & Narváez (eds.), pp. 335–48.

Blum, L. A. (1980). *Friendship, altruism and morality*. London: Routledge and Kegan Paul.

Bond, M. H. (ed.) (1996). *The handbook of Chinese psychology*. New York: Oxford University Press.

Boyes, M. & Walker, L. J. (1988). Implications of cultural diversity for the universality claims of Kohlberg's theory of moral reasoning. *Human Development*, 31, 44–59.

Bukowski, W. M. & Sippola, L. K. (1996). Friendship and morality: how are they related? In W. M. Bukowski, A. F. Newcomb & W. W. Hartup (eds.), *The company they keep*. Cambridge: Cambridge University Press, pp. 238–61.

Colby, A. & Kohlberg, L. (1987). *The measurement of moral judgment*, vol. I. *Theoretical foundations and research validation*. New York: Cambridge University Press.

Cosmides, L. & Tooby, J. (1992). *Cognitive adaptations for social exchange*. In J. Barkow, L. Cosmides & J. Tooby (eds.), *The adapted mind: evolutionary psychology and the generation of culture*. New York: Oxford University Press, pp. 163–228.

Damon, W. (1977). *The social world of the child*. San Francisco: Jossey-Bass.

Döbert, R. (1989). Moralische Erziehung in der Volksrepublik China (Moral education in the People's Republic of China). *Vergleichende Pädagogik*, 25, 246–59.

Eckensberger, L. H. & Zimba, R. F. (1997). The development of moral judgment. In P. R. Dasen & T. S. Saraswathi (eds.), *Handbook of cross-cultural psychology*, vol. III. *Developmental psychology*. Boston: Allyn and Bacon, pp. 299–338.

Edelstein, W. & Noam, G. G. (1982). Regulatory structures of the self and 'postformal' stages in adulthood. *Human Development*, 25, 407–22.

Eisenberg, N. (1982). The development of reasoning regarding prosocial behavior. In N. Eisenberg (ed.), *The development of prosocial behavior*. New York: Academic Press, pp. 219–49.

Fiddick, L. (2004). Domains of deontic reasoning: resolving the discrepancy between the cognitive and moral reasoning literatures. *Quarterly Journal of Experimental Psychology*, 57A, 447–74.

Frankena, W. K. (1973). *Ethics*. 2nd edition. London: Prentice-Hall.

Gerson, R. R. & Damon, W. (1978). Moral understanding and children's conduct. In W. Damon (ed.), *Moral development. New directions for child development*, No. 2. San Francisco: Jossey-Bass, pp. 41–61.

Gibbard, A. (1992). *Wise choices, apt feelings: a theory of normative judgement*. Oxford: Oxford University Press.

Gibbs, J. C. & Widaman, K. F. (1982). *Social intelligence: measuring the development of sociomoral reflection*. Englewood Cliffs: Prentice Hall.

Gilligan, C. (1982). *In a different voice: psychological theory and women's development*. Cambridge, MA: Harvard University Press.

Goodwin, R. & So-Kum Tang, C. (1996). Chinese personal relationships. In Bond (ed.), pp. 294–308.

Gouldner, A. W. (1960). The norm of reciprocity: a preliminary statement. *American Sociological Review*, 25, 161–78.

Hoffman, M. L. (2000). *Empathy and moral development: implications for caring and justice*. Cambridge: Cambridge University Press.

Keller, M. (1984). Resolving conflicts in friendship: the development of moral understanding in everyday life. In W. M. Kurtines & J. L. Gewirtz (eds.), *Morality, moral behaviour and moral development*. New York: Wiley, pp. 140–58.

(1996). *Moralische Sensibilität: Entwicklung in Freundschaft und Familie* (Moral sensibility: development in friendship and family). Weinheim: Psychologie-Verlags Union.

Keller, M., in cooperation with Cecora, L., Eckert, U., Fang, Fu-xi & Fang, Ge (2004a). Self in relationship. In Lapsley & Narváez (eds.), pp. 267–98.

Keller, M. & Edelstein, W. (1990). The emergence of morality in personal relationships. In T. E. Wren (ed.), *The moral domain: essays in the ongoing discussion between philosophy and the social sciences*. Cambridge, MA: MIT Press, pp. 255–82.

(1991). The development of socio-moral meaning making: domains, categories and perspective-taking. In W. M. Kurtines & J. L. Gewirtz (eds.),

Handbook of moral behavior and development, vol. II. *Research*. Hillsdale: Erlbaum, pp. 89–114.

(1993). The development of the moral self from childhood to adolescence. In Noam & Wren (eds.), pp. 310–36.

Keller, M. & Reuss, S. (1984). An action-theoretical reconstruction of the development of social-cognitive competence. *Human Development*, 27, 211–20.

Keller, M., Eckensberger, L. H. & Rosen, K. von (1989). A critical note on the conception of preconventional morality: the case of stage 2 in Kohlberg's theory. *International Journal of Behavioral Development*, 12, 57–69.

Keller, M., Gummerum, M., Wang, X. T. & Lindsey, S. (2004b). Understanding perspectives and emotions in contract violation: development of deontic and moral reasoning. *Child Development*, 75, 614–35.

Keller, M., Lourenço, O., Malti, T. & Saalbach, H. (2003). The multifaceted phenomenon of 'happy victimizers': a cross-cultural comparison. *British Journal of Developmental Psychology*, 21, 1–18.

Keller, M., Edelstein, W., Fang, Fu-xi, Hong, Tang & Schuster, P. (1996). The role of culture in the attribution of moral feelings. Paper presented at the 23rd Annual Conference of the Association for Moral Education, Ottawa, November, 1996.

Keller, M., Edelstein, W., Krettenauer, T., Fang, F. & Fang, G. (2005). Reasoning about moral obligations and interpersonal responsibilities in different cultural contexts. In W. Edelstein & G. Nunner-Winkler (eds.), *Morality in context*. Advances in Psychology 137. Amsterdam: Elsevier, pp. 317–40.

Keller, M., Edelstein, W., Schmid, C., Fang, F. & Fang, G. (1998). Reasoning about responsibilities and obligations in close relationships: a comparison across two cultures. *Developmental Psychology*, 34, 731–41.

Kohlberg, L. (1976). Moral stages and moralization: the cognitive developmental approach. In T. Lickona (ed.), *Moral development and behavior: theory, research and social issues*. New York: Holt, Rinehart and Winston, pp. 31–53.

(1984). *Essays on moral development*, vol. II. *The psychology of moral development: the nature and validity of moral stages*. San Francisco: Harper and Row.

Krappmann, L. (1996). Amicitia, drujba, shin-yu, philia, Freundschaft, friendship: on the cultural diversity of a human relationship. In W. M. Bukowski, A. F. Newcomb & W. W. Hartup (eds.), *The company they keep: friendship in childhood and adolescence*. New York: Cambridge University Press, pp. 19–40.

Krettenauer, T. (2004). Metaethical cognition and epistemic reasoning development in adolescence. *International Journal of Behavioral Development*, 68, 461–70.

Krettenauer, T. & Eichler, D. (2005). Adolescents' self-attributed emotions following a moral transgression: relations with delinquency, confidence in moral judgment, and age. *British Journal of Developmental Psychology*.

Lapsley, D. K. & Narváez, D. (eds.) (2004). *Moral development, self and identity.* Mahwah: Erlbaum.

Ma, H. K. (1988). The Chinese perspectives on moral judgment development. *International Journal of Psychology,* 23, 201–27.

Markus, H. R. & Kitayama, S. (1991). Culture and the self: implications for cognition, emotion and motivation. *Psychological Review,* 98, 224–53.

Nisan, M. (2004). Judgement and choice in moral functioning. In Lapsley & Narváez (eds.), pp. 133–60.

Noam, G. G. & Wren, T. E. (1993) in cooperation with Nunner-Winkler, G. & Edelstein, W. (eds.), *The moral self.* Cambridge, MA: MIT Press.

Nucci, L. P. & Lee, J. (1993). Morality and personal autonomy. In Noam & Wren (eds.), pp. 123–48.

Nunner-Winkler, G. (1993). The growth of moral motivation. In Noam & Wren (eds.), pp. 269–91.

Nunner-Winkler, G. & Sodian, B. (1988). Children's understanding of moral emotions. *Child Development,* 59, 323–38.

Oser, F. & Reichenbach, R. (2005). Moral resilience – the unhappy moralist. In W. Edelstein & G. Nunner-Winkler (eds.), *Morality in context.* Advances in Psychology 137. Amsterdam: Elsevier, pp. 203–24.

Piaget, J. (1965). *The moral judgment of the child.* New York: Free Press. (Original work published 1932.)

Rawls, J. (1971). *A theory of justice.* Cambridge, MA: Harvard University Press.

Richards, D. A. J. (1971). *A theory of reasons for action.* Oxford: Clarendon Press.

Selman, R. L. (1980). *The growth of interpersonal understanding: developmental and clinical analyses.* New York: Academic Press.

Shweder, R. A., Mahapatra, M. & Miller, J. G. (1987). Culture and moral development. In J. Kagan and S. Lamb (eds.), *The emergence of morality in young children.* Chicago: University of Chicago Press, pp. 1–83.

Smetana, J. G. (1982). *Concepts of self and morality.* New York: Praeger.

Triandis, H. C. (1990). Cross-cultural studies of individualism and collectivism. In J. J. Berman (ed.), *Nebraska symposium on motivation 1989,* vol. XXXVII. *Cross-cultural perspectives.* Lincoln: University of Nebraska Press, pp. 41–133.

Turiel, E. (1983). Domains and categories in social cognitive development. In W. F. Overton (ed.), *The relationship between social and cognitive development.* Hillsdale: Erlbaum, pp. 53–90.

(1998). The development of morality. In W. Damon (series ed.) & N. Eisenberg (vol. ed.), *Handbook of child psychology,* vol. III. *Social, emotional and personality development.* 5th edition. New York: Wiley, pp. 863–932.

Youniss, J. (1980). *Parents and peers in social development.* Chicago: The University of Chicago Press.

8. THE MULTIPLICITY OF SOCIAL NORMS

Abu-Lughod, L. (1993). *Writing women's worlds: Bedouin stories.* Berkeley: University of California Press.

Antipoff, H. (1928). Observations sur la compassion et le sens de la justice chez l'enfant. *Archives de Psychologie*, 21.

Asch, S. E. (1952). *Social psychology*. Englewood Cliffs, NJ: Prentice-Hall.

Benedict, R. (1934). *Patterns of culture*. Boston: Houghton Mifflin.

Bok, S. (1978/1999). *Lying: moral choice in public and private life*. New York: Vintage Books.

Clémence, A., Doise, W., de Rosa, A. S. & Gonzalez, L. (1995). La représentation sociale des droits de l'homme: une recherche internationale sur l'étendue et les limites de l'universalité. *Journal Internationale de Psychologie*, 30, 181–212.

Davidson, P., Turiel, E. & Black, A. (1983). The effect of stimulus familiarity on the use of criteria and justifications in children's social reasoning. *British Journal of Developmental Psychology*, 1, 49–65.

Doise, W., Clémence, A. & Spini, D. (1996). Human rights and social psychology. *The British Psychological Society Social Psychology Section Newsletter*, 35, 3–21.

Dworkin, R. (1977). *Taking rights seriously*. Cambridge, MA: Harvard University Press.

Fiddick, L. (2004). Domains of deontic reasoning: resolving the discrepancy between the cognitive and moral reasoning literatures. *The Quarterly Journal of Experimental Psychology*, 57A, 447–74.

(2005). Domains of deontic reasoning: a postscript. Paper presented at the 35th Annual Meeting of the Jean Piaget Society. Vancouver, BC, Canada, June 2005.

Freeman, V. G., Rathore, S. S., Weinfurt, K. P., Schulman, K. A. & Sulmasy, D. P. (1999). Lying for patients: physician deception of third-party payers. *Archives of Internal Medicine*, 159, 2,263–70.

Gewirth, A. (1982). *Human rights: essays on justification and applications*. Chicago: University of Chicago Press.

Haidt, J. (2001). The emotional dog and its rational tail: a social intuitionist approach to moral judgment. *Psychological Review*, 108, 814–34.

Hatch, E. (1983). *Culture and morality: the relativity of values in anthropology*. New York: Columbia University Press.

Helwig, C. C. (1995). Adolescents' and young adults' conceptions of civil liberties: freedom of speech and religion. *Child Development*, 66, 152–66.

(1997). The role of agent and social context in judgments of freedom of speech and religion. *Child Development*, 68, 484–95.

Hyman, H. H. & Sheatsley, P. B. (1953). Trends in public opinion on civil liberties. *Journal of Social Issues*, 9, 6–16.

King, M. L., Jr. (1968). The role of the behavioral scientist in the civil rights movement. *American Psychologist*, 23, 180–6.

Kohlberg, L. (1969). Stage and sequence: the cognitive-developmental approach to socialization. In D. Goslin (ed.), *Handbook of socialization theory and research*. Chicago: Rand McNally, pp. 347–480.

(1971). From is to ought: how to commit the naturalistic fallacy and get away with it in the study of moral development. In T. Mischel (ed.), *Psychology and genetic epistemology*. New York: Academic Press, pp. 151–235.

McClosky, M. & Brill, A. (1983). *Dimensions of tolerance: what Americans believe about civil liberties.* New York: Russell Sage.

Nucci, L. P. (2001). *Education in the moral domain.* Cambridge: Cambridge University Press.

Nucci, L. P. & Nucci, M. S. (1982a). Children's responses to moral and social conventional transgressions in free-play settings. *Child Development,* 53, 1,337–42.

(1982b). Children's social interactions in the context of moral and conventional transgressions. *Child Development,* 53, 403–12.

Perkins, S. A. (2003). Adolescent reasoning about lying in close relationships. Unpublished doctoral dissertation. University of California, Berkeley.

Piaget, J. (1932). *The moral judgment of the child.* London: Routledge and Kegan Paul.

(1951/1995). Egocentric thought and sociocentric thought. In J. Piaget, *Sociological studies.* London: Routledge, pp. 270–86.

Pizarro, D. A. & Bloom, P. (2003). The intelligence of the moral intuitions: comment on Haidt (2001). *Psychological Review,* 110, 193–6.

Protho, J. W. & Grigg, C. M. (1960). Fundamental principles of democracy: bases of agreement and disagreement. *Journal of Politics,* 22, 276–94.

Sarat, A. (1975). Reasoning in politics: the social, political, and psychological bases of principled thought. *American Journal of Political Science,* 19, 247–61.

Smetana, J. G. (1995). Morality in context: abstractions, ambiguities, and applications. In R. Vasta (ed.), *Annals of child development,* vol. X. London: Jessica Kingsley Publishers, pp. 83–130.

(2002). Culture, autonomy, and personal jurisdiction in adolescent–parent relationships. In H. W. Reese & R. Kail (eds.), *Advances in child development and behavior,* vol. XXIX. New York: Academic Press, pp. 51–87.

Smith, L. (2003). From epistemology to psychology in the development of knowledge. In T. Brown & L. Smith (eds.), *Reductionism and the development of knowledge.* Mahwah, NJ: Erlbaum, pp. 201–28.

Stouffer, S. (1955). *Communism, conformity and civil liberties.* New York: Doubleday.

Tisak, M. S. & Turiel, E. (1984). Children's conceptions of moral and prudential rules. *Child Development,* 55, 1,030–9.

Turiel, E. (1983). *The development of social knowledge: morality and convention.* Cambridge: Cambridge University Press.

(1998). The development of morality. In W. Damon (ed.), *Handbook of child psychology.* 5th edition, vol. III: N. Eisenberg (ed.), *Social, emotional, and personality development.* New York: Wiley, pp. 863–932.

(2002). *The culture of morality: social development, context, and conflict.* Cambridge: Cambridge University Press.

(2003). Resistance and subversion in everyday life. *Journal of Moral Education,* 32, 115–30.

(2005). Thought about actions in social domains: morality, social conventions, and social interactions. Unpublished manuscript, University of California, Berkeley.

(2006). Thought, emotions, and social interactional processes in moral development. In M. Killen & J. G. Smetana (eds.), *Handbook of moral development*. Mahwah, NJ: Erlbaum, pp. 7–35.

Turiel, E. & Perkins, S. A. (2004). Flexibilities of mind: conflict and culture. *Human Development*, 47, 158–78.

Turiel, E. & Wainryb, C. (1998). Concepts of freedoms and rights in a traditional hierarchically organized society. *British Journal of Developmental Psychology*, 16, 375–95.

Turiel, E., Perkins, S. A. & Mensing, J. F. (in preparation). *Judgments about deception in marital relationships*. University of California, Berkeley.

Wason, P. (1968). Reasoning about a rule. *Quarterly Journal of Experimental Psychology*, 20, 273–81.

Wertheimer, M. (1935). Some problems in the theory of ethics. *Social Research*, 2, 353–67.

Wikan, U. (1996). *Tomorrow, God willing: self-made destinies in Cairo*. Chicago: University of Chicago Press.

Wynia, M. K., Cummins, D. S., VanGeest, J. B. & Wilson, I. B. (2000). Physician manipulation of reimbursement rules for patients: between a rock and a hard place. *Journal of the American Medical Association*, 283, 1,858–65.

9. CAN PSYCHOLOGY BE A QUANTITATIVE SCIENCE, OR IS KANT RIGHT AFTER ALL?

Borsboom, D. (2005). *Measuring the mind: conceptual issues in contemporary psychometrics*. Cambridge: Cambridge University Press.

Erneling, C. E. & Johnson, D. M. (eds.) (2005). *The mind as a scientific object: between brain and culture*. Oxford: Oxford University Press.

Habermas, J. (1987). *Theorie des kommunikativen Handelns*, vol. I. *Handlungsrationalität und gesellschaftliche Rationalisierung*, vol. II. *Zur Kritik der funktionalistischen Vernunft*. 4th edition. Frankfurt am Main: Suhrkamp.

Heidelberger, M. (2004). *Nature from within: Gustav T. Fechner and his psychophysical worldview*. Pittsburgh: University of Pittsburgh Press.

Kusch, M. (1995). *Psychologism: a case study in the sociology of philosophical knowledge*. London: Routledge.

Lord, F. M. & Novick, M. R. (1968). *Statistical theories of mental test scores*. Reading, MA: Addison-Wesley.

McCarthy, G. E. (2001). *Objectivity and the silence of reason: Weber, Habermas, and the methodological disputes in German sociology*. New Brunswick, NJ: Transaction Publishers.

Molenaar, P. C. M. (2003). *State space techniques in structural equation modeling: transformation of latent variables in and out of latent variable models*. http://www.hhdev.psu.edu/hdfs/faculty/molenaar.html

(2004). A manifesto on psychology as idiographic science: bringing the person back into scientific psychology, this time forever. *Measurement*, 2, 201–18.

Nesselroade, J. R. & Molenaar, P. C. M. (2003). Quantitative models for developmental processes. In J. Valsiner & K. Connolly (eds.), *Handbook of developmental psychology*. London: Sage, pp. 622–39.

Oddie, G. (2005). *Value, reality, and desire*. Oxford: Oxford University Press.

Putnam, H. (2004). *The collapse of the fact/value dichotomy and other essays*. 3rd edition. Cambridge, MA: Harvard University Press.

10. NORMS AND INTUITIONS IN THE ASSESSMENT OF CHANCE

Acredolo, C., O'Connor, J., Banks, L. & Horobin, K. (1989). Children's ability to make probability estimates: skills revealed through application of Anderson's functional measurement methodology. *Child Development*, 60, 933–45.

Bozzi, P. (1990). *Fisica ingenua* (Naive physics). Milan: Garzanti.

Brainerd, C. J. (1981). Working memory and the developmental analysis of probability judgment. *Psychological Review*, 88, 463–502.

Cosmides, L. & Tooby, J. (1996). Are humans good intuitive statisticians after all? Rethinking some conclusions from the literature on judgment under uncertainty. *Cognition*, 58, 1–73.

da Buti, F. (1852–62). *Commento di Francesco da Buti sopra La Divina Commedia di Dante Allighieri* (Francesco da Buti's commentary on Dante's *Divine Comedy*). Pisa: Nistri. (Originally written circa 1385.) Available at http://dciswww.dartmouth.edu

David, F. N. (1962). *Games, gods and gambling: a history of probability and statistical ideas*. London: Griffin.

Dehaene, S. (1997). *The number sense: how the mind creates mathematics*. New York: Oxford University Press.

della Lana, J. (1866–7). *Comedia di Dante degli Allaghieri col commento di Jacopo della Lana bolognese* (Dante's *Comedy*, commentary by Jacopo della Lana from Bologna). Bologna: Tipografia Regia. (Originally written circa 1324.) Available at http://dciswww.dartmouth.edu

Fischbein, E. (1975). *The intuitive sources of probabilistic thinking in children*. Dordrecht: Reidel.

Franklin, J. (2001). *The science of conjecture: evidence and probability before Pascal*. Baltimore: Johns Hopkins University Press.

Gigerenzer, G. (1993). The bounded rationality of probabilistic mental models. In K. Manktelow & D. Over (eds.), *Rationality*. London: Routledge.

Gigerenzer, G. & Hoffrage, U. (1995). How to improve bayesian reasoning without instruction: frequency format. *Psychological Review*, 102, 684–704.

Gilovich, T., Griffin, D. & Kahneman, D. (eds.) (2002). *Heuristics and biases: the psychology of intuitive judgment*. Cambridge: Cambridge University Press.

Girotto, V. (2004). Task understanding. In J. Leighton & R. Sternberg (eds.), *The nature of reasoning*. Cambridge: Cambridge University Press.

Girotto, V. & Gonzalez, M. (2001). Solving probabilistic and statistical problems: a matter of information structure and question form. *Cognition*, 78, 247–76.

(2002). Chances and frequencies in probabilistic reasoning: rejoinder to Hoffrage, Gigerenzer, Krauss, and Martignon. *Cognition*, 84, 353–9.

(2003). Early reasoning about chances and possibilities: historical and developmental evidence. Paper presented at the 16th Jean Piaget Archives Conference, University of Geneva, September.

(2005). Probabilistic reasoning and combinatorial analysis. In V. Girotto & P. N. Johnson-Laird (eds.), *The shape of reason*. New York: Psychology Press.

(in press). Extensional reasoning about chances. In W. Schaeken, G. De Vooght, A. Vandierendonck & G. d'Ydewalle (eds.), *Mental model theory: extensions and refinements*. Mahwah, NJ: Erlbaum.

Hacking, I. (1975). *The emergence of probability*. Cambridge: Cambridge University Press.

Hilton, D. (1995). The social context of reasoning: conversational inference and rational judgement. *Psychological Bulletin*, 118, 248–71.

Howson, C. & Urbach, P. (1993). *Scientific reasoning: the Bayesian approach*. Chicago: Open Court.

Inhelder, B. & Piaget, J. (1964). *The early growth of logic*. London: Routledge & Kegan Paul. (Original work published 1955.)

Johnson-Laird, P. N., Legrenzi, P., Girotto, V., Sonino-Legrenzi, M. & Caverni, J. P. (1999). Naive probability: a model theory of extensional reasoning. *Psychological Review*, 106, 62–88.

Kahneman, D. & Tversky, A. (eds.) (2000). *Choices, values, and frames*. Cambridge: Cambridge University Press.

Kendall, M. G. (1956). The beginnings of a probability calculus. *Biometrika*, 43, 1–14.

Locke, J. (1975). *An essay concerning human understanding*. Oxford: Clarendon Press. (Original work published 1690.)

Neyman, J. & Pearson, E. S. (1967). *Joint statistical papers of J. Neyman and E. S. Pearson*. Berkeley, CA: University of California Press.

Nisbett, R. E., Krantz, D. H., Jepson, C. & Kunda, D. (1983). The use of statistical heuristics in everyday inductive reasoning. *Psychological Review*, 90, 339–63.

Ore, O. (1965). *Cardano, the gambling scholar*. New York: Dover.

Ottimo, A. L. (1827–9). *L'Ottimo commento della Divina Commedia* (Ottimo's commentary on the *Divine Comedy*). Pisa: Capurro. (Originally written circa 1331.) Available at http://dciswww.dartmouth.edu

Piaget, J. & Inhelder, B. (1975). *The origin of the idea of chance in children*. New York: Norton. (Original work published 1951.)

Piaget, J. & Szeminska, B. (1952). *The child's conception of number*. New York: Humanities Press. (Original work published 1941.)

Politzer, G. & Noveck, I. A. (1991). Are conjunction rule violations the results of conversational rule violations? *Journal of Psycholinguistic Research*, 20, 83–103.

Savage, L. J. (1954). *The foundations of statistics*. New York: Wiley.

Sloman, S. A., Over, D., Slovak, L. & Stibel, J. M. (2003). Frequency illusions and other fallacies. *Organizational Behavior and Human Decision Processes*, 91, 296–309.

Tentori, K., Bonini, N. & Osherson, D. (2004). The conjunction fallacy: a misunderstanding about conjunction? *Cognitive Science*, 26, 467–77.

Tversky, A. & Kahneman, D. (1983). Extensional versus intuitive reasoning: the conjunction fallacy in probability judgment. *Psychological Review*, 90, 293–315.

Yost, P. A., Siegel, A. E. & Andrews, J. M. (1962). Nonverbal probability judgments by young children. *Child Development*, 33, 769–80.

Zhu, L. & Gigerenzer, G. (2006). Children can solve Bayesian problems: the role of representation in mental computation. *Cognition*, 98, 287–308.

11. MAKING CONDITIONAL INFERENCES

Barrouillet, P. & Lecas, J. F. (1999). Mental models in conditional reasoning and working memory. *Thinking and Reasoning*, 5 (4), 289–302.

Barrouillet, P., Markovits, H. & Quinn, S. (2002). Developmental and content effects in reasoning with causal conditionals. *Journal of Experimental Child Psychology*, 81, 235–48.

Bjorklund, D. F. & Harnishfeger, K. K. (1990). The resources construct in cognitive development: diverse sources of evidence and a theory of inefficient inhibition. *Developmental Review*, 10, 48–71.

(1995). The evolution of inhibition mechanisms and their role in human cognition and behavior. In F. N. Dempster & C. J. Brainerd (eds.), *Interference and inhibition in cognition*. London: Academic Press, pp. 141–73.

Braine, M. D. S. (1990). The 'natural logic' approach to reasoning. In W. F. Overton (ed.), *Reasoning, necessity and logic: developmental perspectives*. Hillsdale, NJ: Lawrence Erlbaum Assoc., pp. 133–57.

Bucci, W. (1978). The interpretation of universal affirmative propositions. *Cognition*, 6, 55–77.

Cahan, S. & Artman, L. (1997). Is everyday experience dysfunctional for the development of conditional reasoning? *Cognitive Development*, 12 (2), 261–79.

Cummins, D. D. (1995). Naive theories and causal deduction. *Memory and Cognition*, 23 (5), 646–58.

Cummins, D. D., Lubart, T., Alksnis, O. & Rist, R. (1991). Conditional reasoning and causation. *Memory and Cognition*, 19 (3), 274–82.

Dawkins, R. (1999). *The extended phenotype*. Oxford: Oxford University Press.

De Neys, W., Schaeken, W. & d'Ydewalle, G. (2002). Causal conditional reasoning and semantic memory retrieval: a test of the 'semantic memory framework'. *Memory and Cognition*, 30 (6), 908–20.

Dias, M. G. & Harris, P. L. (1988). The effect of make-believe play on deductive reasoning. *British Journal of Developmental Psychology*, 6, 207–21.

(1990). The influence of the imagination on reasoning. *British Journal of Developmental Psychology*, 8, 305–18.

Evans, J. St. B. T. & Over, D. E. (1996). *Rationality and reasoning*. Hove: Psychology Press.

(2004). *If*. Oxford: Oxford University Press.

Gigerenzer, G. & Goldstein, D. G. (1996). Reasoning the fast and frugal way: models of bounded rationality. *Psychological Review*, 103 (4), 650–69.

Hawkins, J., Pea, R. D., Glick, J. & Scribner, S. (1984). 'Merds that laugh don't like mushrooms': evidence for deductive reasoning by preschoolers. *Developmental Psychology*, 20 (4), 584–94.

Inhelder, B. & Piaget, J. (1958). *The growth of logical thinking from childhood to adolescence*. New York: Basic Books.

Janveau-Brennan, G. & Markovits, H. (1999). The development of reasoning with causal conditionals. *Developmental Psychology*, 35 (4), 904–11.

Johnson-Laird, P. N. & Byrne, R. M. J. (1991). *Deduction*. Hillsdale, NJ: Laurence Erlbaum Assoc.

(2002). Conditionals: a theory of meaning, pragmatics, and inference. *Psychological Review*, 109 (4), 646–78.

Kahneman, D. & Tversky, A. (1996). On the reality of cognitive illusions. *Psychological Review*, 103 (3), 582–91.

Kail, R. (1992). Processing speed, speech rate, and memory. *Developmental Psychology*, 28, 899–904.

Klaczynski, P. A. & Narashimham, G. (1998). Representations as mediators of adolescent deductive reasoning. *Developmental Psychology*, 5, 865–81.

Kokis, J. V., Macpherson, R., Toplak, M. E., West, R. F. & Stanovich, K. E. (2002). Heuristic and analytic processing: age trends and associations with cognitive ability and cognitive styles. *Journal of Experimental Child Psychology*, 83 (1), 26–52.

Lea, R. B., O'Brien, D. P., Fisch, S., Braine, M. D. S. & Noveck, I. (1990). Predicting propositional logic inferences in text comprehension. *Journal of Memory and Language*, 29, 361–87.

Leevers, H. & Harris, P. (1999). Transient and persisting effects of instruction on young children's syllogistic reasoning with incongruent and abstract premises. *Thinking and Reasoning*, 5 (2), 145–74.

Markovits, H. (1985). Incorrect conditional reasoning among adults: competence or performance? *British Journal of Psychology*, 76, 241–7.

(1995). Conditional reasoning with false premises: fantasy and information retrieval. *British Journal of Developmental Psychology*, 13, 1–11.

(2000). A mental model analysis of young children's conditional reasoning with meaningful premises. *Thinking and Reasoning*, 6 (4), 335–48.

Markovits, H. & Barrouillet, P. (2002). The development of conditional reasoning: a mental model account. *Developmental Review*, 22 (1), 5–36.

Markovits, H. & Doyon, C. (2004). Information processing and reasoning with premises that are not empirically true: interference, working memory and processing speed. *Memory and Cognition*, 32 (4), 592–601.

Markovits, H. & Handley, S. (in press). Is inferential reasoning just probabilistic reasoning in disguise? *Memory and Cognition*.

Markovits, H. & Quinn, S. (2002). Efficiency of retrieval correlates with 'logical' reasoning from causal conditional premises. *Memory and Cognition*, 30 (5), 696–706.

Markovits, H. & Vachon, R. (1989). Reasoning with contrary-to-fact propositions. *Journal of Experimental Child Psychology*, 47, 398–412.

(1990). Conditional reasoning, representation and level of abstraction. *Developmental Psychology*, 26, 942–51.

Markovits, H., Venet, M., Janveau-Brennan, G., Malfait, N., Pion, N. & Vadeboncoeur, I. (1996). Reasoning in young children: fantasy and information retrieval. *Child Development*, 67, 2,857–72.

Neil, W. T. (1997). Episodic retrieval in negative priming and repetition priming. *Journal of Experimental Psychology: Learning, Memory & Cognition*, 23 (6), 1,291–3,105.

Oaksford, M., Chater, N. & Larkin, J. (2000). Probabilities and polarity biases in conditional inference. *Journal of Experimental Psychology: Learning, Memory & Cognition*, 26 (4), 883–99.

O'Brien, D. P. & Overton, W. F. (1980). Conditional reasoning following contradictory evidence: a developmental analysis. *Journal of Experimental Child Psychology*, 30, 44–61.

(1982). Conditional reasoning and the competence-performance issue: a developmental analysis of a training task. *Journal of Experimental Child Psychology*, 34, 274–90.

Overton, W. F., Ward, S. L., Black, J., Noveck, I. A. & O'Brien, D. P. (1987). Form and content in the development of deductive reasoning. *Developmental Psychology*, 23 (1), 22–30.

Piaget, J. (1970). Piaget's theory. In P. H. Mussen (ed.), *Carmichael's manual of child psychology*, vol. I. New York: Wiley.

(2001). *Studies in reflecting abstraction*. Hove: Psychology Press.

Quinn, S. & Markovits, H. (1998). Conditional reasoning, causality, and the structure of semantic memory: strength of association as a predictive factor for content effects. *Cognition*, 68, B93–B101.

Scholnick, E. K. & Wing, C. S. (1991). Speaking deductively: preschoolers' use of If in conversation and in conditional inference. *Developmental Psychology*, 27 (2), 249–58.

Simoneau, M. & Markovits, H. (2003). Reasoning with premises that are not empirically true: evidence for the role of inhibition and retrieval. *Developmental Psychology*, 39 (6), 964–75.

Sloman, S. A. (1996). The empirical case for two systems of reasoning. *Psychological Bulletin*, 119 (1), 3–22.

Stanovich, K. E. & West, R. F. (2000). Individual differences in reasoning: implications for the rationality debate? *Behavioral-and-Brain-Sciences*, 23 (5), 645–726.

Tipper, S. P. (2001). Does negative priming reflect inhibitory mechanisms? A review and integration of conflicting views. *The Quarterly Journal of Experimental Psychology*, 54A, 321–43.

Venet, M. & Markovits, H. (2001). Understanding uncertainty with abstract conditional premises. *Merrill-Palmer Quarterly*, 47 (1), 74–99.

Wason, P. C. (1968). Reasoning about a rule. *Quarterly Journal of Experimental Psychology*, 20, 273–81.

Wason, P. C. & Shapiro, D. (1971). Natural and contrived experience in a reasoning problem. *Quarterly Journal of Experimental Psychology*, 23, 63–71.

Index

NB page numbers in bold refer to figures and tables